THE
BLESSED EUCHARIST

THE
BLESSED EUCHARIST

OUR GREATEST TREASURE

By

Fr. Michael Müller, C.S.S.R.

PRIEST OF THE CONGREGATION OF THE MOST HOLY REDEEMER

"There hath stood one in the midst of you, whom you know not...the latchet of whose shoe I am not worthy to loose."

—John 1:26-27

TAN BOOKS AND PUBLISHERS, INC.
Rockford, Illinois 61105

Imprimatur: ✠ Martin John Spalding
Archbishop of Baltimore
October 22, 1867

First published by Kelley & Piet of Baltimore, Maryland in 1868. Reprinted in quality paperbound format by TAN Books and Publishers, Inc., in 1973. Retypeset and republished in pocket-size paperbound format by TAN Books and Publishers, Inc., in 1994.

Library of Congress Catalog Card No.: 93-61595

ISBN: 0-89555-507-7

Printed and bound in the United States of America.

TAN BOOKS AND PUBLISHERS, INC.
P.O. Box 424
Rockford, Illinois 61105
1994

An Oblation

I offer Thee this book, O Lord Jesus Christ, Fount of eternal light, in union with that ineffable charity which moved Thee, the only-begotten of the Father, in the plenitude of the Divinity, to take upon Thyself our nature and to become man. I beseech Thee to take it into Thy divine keeping, that it may glorify Thy divine bounty towards us, vile creatures that we are. And since Thou, the Almighty Dispenser of all good things, dost vouchsafe to nourish us during our exile until, beholding Thy glory with unveiled countenance, we are transformed into Thee, grant, I beseech Thee, to all who read these writings with humility, that they may be charmed with the sweetness of Thy charity and inwardly drawn to desire the same for their furtherance in perfection, so that, elevating their hearts towards Thee with burning love, they may be like so many golden censers, whose sweet odors shall abundantly supply all my negligence and ingratitude.

Dear Mother Mary, do thou also pray to thy Divine Son for all those who may read this little book.

Protest of the Author

IN OBEDIENCE to the decrees of Urban VIII of holy memory, I protest that I do not intend to attribute any other than purely human authority to all the miracles, revelations, graces and incidents contained in this book; neither to the titles holy or blessed applied to the servants of God not yet canonized, except in cases where these have been confirmed by the Holy Roman Catholic Church and by the Holy Apostolic See, of whom I profess myself an obedient son; and therefore, to their judgment I submit myself and whatever I have written in this book.

Contents

Preface

My Dear Reader and Brother in Jesus Christ:

Since the spirit of devotion that has urged me to write this book animates you to read it and makes us the happy children of the same loving Father, should you ever hear any person say I might have spared myself the labor, there being already so many learned and celebrated works which treat of this subject, I beg you to answer that Our Lord Jesus Christ in the Adorable Sacrament is such an abundant fountain that the more it flows, the fuller it becomes, and the fuller it is, the more it flows, which signifies that the most Holy Eucharist is so great and so sublime a mystery that the more we say of it, the more remains to be said. If St. Alphonsus could say with all truth of the Passion of Our Lord, "that eternity will not suffice to meditate adequately upon it," we may affirm the same of Jesus Christ hidden in the Blessed Sacrament, and with a thousand times more justice apply to our subject what St. Augustine says in praise of the Blessed Virgin, viz., that all the tongues of men, even if all their members were changed into tongues, would not be sufficient to praise her as she deserves.

Worldly lovers are accustomed frequently to mention and praise those whom they love, that others also may praise and applaud them; how poor and weak should we then consider the love of those who call themselves lovers of the Blessed Sacrament and yet who seldom speak of it or think of endeavoring to inspire others with a love of it. The true lovers of the most Blessed Sacrament do not act thus; they speak of it, praise it everywhere, in public and in private; whenever it is in their power they try to enkindle in the hearts of everyone those ardent flames of love which they themselves burn for their beloved Jesus.

The object of this little book is, then, to make Jesus, in the Blessed Eucharist, more generally known and better loved. Our Divine Saviour is ready to bestow innumerable graces through this Sacrament, which are lost in consequence of the ignorance and indifference of men. When the most Holy Sacrament of the Altar is not revered and loved, scandals will abound, faith will languish and the Church will mourn. On the other hand, if this Sacrament be worthily frequented, peace will reign in Christian hearts, the devil will lose power, and souls will be sanctified. "As many as received Him to them He gave power to be made the sons of God." (*John* 1:12). It has seemed to me that a work explanatory of the prominent points of this mystery, written in a simple and familiar style, would greatly contribute to remove the obstacles to a right appreciation of this wonderful Sacrament of Divine love; and with this conviction I have ventured to lay the following pages before the public, trusting, with the blessing of God, they may prove useful to many souls.

As Almighty God in His goodness imparts His favors to His faithful followers in divers ways—

sometimes by enlightening their minds in a supernatural manner, and even conversing with them familiarly, as it were—and as the nature of this work is intended to be practical, not controversial, I have thought it expedient for the edification of pious souls to introduce into it, after the manner of the Holy Fathers, both some revelations made to certain Saints and several miraculous facts concerning this mystery.

I know there are some persons who, boasting of being free from prejudices, take great credit to themselves for believing no miracles but those recorded in the Holy Scriptures, esteeming all others as tales and fables for foolish women. But it will be well to remember here a remark of the learned St. Alphonsus, who says, "that the bad are as ready to deride miracles as the good are to believe them; adding that as it is a weakness to give credit to all things, so on the other hand, to reject miracles which come to us attested by grave and pious men, either savors of infidelity, which supposes them impossible to God, or of presumption, which refuses belief to such a class of authors. We give credit to a Tacitus, a Suetonius, and can we deny it without presumption to Christian authors of learning and probity. There is less risk in believing and receiving what is related with some probability by honest persons and not rejected by the learned, and which serves for the edification of our neighbor, than in rejecting it with a disdainful and presumptuous spirit." (*Glories of Mary.*) Hence Pope Benedict XIV (*De Canoni. Sanct.*) says: "Though an assent of Catholic faith be not due to them, they deserve a human assent according to the rules of prudence by which they are probable and piously credible."

Now should the Reverend Clergy deem this publication ever so little calculated to promote devotion to the Blessed Sacrament, the compiler will believe himself amply rewarded for his labor if they encourage its circulation.

Michael Müller, C.S.S.R.
St. Alphonsus', Baltimore, Maryland
December 8, 1867

CHAPTER 1

The Doctrine of the Real Presence

A CERTAIN man was once thrown into prison. He there suffered so much from hunger, thirst and cold that at last he was almost dead. One day the king determined to pay a visit to the captive, in order to find out how he bore his sufferings. Having put off his royal apparel, he went in disguise to the prison and asked the poor man how he fared, but the prisoner, being very sad and melancholy, scarcely deigned to answer him. When the king had gone away, the jailor said to the criminal: "Do you know who was speaking to you? It was the king himself." "The king!" exclaimed the captive. "O wretch that I am! If I had known that I would have thrown myself at his feet and clasped his knees, and I would not have let him go until he had pardoned me. Alas! What a favorable opportunity I have lost of freeing myself from this dungeon." It was thus the poor captive lamented in anguish and despair, but all was unavailing.

I think, dear Reader, you understand the meaning of this story. The sufferings of this captive represent the wretchedness of man's condition on this earth. Our true country is Heaven, and as long as we are living on earth, we are captives and exiles. We are far from Jesus Christ, our King; far from Mary, our good Mother; far from the Angels and Saints of Heaven; and far from our dear departed friends. But

1

very many Christians are also, in another respect, like the captive of whom I have spoken. They do not know Jesus Christ, their true King, who not only visits them, but dwells very near them. "But," you will ask, "how can Jesus Christ dwell near them without their knowing Him?" It is because He has put on a strange garment and appears in disguise. Our Lord Jesus Christ abides in two places: in Heaven, where He shows Himself undisguised, as He is in reality; and on earth in the Blessed Sacrament, in which He conceals Himself under the appearance of bread. One day a certain nun said to St. Teresa: "I wish that I had lived at the time of Jesus Christ, my dear Saviour, for then I could have seen how amiable and lovely He is." St. Teresa, on hearing this, laughed outright. "What!" said she, "do you not know then, dear sister, that the same Jesus Christ is still with us on earth, that He lives quite near us, in our churches, on our altars, in the Blessed Sacrament?" Yes, the Blessed Sacrament, or Holy Eucharist, is the true Body and Blood of Jesus Christ, Our Lord, who is truly, really and substantially present under the outward appearances of bread and wine.

This is indeed a great mystery, and the more to confirm your faith in it, I will give you some proofs for it from Scripture and tradition. The first proof is taken from the sixth chapter of the gospel of St. John. Our divine Saviour knew that if He were to teach the Jews and His disciples such a new and wonderful doctrine without having first prepared them for it, there would be scarcely one who would believe Him. When God intends to do something very extraordinary, He generally prepares men for it by revealing to them beforehand what He is about to do. Thus we know that when He intended to destroy the world by the deluge, He made it known through Noah a hundred years before this dreadful event took place. Again, when the Son of God had become man and was about to make Himself known as the Redeemer of the world, He sent St. John the Baptist to prepare the people for His coming. Finally, when He intended to destroy Jerusalem, He foretold it by the prophets; and, Jesus Christ has also described the signs by which men may know when the End of the World is at hand. God acts thus with men because He does not wish to overwhelm them by His strange and wonderful dealings. Hence, when our divine Saviour was about to tell the people that He intended to give them His Flesh and Blood as food for their souls, He prepared them for this mysterious doctrine by working a very astounding miracle.

This great miracle was the feeding of five thousand men with five loaves and two fishes. The people, having witnessed this miracle, were all so full of reverence for Jesus Christ that they wished to take Him by force and make Him king; but Jesus, perceiving this, fled from them. They found Him again, however, on the following day, and then Jesus took occasion from the impression the miracle had made on them to introduce the subject of the heavenly food which He was about to give to the world. "Amen, I say to you," said Jesus, "ye seek Me, not because ye have seen signs, but because ye have eaten of the loaves and have been filled. Labor not for the food which perisheth, but for that which endureth to life everlasting which the Son of man will give you." (*John* 6:26-27). Here He declares that the food He was to give them would confer eternal life. Their curiosity being excited by these words, they desired to know more about this heavenly food and asked what sign He would give them and whether the food He spoke of was better than the manna from Heaven which God had given their fathers in the desert. Then Jesus said to them: "Amen, amen, I say to you, Moses gave you not the bread from heaven; but *My* Father giveth you the *true* bread from heaven; for the bread of God is that which cometh down from heaven and giveth life to the world." (*John* 6:32-33).

In these words He shows the superiority of *this* bread to the manna of the Old Testament, calling it the "*true* bread from Heaven," and saying that it possesses such wonderful efficacy as to give life to the world. The Jews, hearing of such a wonderful kind of bread, said to Him: "Lord, give us this bread always." (*John* 6:34). Whereupon, He replied: "I am the bread of life; your fathers did eat manna in the desert, and died. This is the bread which cometh down from heaven, that if any man eat of it, he may not die. *I* am the living bread which came down from heaven; if any man eat of *this* bread, he shall live forever; and the bread that I will give is My flesh for the life of the world." (*John* 6:52). "He that eateth My flesh and drinketh My blood, hath life everlasting, and I will raise him up on the last day. For My flesh is meat indeed, and My blood is drink indeed. He that eateth My flesh and drinketh My blood abideth in Me and I in him." (*John* 6:55-57). His disciples hearing this, said: "This saying is hard, and who can hear it." (*John* 6:61). Jesus, knowing that His disciples murmured at this, said to them: "Doth this scandalize you?" (*John* 6:62). Observe, He does not say you are mistaken; you do not understand Me. No, on the contrary, He insists still more on the necessity of eating His Flesh and drinking His Blood: "Amen, amen, I say unto you, unless you eat the *flesh* of the Son of man and drink His blood, you shall not have life in you." "Many of His disciples," continues the Evangelist, "hearing this, went away and walked no more with Him."

Jesus, seeing that they would not believe that He was to give them His Flesh and Blood as food for their souls, suffered them to go away offended, and when they were gone, He said to the Twelve: "Will ye also go away?" Then Simon Peter answered in the name of all: "Lord, to whom shall we go? Thou hast the words of eternal life. And we believe and know that Thou art the Christ, the Son of God." (*John* 6:68-70). Remark the noble simplicity of the Apostles' faith.

They believe the words of their Master without the least hesitation; they receive His words in *that* sense in which the others had refused to receive them; they receive them in their obvious meaning, as a promise that He would give them His *real Flesh* to eat and His *real Blood* to drink; they believe with a full faith, simply because He is "the Christ, the Son of God," too good to deceive, and too wise to be deceived; too faithful to make vain promises, and too powerful to find difficulty in fulfilling them. From this time forward the disciples were constantly expecting that Jesus Christ would fulfill His promise.

At length the long-looked-for day came. At the Last Supper Jesus took bread and blessed and gave to His disciples and said: "Take ye and eat, for this is My body." Then taking the chalice, He gave thanks and gave to them, saying: "Drink ye all of this, for this is *My Blood* of the New Testament which shall be shed for many, for the remission of sins." (*Matt.* 26:28). Now in these words we must consider especially the *Speaker.* It was God Himself. It was the same God who created Heaven and earth out of nothing; who, in the beginning, said: "Let light be made," and in an instant the sun, the moon and the stars appeared in the heavens; the same God who once destroyed the whole world by water, with the exception of eight persons; who destroyed Sodom and Gomorrha by fire from Heaven; who, by His servant Moses, wrought so many miracles in the sight of Pharaoh and conducted the Israelites out of Egypt, making a dry path for them in the midst of the Red Sea. It was the same God, Jesus Christ, who once changed water into wine; who gave sight to the blind, hearing to the deaf, speech to the dumb, and life to the dead; Jesus Christ who ascended into Heaven and who, at the end of the world, will come again with great majesty in the clouds of Heaven, to judge the living and the dead. He it was, the great Almighty God, who took bread into His most sacred hands, blessed and gave to His disciples, saying: *"Take ye and eat: For this is My Body."* And no sooner had He said: *"This is My Body,"* than the bread was really changed into His Body. *He* it was who, in the same manner, took the chalice, blessed and gave to the disciples, saying: "Drink ye all of it, for this is My Blood." And no sooner had He said, "This is My Blood," than the wine was really changed into His Blood.

When God speaks, what He commands is done in an instant. As He made the sun, the moon and the stars merely by saying: "Let light be made," so also at the Last Supper, by His word alone, He instantaneously changed bread into His Body and wine into His Blood. To those who doubt this, we may apply the reproof which St. Jane Frances de Chantal once gave to a Calvinist nobleman who was disputing with her father about the Real Presence. She was at that time only five years of age, but hearing the dispute, she advanced to the heretic and said: "What, Sir! You do not believe that Jesus Christ is really present in the Holy Eucharist, and yet He has told us that He is *present*. You then make Him a liar. If you dared attack the honor of the king, my father would defend it at the risk of his life, and even at the cost of yours; what have you then to expect from God for calling His Son a liar?" The Calvinist was greatly surprised at the child's zeal, and endeavored to appease his young adversary with presents; but, full of love for her holy faith, she took his gifts and threw them into the fire, saying: "Thus shall all those burn in Hell who do not believe the words of Jesus Christ."

St. Paul warmly exhorts the Corinthians to flee all communication with idolatry and to abstain from things offered to idols, and he uses the following argument to persuade them: "The chalice of blessing which we bless, is it not the communion of the Blood of *Christ?* And the bread which we break, is it not the communion of the Body of the Lord?" (*1 Cor.* 10:16).

Here he expressly says that in the Holy Eucharist we communicate and partake of the Body and Blood of Jesus Christ. And still further on he says, in the same epistle to the Corinthians: "Whosoever shall eat this bread, or drink the chalice of the Lord unworthily, shall be guilty of the Body and Blood of the Lord." Nay, he goes farther and says: "He that eateth and drinketh unworthily, eateth and drinketh damnation to himself, not discerning the Body of the Lord." (*1 Cor.* 11:29).

How could the Apostle declare that anyone who received Holy Communion unworthily would eat and drink eternal damnation, if such a one did not really receive Our Lord? Would it not be absurd to say that a man would incur eternal damnation by merely eating a piece of bread or drinking a few drops of wine? But because the Apostle, taught by Jesus Christ Himself, knew that he who receives Holy Communion receives Our Lord Himself, he declared that to receive it unworthily was to be guilty of the Body and Blood of Jesus Christ and consequently to deserve Hell-fire.

Moreover, all the Fathers of the Church teach the same doctrine as St. Paul. St. Ignatius, Bishop of Smyrna, who lived in the first century, wrote as follows to the faithful of that city: "Because the heretics refuse to acknowledge that the Holy Eucharist contains the same flesh which suffered for our sins and was raised again to life by God the Father, they die a miserable death and perish without hope."

Tertullian says: "Our flesh is nourished with the Body and Blood of Jesus Christ so that our souls are filled with God Himself." "Who," asks St. John Chrysostom, "will give us of His flesh that we may be filled?" (*Job* 31:31). This Christ has done, allowing Himself not only to be seen, but to be touched too, and to be eaten, so that our teeth pierce His

Flesh, and all are filled with His love.

Parents often give their children to others to nurse them: not so do I, says Christ—I nourish you with My Flesh and place Myself before you. I was willing to become your brother; for your sake I took Flesh and Blood; and *again I deliver to you that Flesh and Blood* by which I became so nearly related to you." (*Homil.* 46). In like manner do all the Fathers of the Church speak that have written upon this subject.

But you will ask: "*How* is Our Lord present in the Holy Eucharist?" I answer: "Jesus Christ is truly, really and substantially contained under the outward appearance of bread and wine, i.e., He is present whole and entire, His Body and soul, His Flesh and His Blood, His whole humanity and His whole divinity. This is clear from what Our Lord said at the institution of this holy mystery: "This is My Body," that is to say, this which I hold in My hand is the same body of Flesh with which you see Me clothed, the same Body that I have borne for thirty-three years, the very Body that shall be tomorrow nailed to the Cross.

Moreover, as in Him the human nature was inseparably united to the divine, He Himself—His whole humanity and divinity—was contained under that outward appearance of bread. "How is this possible?" you ask. I answer: "By the Almighty power of God." Is it not as easy for Him to change bread into His Body and wine into His Blood as it was for Him to create Heaven and earth out of nothing? It happened once in the Netherlands that two ladies, a Catholic and a Protestant, were disputing on the subject of the Real Presence. The Protestant asserted that the Real Presence was impossible. The Catholic asked her: "Have you Protestants any creed in your religion?" "Oh, to be sure," said the Protestant; and she began to recite: "I believe in God the Father Almighty, Creator of heaven and earth." "Stop," said the other; "that is enough. You say that you believe in an all-powerful God; why then do you not believe that He can change bread into His Body and wine into His Blood? Is that difficult for Him who is Almighty?" The Protestant had nothing to answer.

A similar argument was once made use of by a pious painter named Leonardo. He one day met in an inn two men, one of whom was a Lutheran and the other a Calvinist. They were ridiculing the Catholic doctrine about the Blessed Sacrament. The Calvinist pretended that by these words, "This is My Body," it was only meant that the bread *signifies* the Body of Christ; the Lutheran, on the other hand, asserted that this was not true, but that they meant that bread and wine, in the moment of their reception, became, by the faith of the recipient, the Body and Blood of Christ. While this dispute was going on, Leonardo took a piece of paper and drew the image of Our Lord Jesus Christ, with Luther on the right hand and Calvin on the left. Under the image of our Saviour, he wrote the words: "This is My Body." Under the figure of Calvin he wrote: "This *signifies* My Body"; and under that of Luther: "This becomes My Body in the moment that you eat it." Then handing the paper to the two disputants, he said: "Which of these three is right, our Saviour, or Calvin, or Luther?" They were struck at the force of the argument, and ceased to scoff at the Catholic doctrine.

Indeed, this objection to the Real Presence is but a proof of the blindness into which men fall when they are led astray by pride and instigated by the devil. The devil has had from the beginning a special hatred for this doctrine. In the early ages of the Church, he incited Simon the Magician and the Manichaeans to deny it, and in later times, he seduced Berengarius to follow their example; but he never succceded so well as with Luther, Calvin, Zwingli and the other heresiarchs of the sixteenth century.

Luther acknowledges himself that the devil once appeared to him in a visible shape and told him to abolish the Sacrifice of the Mass and to deny the Real Presence of Our Lord in the Blessed Sacrament. And indeed, this is not strange. The devil knows that, according to the promise of Jesus Christ, they who receive Holy Communion worthily will not fall into his power but will obtain eternal life, and on this account he either tempts men to disbelieve the mystery, or he suggests every sort of pretext to keep them from receiving it. But he himself believes it and trembles. Would to God that all men had so strong a faith! After Our Lord had changed bread into His Body and wine into His Blood, He added the words: "Do this in remembrance of Me."

Now, by these words, He commanded the Apostles and their lawful successors, the Catholic bishops and priests, to consecrate, i.e., to change bread and wine into His Body and Blood. "Do this," He says—that is to say, "do this which I have done; as I have changed bread and wine into My Body and Blood, so do you also in My name change bread and wine into My Body and Blood."

This change takes place in the Sacrifice of the Mass at the Consecration. The moment the priest pronounces the words of the Consecration over the bread and wine, that very instant Jesus Christ is present as truly as He is in Heaven, with His Body and Soul, His humanity and divinity. After Consecration nothing remains of the bread and wine, except the sensible qualities or appearances. If, for instance, the bread is round, its roundness remains after the Consecration; if it is white, its whiteness remains; if it has a certain taste or quality before, that taste or quality continues; and so with the wine; the particular taste, color and every other sensible quality is just the same after the Consecration as it was before it. In a word, whatever is capable of being perceived by the senses remains, but the *substance*, which is perceived by the understanding alone, and not by the senses, is changed.

But you will perhaps ask: "Why does Our Lord hide Himself under the outward appearances of bread and wine? Why does He not manifest Himself under the sensible qualities of His Body, with His wounded hands, His merciful countenance, His radiant majesty?" Now, Our Lord does so chiefly for two reasons: The first is that we may not lose the merit of faith. Were we to see Jesus Christ as He is seen by the blessed in Heaven, we could no longer make an act of faith in His Real Presence, for "faith is the belief in things which we do not see." (St. Paul).

Now Our Lord wishes to bestow on us after this life a great reward for our faith, as He Himself has said: "Blessed are they that do not see and yet believe." Many of the Saints, in order not to lose the merit of their faith, have gone so far as to beg Our Lord not to favor them with those consoling manifestations of Himself in the Blessed Sacrament which He has sometimes granted to His chosen servants. One day, when St. Louis, King of France, was invited to go to a church in which Our Lord appeared in the Holy Eucharist under the form of an infant, he replied: "I will not go to see my Lord in the Holy Eucharist because I *believe* that He is present there as firmly as if I had seen Him. Let those go and see Him who do not believe."

Surius relates, in the life of St. Hugo, that a priest of a certain village in England, on breaking the Sacred Host one day at Mass, saw blood issuing from it; whereupon, filled with reverential awe, he determined to lead a holier life in the future, and in fact he soon became renowned for his sanctity. St. Hugo happening once to stop at this village, the priest related this miracle to him and offered to show him the cloths which were yet stained with the miraculous blood; but the holy bishop refused to look at them and would not even allow his attendants to do so, saying that such wonders and sensible proofs were only for those who did not believe. And when he noticed that some of his attendants had a desire to see them, he reprimanded them sharply and said that this desire proceeded not from piety but from curiosity and that it was more perfect to believe without seeing, as Our Lord Himself assures us. "Blessed are they that have not seen and yet believe." (*John* 20:29).

The second reason why Our Lord hides Himself is that He might inspire us with confidence. If He were to show Himself in all His glory, as He appears to the Angels and Saints in Heaven, who would dare to approach Him? Surely no one. But Jesus most earnestly desires to unite Himself intimately to our souls, and therefore He conceals Himself under the outward form of bread, that we may not be afraid of Him. "Our great King," says St. Teresa, "veils Himself that we may receive Him with greater confidence."

In order to enliven our faith in His Real Presence, Our Lord has frequently manifested Himself in a sensible manner in the Holy Eucharist. Church history abounds in instances of the kind. The first that I shall relate is that of a miracle which occurred in the church of St. Denis in Douay and is recorded by Thomas Cantipratensis, an eye-witness. A certain priest, after having distributed Holy Communion to the faithful, found one of the Sacred Hosts lying on the floor. Full of consternation he knelt down to take it up, when the Host arose of its own accord and placed itself on the purifier. The priest immediately called those who were present, and when they came near the altar, they all saw in the Sacred Host Jesus Christ under the form of a child of exquisite beauty. "On hearing the news," says our author, "I too went to Douay. After I had declared to the dean the object of my visit, we went together to the church, and no sooner had he opened the ciborium wherein the miraculous Host was contained than we both beheld our Divine Saviour." "I saw," says Thomas, "the head of Jesus Christ, like that of a full grown man. It was crowned with thorns. Two drops of blood trickled down His forehead and fell on His cheek. With tearful eyes I fell prostrate before Him. When I arose again, I no longer saw either the crown of thorns or the drops of blood, but only the face of a man whose aspect inspired great veneration." This miracle gave rise to a confraternity in honor of the

Most Holy Eucharist, to which several popes, especially Paul IV and Clement XIV, granted numerous indulgences. (P. Favre, *Le Ciel Ouvert*).

In the village of *Les Ulmes de St. Florent*, in the diocese of Angers, the following miracle occurred on the second of June, 1666, the Saturday within the octave of the feast of Corpus Christi. The people were assembled in the church for Benediction, and when the priest had intoned the hymn, *"Verbum Caro, panem verum,"* there appeared in place of the Host the distinct figure of a man. He was clothed in white, and His hands were crossed on His breast; His hair fell upon His shoulders, and His countenance was resplendent with majesty. The curate then invited all his parishioners to come and witness the miracle: "If there be any infidel here," said he, "let him now draw near." Everyone approached and gazed upon this beautiful vision for about a quarter of an hour, after which the Host resumed its former shape. The Bishop of Angers, Mgr. Henry Arnaud, after having examined the testimony in favor of this miracle, caused it to be proclaimed throughout the whole of France.

The Blessed Nicholas Fattori, a Franciscan friar, remarkable for his piety and purity of heart, often saw Jesus Christ in the Consecrated Host in the form of an infant. On touching the Blessed Sacrament, he seemed to feel, not the mere Eucharistic species, but the very Flesh of Jesus Christ. On this account, he used to present his fingers to those who wished to kiss his hand, saying: "Kiss these fingers with great respect, for they are sanctified by real contact with Jesus Christ Our Lord and Sovereign Good." It is also related that, when this holy man was in the presence of the Blessed Sacrament, he used to rejoice as a child does in the presence of its mother.

Our Lord in His great mercy has even gone so far as to manifest Himself to His enemies, to the unbelievers.

In the life of St. Gregory the Great, written by Paul the deacon, it is related that a noble matron of Rome, who was accustomed to prepare the hosts for the Holy Sacrifice of the Mass, went one Sunday to receive Holy Communion from the Holy Pontiff. When he gave her the Blessed Eucharist, saying, "May the body of Our Lord Jesus Christ preserve thy soul unto life everlasting," she laughed outright. Seeing this, the Sovereign Pontiff did not give her the Blessed Sacrament, but replaced it on the altar, and when the holy mysteries were ended, he asked the lady why she laughed when about to receive the Body of the Lord. "Why," said she, "I laughed because I saw that what you said was the Body of the Lord was one of those very wafers which I had made with my own hands." Upon this the Pope ordered all present to pray that God, in confirmation of the truth, would cause all to see with the eyes of the body what the unbelief of this woman had prevented her from seeing with the eyes of the soul. Accordingly, when the holy Pontiff and all present had prayed for a while, the corporal was removed, and in sight of the multitude who pressed round to witness the miracle, the Holy Host was visibly changed into flesh. Then, turning to the woman, the Pope said: Learn now to believe the words of the *Eternal Truth* who declares: "The bread which I give is My Flesh, and My Blood is drink indeed." And having besought God once more to change the Host into its original form, he gave her the Holy Communion. This woman never again doubted of the Real Presence and soon made great progress in virtue.

I shall adduce only one more instance, which is related by St. Alphonsus in his History of Heresies. It occurred about the time in which Wickliffe began to deny the Catholic doctrine of the Real Presence. Some Jews procured a Sacred Host through a servant girl whom they had bribed to receive it unworthily. They then carried it to an inn where they cut it into several pieces. Immediately a great quantity of blood issued from each of the particles, but this miracle did not convert those unhappy wretches. They now concealed the particles in a meadow near the city of Posen. Some time afterwards, a cow-herd, on crossing this meadow, saw the small particles of the Host rising into the air and shining like fiery flames; he saw, moreover, that the oxen fell on their knees as if in adoration. The cow-herd, who was a Catholic, told his father what he had seen, and the father, having also witnessed the miracle, acquainted the magistrate of the fact. Thereupon a great concourse of people flocked to the place to witness the miracle. In fine, the Bishop, with the clergy of the city, went in procession to the place, and having deposited the holy particles in a ciborium, they carried them to the church. A small chapel was built on the spot where this miracle occurred. This chapel was afterwards enlarged and converted into a magnificent church by Wenceslaus, King of Poland; and Stephen, the Archbishop, testifies to his having seen in this church these bloody particles.

You might be inclined to infer from this narrative that Our Lord's Body is really broken and His Blood really shed whenever the Host is cut or divided, but this is not the case. In the Blessed Sacrament Our Lord's body remains whole and entire in each particle, as it was in the entire Host. The Fathers of the Church explain this by the comparison of a broken mirror, for just as each part of the mirror reflects the entire image which the whole reflected before it was broken, so also does each particle of the Host contain Christ's Body entire, as the whole Host did before it was broken. And what is true of the Host is true also of the chalice; Our Lord is present under each drop of Blood as truly as under the whole species in the chalice.

Whenever, therefore, the Host is broken or the Blood spilt, it is not Our Lord's Body and Blood that are broken and divided, but only the sacred species. Moreover, Our Lord's Blood, as well as His Body, is present under the form of bread, and His Body, as well as His Blood, is present under the appearance of wine. At His Resurrection, Our Lord's soul was reunited to His Body and Blood, never again to be separated; so that where His Body is, there also is His Blood, His Soul, and His Divinity; and where His Blood is, there also are His Body, Soul and Divinity. In a word, Christ is entirely present under the species of bread, as well as in the least particle of it, and He is also entirely present under the species of wine, as well as in the least particle of it. On this account, the Church, moved by several weighty reasons, communicates the faithful under the form of bread only, knowing that they are thereby deprived of no part of the Sacrament, but that they receive the Blood of Jesus Christ as truly as if they drank it out of the chalice.

That Our Lord's Blood is contained along with His Body in the Sacred Host is proved, not only by the authority of the Church and the Scriptures, and by the arguments from reason which I have just stated, but also by numerous miracles. Some of those which I have already related prove this doctrine. I will, therefore, add but one more.

It is related in the chronicles of the Hieronimites that a religious of that order, named Peter of Cavanelas, was much tempted by doubts about the presence of Blood in the Sacred Host. It pleased God to deliver him from the temptation in the following manner: One Saturday, as he was saying Mass in honor of our Blessed Lady, a thick cloud descended upon the altar and enveloped it completely. When the cloud had disappeared, he looked for the Host he had consecrated, but could not find it. The chalice, too, was empty. Full of fear, he prayed to God to assist him in this perplexity; whereupon, he beheld the Host upon a paten in the air. He noticed that Blood was flowing from it into the chalice. The Blood continued to flow until the chalice was as full as it had been before. After his death, this miracle was found recorded in his own handwriting. At the time it happened, nothing was known about it, as Our Lord enjoined secrecy upon him. Even the person who served his Mass knew nothing about it; he only noticed that the priest shed many tears, and that the Mass lasted longer than usual.

Ah, how mysterious, yet how divine and how consoling is the doctrine of the Real Presence! Indeed, it is one of the most wonderful and most consoling of all doctrines. It is the center of Catholic devotion and has ever been the object of the most rapturous contemplation of the saints. But I have not yet mentioned a fact which, I believe, will increase your appreciation of this mystery. It is, in some respects, more wonderful than any I have yet mentioned, and with it I will conclude my instruction.

There have been many holy persons who have had a supernatural instinct by which they were sensible of the presence of Jesus Christ in the Blessed Sacrament, even when it was hidden and at a distance from them; they could also distinguish a consecrated Host from an unconsecrated one. Goerres, in his celebrated work entitled *Christian Mysticism*, notices this fact and thus prefaces the enumeration of the few cases which he cites: "In reference to the holiest of all things, the Sacrament of the Eucharist, we find that those Saints who have succeeded in raising themselves to the higher regions of spiritual life were all endowed with the faculty of detecting the presence of the Blessed Sacrament, even when it was hidden and at a considerable distance. Blessed Ida of Louvain was always sensible of the presence of Our Lord at the precise moment of Consecration. Once, when the server at Mass had by mistake given the priest water instead of wine, so that there was no consecration, St. Coleta, though kneeling at a distance, perceived it by a supernatural instinct.

The Cistercian nun Juliana always knew when the Blessed Sacrament was moved from St. Martin's Church at the close of the service, and each time she used to be overwhelmed with sadness. This was frequently witnessed by her friend Eva. *(Ibid.)* One day the Franciscans of Villonda invited the holy Carmelite Cassetus to visit them, and in order to try him, they took the Blessed Sacrament out of the tabernacle in which it was usually kept and placed it elsewhere. They put no light before it, but left the lamp burning as usual before the customary altar. On entering the church, the companion of Cassetus turned towards the high altar, but Cassetus immediately pointed out the spot where the Blessed Sacrament had been placed, saying: "The body of Our Lord is there and not where the lamp is burning; the brothers whom you see behind the grating have placed it there in order to try us." *(Ibid.)*

St. Francis Borgia had the same gift, and on entering a church, he always walked straight to the spot where the Blessed Sacrament was kept, even when no external sign indicated its presence. In 1839, Prince Licknowsky visited Mary Moerl, the celebrated Tyrolese virgin upon whom God bestowed so many miraculous gifts. While she was kneeling in ecstasy on her bed, he observed that she moved round towards the window. Neither he nor any of those present could tell the cause of this. At last, on looking out, they saw a priest passing by, carrying the Viaticum to the sick, without bell or chant or any sound that could give notice of its approach. *(Catholic Magazine)*.

In the life of St. Lidwina of Holland, it is recorded that the priest, in order to try her, gave her an unconsecrated host, but the Saint perceived that it was only bread and said: "Your Reverence will please give me another host, for that which you hold in your hand is not Jesus Christ."

Blessed Margaret of the Blessed Sacrament, a Carmelite nun who lived in France, was one day suffering great pain. Her sisters, wishing to ascertain whether she would really find relief in the presence of the Blessed Sacrament, to which she had a singular devotion, carried her at first to various places in which the Holy Eucharist was *not* kept and exhorted her to pray to Jesus Christ; but she answered in a plaintive voice: "I do not find my Saviour here," and addressing herself to Him, she said: "My Lord, I do not find here Thy Divine Truth," after which she besought her sisters to carry her into the presence of the Blessed Sacrament. (Her life by P. Poesl, C.S.S.R.).

When St. Louis, King of France, was on his death-bed, he was asked by the priest who brought him the Viaticum whether he really believed that Jesus Christ, the Son of God, was present in the Host. The Saint, collecting all his strength, answered with a loud voice: "I believe it as firmly as if I saw Him present in the Host, just as the Apostles saw Him when He ascended gloriously into Heaven." Now, if you would have such faith as this great Saint, make use of the following means: First, make many acts of faith in the Real Presence of Jesus Christ in the Blessed Sacrament. Make them at home; kneel down in your room; turn toward some church in which the Blessed Sacrament is kept and say: "My Jesus, I firmly believe that Thou art present in that church; I sincerely wish to be with Thee; but since this is impossible, I beseech Thee to give Thy blessing to me and to all men."

Make such acts of faith when you are abroad or when you are at your work; turn from time to time towards the Blessed Sacrament and say: "My amiable Saviour, bless me and everything that I do; I will do and suffer everything for love of Thee." Make such acts of faith on your way to church. Say to yourself: "I am going to visit the King of Heaven and earth; I am going to see my good Jesus, my amiable Saviour, who died on the Cross for me, a wretched sinner; I am going to visit the best of fathers, who even considers it a favor when I have recourse to Him in my necessities."

Finally, excite your faith when you are in church. Kneel with profound reverence and adore your God and Creator, saying: "My God, I firmly believe that Thou art in this tabernacle. I believe that in the Blessed Sacrament the same God is present who created Heaven and earth out of nothing; the same God who became an infant for my sake; who, after His death and Resurrection, ascended into Heaven, and now sits at the right hand of God the Father Almighty; the same who, at the end of the world, will come in great majesty to judge the living and the dead."

This, then, is the first rule—to make many acts of faith. The second is to keep yourself free from sin; for God will not bestow the gift of a lively faith on a soul that is dead in sin. The third and most efficacious means to gain a strong faith in the Real Presence of Jesus Christ in the Blessed Sacrament is to pray for it. "He that asketh receiveth." Hence, if you wish to have a lively faith in this mystery, a faith that will make you exult when in the presence of the Holy Eucharist, or even when you think of it, ask it of Jesus Christ, and be assured that you will receive it. But since this lively faith is a gift of inestimable value, Jesus Christ wishes that we should ask for it again and again without ceasing. Pray for it therefore until you have obtained it, and when you have obtained this great gift, continue to pray that it may never be taken from you. Make this prayer especially during Mass. Hear Mass frequently and, especially in the time between the Consecration and the Communion, beseech Jesus Christ to grant your petition, and doubt not in the least that you will obtain it.

A young cleric once heard a missionary preach on the Real Presence, and on the great love of Jesus Christ in the Blessed Sacrament. The preacher spoke with as lively a faith as if he saw Jesus Christ with his eyes. The young man was struck at this, and said to himself: "Oh my Lord! What shall become of me? I, too, must one day preach on Thy presence in the Holy Eucharist; but how feeble will my words be in comparison with the words of this pious priest!" The young man related this afterwards, and he added that, from that time forward, he had always begged of Jesus Christ the gift of a lively faith in the Real Presence and that he had done so frequently during Mass, particularly at the time of the elevation. By this means his faith became so strong that he afterwards besought Our Lord *not* to appear to him in any sensible manner, and he could find nowhere so much joy and contentment of heart as in a church where the Blessed Sacrament was preserved.

Often call to mind the wonders which Jesus Christ has wrought in this mystery of love; make many acts of faith in His Real Presence; lead a very chaste life; often beseech Jesus Christ to give you a lively faith, especially when you have received Holy Communion; and then rest assured that your faith will become strong and lively, like the faith of a Saint, and your happiness will be unbounded. In days of yore, God complained that the Jews did not know Him: "The ox knoweth his owner, and the ass his master's crib:

but Israel hath not known Me, and My people hath not understood." And when our Divine Saviour came on earth, He repeated the same reproach. When Philip said to Our Lord at the Last Supper: "Lord, show us the Father, and it is enough for us," our Saviour reproached him, saying: "Have I been so long with you and you have not known Me? Philip, he that seeth Me, seeth the Father also."

In the same manner does our dear Saviour, hidden under the Sacramental veils, seem to reproach us: "I, your God and Redeemer, have been so long with you in the Blessed Sacrament, and yet you do not know Me? Do you not know that when you see the Blessed Sacrament, you see Me, your Jesus? Do you not know that, when you are in the presence of the Blessed Sacrament, you are in *My* Divine Presence?" Alas, this reproach is but too just! How true are the words of the Evangelist: "He was in the world, and the world was made by Him, and the world knew Him not. He came unto His own, and His own received Him not." May you, my dear reader, never deserve this reproach, but rather, may you be of the number of those of whom the same Evangelist says: "But as many as received Him (that is, with a lively faith), to them He hath given power to be made the sons of God." May you live on earth as a child of God, and after death may you be received into the kingdom of your heavenly Father, where, in reward for your faith, you will see, face to face, Him whom you have adored in the Blessed Sacrament and will hear from His lips the consoling words: "Come, My well-beloved, blessed art thou, because though thou hast not seen, thou hast yet believed."

CHAPTER 2

On the Reverence Due to
Jesus Christ in the Blessed Sacrament

A YOUNG Portuguese traveled to India to seek his fortune. In a few years he returned to Europe, accompanied by several of his own vessels, laden with wealth, the fruits of his toil and researches. Having arrived at his native place, "Stay," said he to himself, "I must play a little deception on my relations." He put on soiled garments and a torn cloak and hastened to the house of his cousin Peter. In this disguise he claimed relationship: "I am your cousin John," said he. "I have passed several years in India; I now return to visit my friends and native land once more. You see my position, and thus by ties of kindred, I crave hospitality at your hands." "Ah! Would to Heaven I could accommodate you, my dear John," replied Peter. "Excuse me, my house is wholly occupied." John, playing his role, proceeds to another friend's house; makes the same advance, realizes the same reply; and thus to a third and fourth.

His poverty-stricken appearance had thus driven him from door to door. Ah, poor deluded friends, little did you imagine that, under that tattered garment, a man of wealth lay concealed! John hastened back to his ships, cast aside his beggar's dress, robed himself in costly attire, and followed by a multitude of servants, proceeded at once to purchase a princely dwelling in the very heart of the city. His fabulous wealth, his lordly retinue, his high-blooded steeds were the talk of the town and neighborhood. The news soon reached the ears of his friends. Picture to yourselves, if you can, their wondrous amazement! How changed would their conduct now be if the opportunity could but present itself anew! Listen to the altered tone of their language: "What is the meaning of all this?" said one to the other. "Could you have supposed this for a moment? Had I but known this before, my friend would have met with very different treatment at my hands; but alas, it is now too late! We have repulsed him forever."

The foregoing story serves as an illustration of what takes place between Christians and their Lord. This man went to his friends as a beggar, attired in poor, tattered garments, disguising thus his affluence and power. In the Holy Sacrifice of the Mass, does not our Blessed Lord act in the same manner? Does He, whilst silently remaining enclosed in our Tabernacles, by day and by night, display His heavenly glory and brightness? No. But He there remains, as it were, in a poor, miserable dress, under the humble appearance of bread.

This stranger came to his friends a second time in rich and royal attire, escorted by numerous attendants. Jesus Christ will come again, at the end of the world, enthroned on the clouds of heaven, in great power and majesty. Myriads of Angels and blessed spirits will surround Him on every side, for wealth, glory and power are His. To whom can we compare those unkind friends of our narrative? Unfortunately, to a very great number of Christians of the present day. How is that, you will perhaps ask me? Because, as they paid little or no attention to their relative in his poverty, so in the same manner, a great many Christians pay little or no reverence to Jesus Christ, when humbly concealed in the Sacrament of His love. After this conduct of Christians, let us not be astonished if we hear of infidels or heretics treating Our Lord with irreverence in the Holy Eucharist.

Once a Jewess pushed her temerity and hardihood so far as to receive Holy Communion with the Christians. Her audacity was immediately detected, although when she had received the Sacred Host, she bowed down most profoundly, covering her face with her hands as though wrapped in the purest devotion. Well, you will say, "How did she betray herself?" Those who were near her noticed that she was keeping the Sacred Host in her mouth and treating it with irreverence. She acted thus in order to ridicule and dishonor Jesus Christ, the God of the Christians. The observers of this conduct concluded that she must be either a sorceress or, as was really the case, an unbelieving Jewess.

In what does her conduct differ from that of many people of our day? Do we not see men who hardly bow their head, much less bend the knee when passing before that Most August Sacrament? Women enter the church who, by their dress and thoughtlessness, cannot claim any high prerogative in the modesty of their sex. Men even grant full liberty to their wanton gaze, heedless of the penetrating eye of their God, who fills that temple and whose sight has already pierced their souls. When, at processions intended to honor the Blessed Sacrament, I see such behavior, I must conclude that this is the result of the most complete indifference towards Jesus Christ or a total forgetfulness of His Presence. What then? Shall I call these persons Jews? Shall I call them sorcerers? No. But I think I shall not be far astray in saying that they have not a lively faith. They may be Catholics, if you will, but certainly, their faith is not practical. They do not *realize* that Jesus Christ is present in the tabernacle and in the monstrance. They are deceived by their senses.

In the monstrance, or in the hands of the priest at Mass, they see nothing but the white host, and their thoughts penetrate no further. But if they only reflected on what their faith teaches, *viz.,* that under that little host Jesus Christ conceals His heavenly splendor and glory, how different would be their deportment! How different their thoughts and feelings! Would you know how they would act if their faith were real and lively? Go to the palace of a king. Mark the silent expectation in that splendid apartment! What mean those movements so circumspect? That tread so noiseless? That voice so subdued? Ah, 'tis the royal antechamber! There a loud word is an impertinence; there unbecoming attire is a crime. But hark! Even that stealthy conversation is hushed; every eye is turned to one point; each one assumes the most respectful attitude; the curtain is drawn; and the obsequious courtiers stand in the presence of their King. What an unpardonable breach of decorum would it not be for anyone to remain sitting at a moment like this! Yes, to talk, to laugh or to remain with head covered!

Now, if such honor is paid to earthly princes, what reverence is not then due to Him Who is "King of kings and Lord of lords?" St. John Chrysostom is indignant with us for even making the comparison, and it is with reason. For what is an emperor when compared to the King of Heaven and earth? He is less than the blade of grass when compared to the whole universe.

Whenever the Blessed Sacrament is exposed in the tabernacle, borne in procession or carried as Viaticum to the sick; whenever the Sacred Host is raised at the Consecration in the Mass, our infallible faith says to us: *Ecce Rex vester!* "Behold your King!" Behold your Redeemer, your Judge, your Creator, your God!

If then in the presence of the Most Holy Sacrament I feel no devotion interiorly and show no modesty exteriorly, what will you think of me? You will say with truth and justice that: "That man does not believe that his God is present there"; or again, "That man's faith is cold and dead."

Who could believe that Jesus Christ is present in this Sacrament and fail in reverence towards it? What reverence did not the Jews pay to the Ark of the Covenant! No one dared to approach it, yet fifty thousand persons who, through curiosity, ventured to gaze thereat, were instantly struck dead as a punishment for their rash act! Yet, what did the Ark contain? Only the Ten Commandments of God.

But in the Holy Eucharist, faith tells us that God Himself is present, He who made all things out of nothing and could destroy them in a moment. He who at the last day will come on the clouds of Heaven to judge the living and the dead.

Only let Catholics believe this with a lively faith, and our churches will be filled with worshippers, whose deportment will correspond to their belief. The modest attire, the guarded eye, the bended knee, the meekly folded hands will bespeak the conviction of their hearts. Only let Catholics have a lively faith in this mystery, and Jesus Christ will seldom be left alone. At all hours, His children will come to present themselves before Him, as subjects before their prince, as slaves before their master, as sick men before their physician, as children before their father, in a word, as friends before their beloved friend.

Only let a congregation be animated with a lively faith in this doctrine of our holy religion, and each mind will be filled with amazement, the spirit will be recollected, the soul moved to contrition, the affections inflamed, the eye melted to tears of tenderness and the voice broken with sighs like those of the poor publican: *"O God, be merciful to me, a sinner!"* Or like unto that of St. Peter, *"Depart from me, O Lord, for I am a sinful man!"* Thus reverence is nothing more than a lively faith. The reality of the Divine Presence in the Blessed Sacrament is the true rule of our deportment before it. The Catholic has within himself the rule of decorum. He needs nothing else to teach him what is proper or improper in church, besides the dogma which assures him that he is in the presence of his God. If then he be but a little recollected, he will be, almost necessarily, respectful.

This then is the great means of preserving a reverent deportment, to remember Who He is that is enclosed in the tabernacle and *what* we are, *viz.:* that our Divine Saviour is in our midst and that we are His creatures and subjects come to worship Him. But although our faith is sufficient to teach us how we ought to behave before Our Lord, yet because it is sometimes difficult to keep in mind the truths of faith and because examples are always more powerful than a bare precept, I will set before you some striking examples, which may serve to impress upon your mind the duty of reverence towards the Blessed Sacrament.

First, I will propose the example of the Angels. St. Basil and St. John Chrysostom testify to having seen at the time of Mass, or when the Blessed Sacrament was exposed, many hosts of Angels in human form, clothed with white garments and standing round the altar as soldiers stand before their king. But what was their attitude and deportment? Their heads were bowed, their faces covered, their hands crossed, and the whole body so profoundly inclined as to express the deepest sense of their own unworthiness to appear before the Divine Majesty. Oh, would we but think of this! The Angels, those pure spirits, shrink before the Infinite Holiness of God, and we allow vain, worldly and even sinful thoughts to insinuate themselves into our minds in His Presence!

The Angels tremble before His Greatness, and we fear not to talk and laugh in His Presence! The Angels, those princes of Heaven, are all humility and modesty, and we, the dust of the earth and miserable sinners, all impertinence and pride! The Angels veil their faces before His splendor, and we do not even so much as cast down our eyes, but rudely stare and gaze around! The Angels bow down to the earth, and we will not bend our knee! The Angels, full of awe, fold their hands upon their breasts, and we allow ourselves every freedom of attitude and movement!! Oh, what a subject of confusion! What humiliating reflections! What an impressive lesson!

Secondly, I will take you from the princes of Heaven to the princes of the earth, and teach you a lesson from the example of kings and nobles. There are many beautiful examples on record of the homage which kings and emperors have paid to the Saviour of mankind, so humbly hidden in the Blessed Sacrament. Philip II, King of Spain, always dispensed with regal pomp and pageantry when he assisted at processions of the Blessed Sacrament, and as an ordinary personage, mingled with the common throng. Inclemency of weather deterred him not from paying this tribute of honor to his Lord. One day, as he was devoutly accompanying the Blessed Sacrament with uncovered head, a page held his hat over him, to shield him from the burning sun. "Never mind," said Philip, "the sun will do me no harm; at such a time as this we must regard neither rain nor wind, heat nor cold."

On another occasion, whilst the Blessed Sacrament was being carried a great distance to a sick person, Philip accompanied it all the way on foot. The priest, observing this, asked him if he were not tired. "Tired!" replied he, "Behold, my servants wait upon me both by day and by night, and never yet have I heard one of them complain of being tired! Shall I, then, complain of fatigue when I am waiting upon my Lord and my God, Whom I can never sufficiently serve and honor!"

Rudolph, Count of Hapsburg, whilst hunting one day, observed a priest carrying the Viaticum to the sick, whereupon he immediately alighted, and insisted on the priest mounting in his place. The offer was accepted. The priest, having gone through his sacred and pastoral duty, returned the animal, with many marks of gratitude, to the Count. But this noble and Christian Count could not be prevailed upon to accept it. "No," said he, "keep it, for I am not worthy to ride upon a horse which has borne my Lord." (Heiss's *History of Austria*).

Whilst the Lutheran heresy was spreading its ravages throughout Germany, Charles V, of Spain, hastened to Augsburg to assist at the diet convened there to stem the pernicious influence of this heresy. The feast of Corpus Christi fell at that time. It was celebrated with every possible pomp and magnificence; the Emperor Charles assisted thereat with the most edifying devotion. At the procession, the Prince Bishop of Mayence carried the Most Adorable Sacrament, being supported on the right by Ferdinand, the Roman King, on the left by Joachim, Elector of Brandenburg. The canopy was borne by six princes, namely, Louis, Duke of Bavaria; the son of the Elector of Brandenburg; George, Duke of Pomerania; Philip, Count Palatine of Werdelburg; Henry, Duke of Brunswick; and the Duke of Mecklenburg. When these six princes had carried it as far as the Chapel on Mount Berlach, six others took it and carried it to a place called the Holy Cross, whence six others bore it to the Cathedral. The Emperor Charles, torch in hand, on foot and with uncovered head, accompanied by several Archbishops, Bishops and many persons of high rank, followed the procession during the whole route.

Such noble traits of devotion are not confined to days gone by; in our own times, we see princes who have inherited from their fathers this true devotion to the Most Holy Sacrament. Of the present

Emperor of Austria it is related that, one day as he was riding through the streets of Vienna, at the signal announcing that the Blessed Sacrament was being carried to the sick, he immediately stopped his carriage, alighted, and on bended knees, there devoutly adored his Lord and God. The same is said of that excellent princess, the late queen of Belgium.

Now, these instances of reverence are not mentioned as being great in regard to the Blessed Sacrament. Before Him who dwells concealed under that veil, princes are as nothing. Why then should we be astonished at this? Why look on this tribute of devotion as something extraordinary? 'Tis true, these princes are as nothing before Our Lord, but they are great and mighty when confronted with us and may well serve to remind us of the obligation which Faith imposes upon us. If then those whose position bespeaks honor and ease cheerfully submit to humiliation, inconvenience and pain at the call of Religion, what ought we not to do? We cannot boast of high position to make us proud, luxury to make us effeminate or gentle care to make us tender. On the contrary, our position bows us to humility; our necessity and poverty bend us to labor; our life accustoms us to forgo our ease. This being the case, while we honor the great ones of the earth, shall we refuse to join with them in worshiping Him who is the source of all greatness, and who is above all?

We have seen that reverence towards the Blessed Sacrament is enjoined upon us by faith and reason, and preached to us by Heaven and earth. I will add then but one more reflection: It is urged upon us by the teaching of our Holy Mother the Church.

To what tend all her beautiful ceremonial, her

minute ritual and her costly ornaments, but to inspire or express reverence for her Divine Spouse? Why is the priest who celebrates Mass and the faithful who are communicated required to be fasting, but on account of the greatness of the Guest they are about to receive? The incense, the lights, the flowers, the vestments of the priests, the numerous attendants, the genuflexions, are not all these to honor Him who has so greatly humbled Himself for the love of us? And not content with her daily homage, she has appointed a festival in the year for the express purpose of repairing the injuries which Jesus Christ has received from men, either at the time of His visible sojourn on earth or since the establishment of His Religion.

What is the procession of Corpus Christi but a reversal of the judgment which an unbelieving world passed upon Our Lord and a compensation for the outrages which it has inflicted on Him? As He was once in the most ignominious manner led as a malefactor through the streets of Jerusalem, from Annas to Caiphas, from Caiphas to Pilate, from Pilate to Herod, from one tribunal to another, so is He, on this day, borne in triumph through the streets, as the Spotless Lamb of God and man's Highest Good.

As His sufferings had no other witnesses than envious and mocking Jews, so now on this day, every knee bends in adoration before Him. As the executioners once led Him forth to death, so in this procession, the great ones of the world mingle with the throng to do Him reverence. As then His ears resounded with the most scornful and outrageous blasphemies, so now on this great festival, the

Church greets Him with every kind of musical instrument and song of praise. The crown of thorns which once pierced His brow is now exchanged for the wreath of flowers around the monstrance, while civil magistrates with their insignia and troops of heroes with glittering arms and waving banners replace the fierce Roman soldiers who once kept watch around His dark and silent tomb. The Cross which Jesus bore with sorrow and sweat up the rugged hill of Calvary is on this His day of triumph carried before all as the sign of victory. Jesus Himself, who was lifted up upon it, is now in the Blessed Sacrament raised aloft to impart His Benediction to His kneeling and adoring people.

If such be the spirit of the Church, what should be the practice of her children? Are we Catholics? Where then is our faith?

It is Jesus our Saviour who remains enclosed in the tabernacle, and who is lifted on high in the monstrance. It is the true Eternal God whom we receive in Communion. We must show by our works that we believe this. I do not say that we are bound, as the early Christians, to prostrate ourselves to the earth and press our foreheads in the dust. I do not say that we are bound to imitate St. Vincent de Paul and bend the knee when it costs us the most excruciating pain to do so.

Nevertheless, we are bound at least to avoid offending our Divine Lord and dishonoring Him to His face. We are bound, when about to receive Holy Communion, carefully to prepare ourselves by a good Confession and thus avoid the dreadful peril of receiving Him in a state of mortal sin. We are bound to lay aside all unbecoming attire and scandalous behavior, especially in the House of God, and to be modest, reverent and humble in attitude and deportment. We ought to regard all our members as in some way consecrated by Jesus Christ, whom we so often receive, or at least whom we visit in the Church. It is not fitting that the feet which have borne us to the altar of God should carry us into evil company; that those eyes which, in the morning at Mass, have looked upon the Immaculate Victim, should through the day look at that which is unclean; that the tongue which has been the throne of God should utter blasphemous, impure or calumnious words; that the heart which has been united to the Infinite Purity and Beauty should be polluted by the stain of sin. But alas, how often such indecencies are perpetrated!

When one thinks of the offenses which Jesus Christ receives in this Sacrament, of the sacrilegious Communions which those make who receive in mortal sin, or in the proximate occasion of sin, of the neglect of so many to receive Holy Communion for a long time, and the insufficient preparation they do make when they receive, all this is enough to make the true Christian shudder with horror. Yes, we are inclined to believe [that] as of old God repented that He had made man because his heart was bent on wickedness, so now Our Lord must surely repent of having instituted this Sacrament and must even wish to take away from His priests the power which He gave them of consecrating His Body and Blood.

But no, such a thought does an injustice to His love. Jesus Christ will never withdraw the power which He confided to His Church of changing bread and wine into His Most Adorable Body and Blood.

He will continue to suffer patiently and silently till the End of Time for the sake of those faithful souls who give Him pleasure by the devotion and love with which they receive or visit Him. Let us seek to be of that number. *Accedamus cum vero corde in plenitudine fidei.* "Let us approach Him with an upright heart and a lively faith."

One day He will throw off His disguise and appear in His heavenly might and splendor. Oh, how happy will they be then who have kept Him company in His humiliation! They will not be confounded, but will "stand before Him with great constancy." They will "see His face" and rejoice forevermore.

CHAPTER 3

On the Love of Jesus Christ in the Blessed Sacrament

ONE DAY two men who were disputing about the possession of a piece of land came to the Emperor Otho that he might decide on the affair in question; each of them said: "The land belongs to me." And what do you think the Emperor did, when he found himself unable to settle the dispute? He gave to the one, out of his own purse, as much money as the piece of land was worth, and to the other the land itself, and thus satisfied both.

A similar, but far more wonderful act of liberality took place at Jerusalem eighteen centuries ago [now nineteen]. This happened in the following manner: Our Divine Redeemer having lived on this earth more than thirty years and the time having come for Him to leave it, there arose, as it were, a dispute between Heaven and earth. The Angels wished to have their Lord and their God with them in Heaven again, after He had been for so long a time with men on earth. Men, on the other hand, especially the Apostles, desired to detain their Divine Master, Jesus Christ, with them on earth. They felt very sad when He told them that the time had come for Him to leave them. Now, how did our sweet Lord act in order to settle this dispute? He found out a means to satisfy both men and Angels. He satisfied the Angels by ascending to Heaven; He satisfied men by remaining invisibly with them in the Blessed Sacrament and by giving power to the Apostles and their lawful successors to change bread into His Body and wine into His Blood.

What could have induced Our Dear Lord, Christian soul, to stay with us on earth in the Blessed Sacrament? Was it to gain honor? Alas, Our Good Lord receives the same treatment in the Blessed Eucharist which He received during the thirty-three years that He lived upon earth! When upon earth, He was made light of, and it was said of Him: "Is He not the son of a carpenter?" "Why do you listen to Him?" said the Pharisees. "Do you not see that He has a devil, that He is possessed, that He is a wine-drinker and a friend of sinners?" They bound Him, scourged Him, crowned Him with thorns, and at last making Him carry His own Cross, they crucified Him. Such was the honor which Jesus Christ received when living among men! And has He not been treated in the same manner in His Sacrament, from that time to the present day? Instead of being honored by all men, as He deserves, He is dishonored and insulted. Some do not think of Him for weeks together; others walk carelessly into the church, almost like men without faith, and make their genuflexion before Him as if they wished to mock Him; others behave in church as if they were in their own houses. In many churches there is not even a lamp kept burning; and how often has it happened that the consecrated Hosts have been trodden under foot or thrown into the fire by heretics, Jews and other bad men?

Such has been the treatment He has met with—

contempt, mockery and insult, or coldness and indifference towards His Divine Majesty! Certainly the expectation of being honored could not have induced Him to remain with us! What then induced Him to stay with us in the Holy Eucharist? Was it to seek or to increase His own happiness? By no means. His happiness is so great that it cannot be increased. He has risen from the dead; He is glorified; He sits at the right hand of God the Father and has all power in Heaven and on earth. The Angels serve Him; men are His subjects, whom He will judge and reward according to their deserts; the devils tremble at His presence; every knee must bend before Him, of those that are in Heaven, on earth and under the earth, in Purgatory and in Hell. What then is wanting to His happiness? Nothing! Since, therefore, Our Lord cannot become happier by remaining with us and since He does not receive due honor among us, what, I ask once more, could have induced Him to abide here so long, to remain on earth for eighteen hundred years, yea, even until the end of the world, to be present in the Blessed Sacrament in every place, in every parish church in America, Europe, Africa, Asia, Australia, in the isles of the sea, and even sometimes in the midst of the ocean itself? Ah, Christian soul, there was no other motive than love, the great, the excessive love of Jesus Christ towards men!

Yes, it was love, love alone, nothing but love, which induced Jesus, our Redeemer, to remain among us in the Blessed Sacrament. O Jesus, O most sweet Jesus, hidden under the sacramental species, give me now such love and humility, that I may be able lovingly to speak of this invention of boundless love, that all who hear of it, may begin to love Thee in reality.

O Mary, Mother of Jesus Christ, and our dear Mother; O all ye holy Angels, who, by your adoration in our churches, make up for the little love which your God and our Saviour receives from men, obtain for us the grace to comprehend a little the love of Jesus Christ in the most Holy Sacrament.

In order to conceive in some measure the love of Jesus Christ in this wonderful Sacrament, let us consider first *the time* at which He gave Himself to us as our food and drink. Jesus might have instituted this Sacrament when, in the twelfth year of His age, He traveled to Jerusalem, or at the wedding in Cana, or when He was thirty years old and began to teach publicly, or He might have instituted it after His Resurrection. But He chose, for the time of its institution, the last moment of His earthly career.

Why did He wait so long? Why did He not institute it sooner or later? Why not after His Resurrection? Why just at the moment when He was about to take leave of the Apostles and quit the earth? He instituted this Sacrament at the last moment of His life in order that men might the better see the excess of His love. Do you ask how this is? To make it clearer, imagine a father who has in store costly presents of gold and jewels which he intends to give to his children in order to show them how much he loves them. What time do you think this father will choose for bestowing these gifts as being best calculated to make a deep impression on them? He will wait until he is on his deathbed, and then he will give them, that they may be the last memorials of his love.

Behold, our Divine Saviour thought and acted in the very same manner. He thought, I have already given men so many proofs of My love towards them: I have created them; I preserve their lives; I have become man—for their sake I became a child; I have lived among them for more than thirty years; I am yet to suffer and die for them on the cross and to re-open Heaven for them; what can I do more for them? Ah! I can make them one more present; I will give them a most precious gift; I will give them all that I have, so that they may not be able to charge Me with having done less for them than I might have done. I will give them Myself as a legacy; I will give them My Divinity and My Humanity, My Body and My Soul, Myself, entirely and without reserve. I will make them this present at the last moment of My life, at a time when men are accustomed to bequeath to those whom they love that which they value the most.

At the very moment when they are seeking to betray Me, at the very moment when the Pharisees and Jews are planning to remove Me out of the world, I will give Myself to men on earth to be their food and drink, to abide with them in the Blessed Sacrament in a wonderful manner, to be always in their midst, by dwelling in their churches. Instead of withdrawing My love from them on account of their ingratitude, I will manifest it to them the more.

Wonderful manner! Who could ever have imagined that God would go so far in His love for ungrateful men as to give them His own Flesh and Blood as the food of their souls? What man or Angel would ever have conceived such a thing? And supposing it had occurred to some man or Angel to wish that God might do so, who would have dared to express such a wish or to ask such a thing of God? Would not the thought have been immediately banished from the mind as sacrilegious? Now, what the Angels could never have conceived nor men dared to ask, the immense love of God has given us unasked.

Hence Our Lord was right indeed to say to His Disciples when they became sad on account of His having told them of His approaching departure from them: "Let not your hearts be troubled; I will not leave you orphans." A good mother on her deathbed says to her weeping children: "Dear children, I must now die and leave you. I recommend you to God and to the protection of your Blessed Mother Mary. Avoid sin and act always as good children, that I may be so happy as to see you again in the other world."

But Jesus does not speak thus to His Apostles. He says: "You need not be sad because I am about to leave the world. I will remain always with you in My most Holy Sacrament. I will give you a power than which there is no greater in Heaven or on earth, that of changing bread into My Body and wine into My Blood. In virtue of this power, you can always have Me with you. You need only pronounce the words of Consecration over the bread and wine, and in that very moment I will be with you and you will hold Me in your hands. O Love! O Love of God toward us! O Jesus, Thou lovest us too much! Thou couldst not endure that we should be left alone in this world; and that even death might not be able to separate Thee from us, Thou didst leave Thyself to us as our food in the Blessed Sacrament.

Secondly, in order that we may see the love of

Jesus in the Holy Eucharist still more clearly, let us consider with a lively faith *whom* we have in our midst. Dear Christian, consider [that] if Jesus Christ had left a Saint or an Angel with us in His stead after His death, or if He had given us His own Mother to remain with us and keep us company, would it not have been a very great proof of His love towards us? But He has left neither Saint nor Angel, not even His own Mother, for it was too little for His love. He Himself would be ever with us.

Yes, indeed, the good God, the holy and merciful God is among us—the Almighty God who created us and the whole world out of nothing and who still continues to preserve us. That same God is in our tabernacles who saved Noah from the deluge; who gave manna from Heaven to the Jews; who, amid lightning and thunder, gave the Ten Commandments to Moses on Mount Sinai; who, at Babylon, delivered the three youths from the flames of the burning furnace; who saved the life of Daniel in the den of lions.

That same Jesus is with us in our churches who at His birth was laid on straw and adored by the Magi, who fled into Egypt, who was sought for by the Blessed Virgin and found in the Temple, who changed water into wine, who restored sight to the blind, made the deaf to hear and the dumb to speak. Beloved Christian, you esteem Simeon happy in having been permitted to take the Infant Jesus in his arms; and were you to receive a grace like him, no doubt you would exclaim: "Now dost Thou dismiss Thy servant, O Lord, according to Thy word, in peace: because my eyes have seen Thy salvation."

You consider Zacheus happy because Our Lord

vouchsafed to enter his house and eat with him; you deem St. John happy because he rested on the breast of our Saviour at the Last Supper; and, above all, you regard St. Joseph and the Blessed Virgin Mary so very happy because they nourished and supported Our Dear Lord. But are you not as happy as they? Are you not even happier? You do not hold Our Lord in your arms as Simeon did, but you receive Him into your heart in Holy Communion; you do not rest on the bosom of Our Lord like St. John, but the Saviour Himself rests in your heart after Holy Communion; you do not nurse and support Our Lord like St. Joseph and the Blessed Virgin, but you have a still greater happiness, for the Saviour Himself nourishes you and gives Himself to you as your food. O Love! O Love! O who can understand the love of God for men!

What would you say if a shepherd suffered himself to be slain in order to save his sheep? What would you say if, in those times of horrible famine which history here and there records, when the cravings of hunger silenced the voice of nature and men fed on each other's flesh, a king had loved a beggar so much, or a lord his servant, as to give himself as food in order to save the poor sufferer from starvation? Do you think that any shepherd or king or lord could really be found who would act thus? Certainly not. Again, a mother's love is proverbial, and mothers are often found who love their offspring so much that they will deprive themselves of a morsel of their scanty bread to give it to their hungry children, and yet it has sometimes happened that even mothers have devoured their own infants in time of famine.

Now, while no shepherd loves his sheep so much as to give his own life for them; while no king ever loved a beggar so much as to suffer, for his sake, the loss of life or limb; while even a mother can grow cruel towards the fruit of her womb, Jesus, our God and our King, has loved us so much as to give Himself to us whole and entire. His Flesh and Blood, His Humanity and Divinity really and substantially.

"I am the good Shepherd," says Jesus; "a good shepherd gives his life for his sheep." He seems to say to us: "I give My life for you, each day, at each Holy Mass, at each Holy Communion. I am the God of Supreme Wisdom, but I cannot find a more adequate pledge of My love. I am Almighty, but My omnipotence is not able to do anything greater; I am love itself, but I cannot give you anything more consoling!" It is so, sweet Lord, I acknowledge Thy infinite love, and full of amazement at Thy immense charity, I find no better words to express my wonder than those of Thy saints: "Lord, Thou hast become foolish from love towards us." (St. Mary Magdalene de Pazzi). "He has given Heaven; He has given earth; He has given His Kingdom; He has given Himself—what more has He to give? O my God! (Allow me to say it) How prodigal art Thou of Thyself!" (St. Augustine).

Thirdly, an especial mark of the love of Jesus Christ in the Blessed Sacrament towards us is the *manner* in which He gives Himself to us. He is with us, but under strange forms. Now, someone may say: "Would not the love of Jesus Christ have seemed greater if He had remained with us visibly, so that we might have seen Him and conversed with Him as one friend does with another?" No, dear Christian, it would not have seemed so great. Just because He conceals Himself from our eyes, He gives a new proof of His love and shows that He thinks of us all, of sinners as well as of the just.

"How so?" you ask. I will tell you how. First, then, with regard to sinners, Jesus renders them a great favor by concealing Himself. You know that the best remedy for weak eyes is to exclude the light. We cannot look at a very bright object without our eyes being dazzled. None of us could look steadily at the sun at noon; if we should do so, we would become blind. We read in Holy Scripture that Moses once conversed with God on a mountain and that afterwards, when he came down to the Jews, his countenance was so radiant with light that they were unable to look upon him, and he was obliged to put a veil over his face when he spoke to them.

Suppose now, beloved Christian, that Jesus Christ were to manifest Himself on our altars in His heavenly splendor and glory, and one yet at enmity with God should come into the church; how would he feel? Would he not be overwhelmed with awe and terror? Yea, a mortal agony would seize the poor wretch at the sight of Jesus Christ. When Adam and Eve had sinned, they heard the voice of the Lord, who was walking about in Paradise, and they hid themselves from the Lord in the midst of the garden. The mere sight of an offended God was insupportable to them. Cain, too, acted in the same manner after having killed his brother. "And Cain fled from the face of the Lord." Oh, it is terrible for man to appear before God with a conscience laden with sin!

If in our day Jesus Christ were to show Himself openly, sinners would flee from the church in order to avoid the angry countenance of their Judge. If one conscious of sin should dare to remain and brave the displeasure of his offended Lord, his heart would die within him before the angry glance of those eyes which are "as a flame of fire." One single indignant look that Philip II, king of Spain, cast upon two of his courtiers, who behaved irreverently in church, was enough to drive one of them out of his senses and to kill the other. How then could a sinner endure the eye of Jesus Christ?

We may judge, in some measure, from what took place when the Bethsamites looked upon the Ark of the Covenant with irreverent curiosity. More than fifty thousand were instantly punished with death for having gazed at the Ark of the Covenant of the Lord in which the Ten Commandments of God were preserved. "And the men of Bethsames said: 'Who can stand before the face of the Lord, of that Holy God?'" Who then does not see that it is a great grace and benefit for us and all sinners that Jesus Christ should veil Himself from our view under the appearances of bread and wine? Oh, how considerate and amiable is the heart of Jesus Christ! He does not wish openly to meet with one who is His sworn enemy and who, on that account, deserves nothing else but His wrath and vengeance. He works one of His greatest miracles and draws near to him without being seen. He keeps Himself hidden under the poor veil of bread that the sinner may not tremble and fear before His majesty and brightness, but may approach Him with confidence to ask the pardon of his sins and grace not to relapse into them again.

But not only to sinners does Jesus Christ show special love by concealing Himself in the Blessed Sacrament, but also to the just. These, indeed, would not, like sinners, be conscience-stricken at the sight of Jesus Christ in the Holy Eucharist, but they would nevertheless be almost *beside* themselves with amazement, and instead of entertaining a confident and childlike love and affection for Him, they would feel an excessive and oppressive fear of Him. As soon as the Queen of Saba saw Solomon sitting on his throne in all his regal splendor, she became breathless and fainted away. This was natural. That which is too splendid repels rather than attracts, and while an ordinary brightness pleases the eye, an intense, excessive brightness dazzles and blinds it.

Oh, what would happen if the Son of God were to appear on the altar in His Divine Majesty, surrounded with heavenly light and glory? What eye could behold His brightness? For if even the few rays of light which our Divine Saviour suffered to beam from His face on Mount Thabor caused His disciples—intimate and familiar as they were with Him—to fall to the ground in amazement and dismay, who could bear in its full intensity the glory of His countenance as it appears to the eternal but insatiable gaze of the Elect and which forms the heaven of Heaven itself? Ah, in the glorious presence of Christ, even the just would be awe-stricken! Nay, they would perhaps die from distress and fear.

At all events, they would not dare to approach their Divine Saviour with love and affection. No one would venture to draw near to Him in order to converse with Him and to explain to Him his wants. The unfathomable mystery of the Blessed Sacrament would no longer be *amor amorum* (i.e., "love of all loves," as St. Bernard calls it); it could no longer be called a pledge of love between God and man; but it would be a Sacrament of Glory and Majesty before which we should be obliged to bend the knee, not in love and confidence, but in fear and trembling. But no, our Divine Saviour, who loves us so excessively, would in this Sacrament deal in all kindness with just and pious souls and would treat with them, not as a God of Majesty with His subjects, but as a good father with his beloved children, as a brother with his brothers, a friend with his confidential friend, a bridegroom with his bride.

Comedite, amici, et bibite et inebriamini, carissimi, says He to us. ("Eat, my friends, and drink and be inebriated, my well-beloved!") *Venite ad me omnes, qui laboratis et onerati estis, et ego reficiam vos*. ("Come to Me, all ye that labor and are heavy laden, and I will refresh you." *Matt.* 11:28). *Venite omnes,* "come ye all," without exception; come ye poor and suffering; come ye rich and prosperous; come ye despised; come ye honored ones of the earth; come ye servants and slaves; come ye princes and masters; come ye husbands and wives; come ye parents and children; come ye young men and young women; come ye great and small; come all, without any exception; come ye My beloved children whom I have redeemed; expose to Me your wants and your troubles! *Ego reficiam vos,* "I will refresh you," I will console you. *Venite,* "come," then, come without fear! I am waiting for you at all hours.

Consider it well, dear Christian, in order that we may approach Him with childlike confidence; the most amiable and sweet heart of Jesus Christ invented this wonderful Sacrament, manifesting His love by concealing His Majesty and keeping Himself hidden under the appearance of bread, as under a veil, which He suffers no single beam of His Divinity to pierce, lest He might so awe us as to prevent our confidential intercourse with Him. "It is on account of our weakness," says Hugo of St. Victor, "that He does not show Himself in the brightness of His Majesty." He acts towards us as a prince or a king who, having put aside his garments of state, appears in the company of his subjects without the emblems of his rank, not expecting from them the exact observance of court etiquette or demonstrations of so great respect, but intending, on the contrary, to make merry and rejoice with them in all confidence and familiarity.

O good Lord, O great God, how humbly dost Thou hide Thyself for our sake! But alas, how much is Thy bounty and love abused! Not only do sinners despise Thee in this Thy Sacrament of love, because they see Thee not, but the good also, the just, treat Thee with indifference and coldness. Thou hast been so long with them, and they with Thee, and for want of a lively faith, they have not known Thee. So long hast Thou been with us, and there are so few who know it, so few who are penetrated with a sense of their unspeakable happiness. I hear Thee complain of us, O dear Jesus, as Thou didst one day complain to the Blessed Margaret Alacoque [St. Margaret Mary], when showing to her Thy heart crowned with thorns: "Behold this heart of Mine so full of love for men that it has shed its last drop of blood for them and has given them My own Flesh and Blood as food and drink for their souls, and consider how this heart receives from most men in return for so great a love nothing but ingratitude and contempt!

But what grieves Me most is that I am thus treated even by good and just souls.''

Do you not understand, dear Christian, the just complaint of your Divine Saviour? Is your heart not touched by it? ''Behold,'' says He, ''behold this heart which loves men so excessively, this heart which is always pouring out graces upon them, this heart so full of pity to receive sinners, to help the poor and indigent, to cure the sick, to console the afflicted, to hear the prayers of all men, at what time soever they come to ask—this heart is not known; it is despised and (what is the most piercing grief) even by those souls into which I have so often entered in Holy Communion.''

Ah, dear Christian, have you a heart? Well, if it be not of stone or iron, let it be touched by this touching complaint of the heart of Jesus Christ in the Blessed Sacrament. Give to your God and Saviour what is due to Him. Repay Him for the benefit of your creation; repay Him for the benefit of your redemption; for the benefit of the preservation of your life; for the pains of His scourging; for the agony of His crucifixion; but, above all, repay Him, yes, in some measure, repay Him for the excessive love and affection which He bears you in the Blessed Sacrament. ''But how,'' you will ask; ''how shall I pay my Jesus for His love to me? What can I give Him in return?'' Nothing but *love*. Love demands love and is contented only with love. But it must be *true love*, that is, such love as animates you to keep His Commandments and to avoid sin; such love as impels you to receive Him often in Holy Communion and still oftener to visit Him in the church. Ask of Him then so to detach your heart from all creatures that you may live only for Him, who came down from Heaven to live and die for you. So doing, you may expect with all confidence that in your last hour your dear and amiable Saviour, whom, having not seen, you have loved, will come to meet you, calling you to Him by these sweet and consoling words: "Come, thou good and faithful servant, come; because thou hast been faithful in little things, I will place thee over many." "Come and see what thine eye has never seen; come and hear what thine ear has never heard; come and enjoy what on earth thy heart has never conceived; come, enter into the joy of thy Lord forever and ever."

CHAPTER 4

On Visiting Jesus Christ In the Blessed Sacrament

"WHERE is the new-born King of the Jews?" inquired the three Magi of Herod, king of Jerusalem. "Where is He?" they repeat in their great desire to find Him. "We have seen His star in the East, and we have come to adore Him. Ah, tell us where He is; we desire so much to see Him; we have made so long a journey in order to become acquainted with Him!" What a joy must it not have been for these three holy kings to learn that the Saviour of the world was born in Bethlehem; with what speed must they not have gone thither to find out their true King, who had caused the wonderful star to appear which led them to His abode.

Beloved Christians, you have heard and read this incident among the many wonderful events in the life of our God and Saviour. On hearing or reading the account, you have perhaps even earnestly desired to have lived at the time of the Apostles in order that you might have had the happiness of seeing your Lord and Saviour. But you ought to know that you are happier now than if you had lived at the time of the Apostles, for you might have been obliged to travel very far and make many inquiries to find out the place of His abode. But now there is no need of traveling far or of making many inquiries to find

Him. He is, as we know by faith, in our churches, not far from our homes. The Magi could find Him in one place only; we can find Him in every part of the world, wherever the Blessed Sacrament is kept. Are we then not happier than those who lived at the time of our Saviour Himself? Yes, we are happier than they; no faithful soul can doubt it. But can we say also that we know how to avail ourselves of this happiness?

Alas! How many are there perhaps who must confess that up to this day they have never visited Jesus Christ in the Blessed Sacrament, resembling Jutta, the niece of the Empress, St. Cunegunda, of whom it is related that she stayed at home, without any plausible reason, while the Blessed Sacrament was exposed in the church. St. Cunegunda, inflamed with holy indignation at this indifference, gave her niece a severe slap in the face. The Lord, in punishment of Jutta's indifference toward Him, allowed the print of Cunegunda's fingers to remain indelibly stamped on her face. This was a life-long monitor for her. Such a monitor, however, is not given to everyone to remind him of his duty towards Jesus Christ in the Blessed Sacrament; I will therefore set forth some reasons which ought to induce every faithful soul to show for the future more fervor, gratitude and love for her Divine Saviour by often visiting Him in this mystery of love, and by asking of Him graces, not only for herself, but especially for all those who are cold and indifferent towards the excessive love and patience of their God hidden under the sacramental species.

If there be one consideration which, more than all others, ought to induce you often to visit Jesus

Christ in the church, it is the thought of the excessive love which He bears to us in this adorable mystery of His love. "It is my delight to be with the children of men," says our Divine Saviour in Holy Writ. Oh, what great condescension it would be for a king to invite a poor man to come to his palace and to keep company with him! But Jesus Christ, the King of Heaven and earth, says: "Come all ye that labor and are burdened, and I will refresh you." (*Matt.* 11:28).

Ought we not to look upon it as a great grace and favor to be invited into His presence? Surely, we ought to find our delight in His company since He is delighted to be in ours. We ought to go to Him frequently and say to Him: "My Jesus, why dost Thou love me so much? What good dost Thou see in me that Thou art so enamored of me? Hast Thou already forgotten the sins by which I have offended Thee so grievously? Oh, how can I love anything else than Thee, my Jesus and my All? No one has ever done so much to make me happy as Thou hast done, O amiable, O most amiable Jesus! Never let me love anything but Thee."

If you had a friend who always wished you well and who had promised to help you in all your wants and who would even take great pleasure in the opportunity of bestowing a benefit upon you, you would undoubtedly be acting ungratefully if you did not have recourse to him in your necessities. But where, I ask, can you find a better, a more faithful, or a more liberal friend than Jesus Christ in the Blessed Sacrament—one who more sincerely wishes you well, one who consults more your advantage and happiness, one who grants your petitions with greater readiness and pleasure? Ought you not, then, to feel drawn to go after your King and best Friend in order to show your gratitude to Him?

What would you say if a rich man should come and take up his abode in the neighborhood of a poor beggar for no other purpose than to make it more easy for the poor man to receive from him relief in all his necessities? What would you say of such a lord? "Oh!" you would exclaim, "how good, how exceedingly good he is! He deserves to be honored, esteemed, praised and loved by all men. How happy is the poor man who has such a lord for his friend!" But while in fact none of the rich of this world has ever gone so far in love to the poor, Jesus Christ, the King of Heaven and earth, has gone so far in His love for us poor sinners; He takes up His abode in our churches for the convenience of each one of us. Oh how happy we are! Would to God that each of us availed himself of this happiness by frequently visiting Jesus Christ in the Blessed Sacrament. Thus at least the Saints have ever shown their gratitude.

St. Mary Magdalene de Pazzi, as we read in her life, visited Jesus Christ in the Blessed Sacrament thirty times a day. The Countess of Feria, a fervent disciple of the venerable Father Avila and afterwards a nun of the Order of Poor Clares, was called the Spouse of the Blessed Sacrament, from her fervent and lengthened visits to it. Being once asked what she did during the many hours which she spent before its Sacred Presence, she replied: "I could remain there for all eternity! Is there not there the very essence of God, which is the food of the blessed? Good God! They ask what we do before Thee? What is there that we do not do? We love, we praise, we give thanks, we entreat. What does a beggar do in the presence of a rich man? What does the sick man do when he sees his physician? Or one who is thirsty at a running spring? Or a starving man at a plentiful table?''

St. Elizabeth of Hungary was accustomed, even in her childhood, often to visit Jesus Christ in the Blessed Sacrament. If she found the church closed, she would affectionately kiss the lock of the door and the walls of the church for love of Jesus Christ in the Most Holy Eucharist.

St. Alphonsus, being unable on account of his advanced age to walk to the church, had himself carried thither in a chair in order to pay his accustomed visit to his beloved Saviour.

Father Louis la Nusa, a great missionary of Sicily, was, even when a young student in the world, so much attached to Jesus Christ that it seemed as if he could hardly tear himself from the presence of his beloved Lord on account of the great delight he found there, and being commanded by his director not to remain before the Blessed Sacrament longer than an hour at a time, when that period had elapsed, it was as great a violence to him to separate from the bosom of Jesus as for an infant to tear itself from its mother's breast. The writer of his life says that when he was forced to leave the church, he would stand looking at the altar and turning again and again as if he could not take leave of his Lord, whose presence was so sweet and so consoling.

Father Salesio, of the Society of Jesus, felt consolation in even speaking of the Blessed Sacrament. He never could visit it often enough. When summoned to the gate, when returning to his room, or passing from one part of the house to another, he made use of all these opportunities to repeat his visits to his beloved Lord, so that it was remarked that scarcely an hour of the day elapsed without his visiting Him. Thus at length he merited the grace of martyrdom at the hands of heretics while defending the Real Presence in the Most Holy Sacrament.

Oh, how do these examples of the Saints confound us, who have so little love for Jesus Christ and are so negligent in visiting Him! But someone may say, "I have too much to do; I am busy; I cannot find time." Dear Christian, do not say, "I have too much to do," but say, "I have too much love and affection for the goods of this world and too little love for Jesus Christ." You find time to eat and to drink; you find time to rest and to sleep; you find time to talk and to laugh; time to amuse yourself; time for all your temporal affairs; time even to sin. And how is it that you find time for all these things? It is because you like them.

If you appear but seldom before Jesus Christ in the Blessed Sacrament, it is an evident sign that you love Him but little. Love Him a little more, and you will find time to visit Him. Do not say, "I am busy." The Saints, too, were very busy, perhaps more so than you are, and yet they found time enough to visit their Lord. Do you imagine that you have more to think of than St. Wenceslaus, King of Poland, or St. Louis, King of France? And yet because they tenderly loved Jesus Christ their King, they found time every day to pay a visit to Him. Be sure, if you do not visit Jesus Christ at all, or if you visit Him but seldom, your love and affection for Him are not great. I repeat then once more: Love your Lord and God in the Blessed Sacrament a little more, and I am sure you will be found oftener before the altar.

Again, do not say, "I have too much to do." It is for this very reason that you should feel obliged to visit your Saviour. For the laboring and heavy laden are invited by Jesus Christ to come to Him: "Come to Me all ye that labor and are heavy laden, and I will refresh you." "Instead of being kept away from Me by your numerous toils and labors," He seems to say to you, "you should rather feel drawn to Me, in order to speak to Me about them. Come and tell Me all your troubles, recommend to Me all your affairs, and I will bless them that they may succeed."

The Saints understood this well; they knew and were persuaded that on God's blessing depends everything; they knew that if God did not bless their temporal affairs, they would not succeed, nay, that they would even be injurious and hurtful to their souls. Whenever St. Vincent de Paul had to transact any important business, he would go before the Blessed Sacrament and recommend the affair to Jesus Christ, beseeching Him confidently to give it His blessing, and after having performed it, he went again to the church to thank Jesus Christ for its success. Before the Blessed Sacrament St. Francis Xavier, too, found strength for his toils in India. While his days were passed in saving souls, he passed much of the night in prayer before the Blessed Sacrament.

St. John Francis Regis used to do the same; and if he found the church closed, he would console himself by kneeling at the door, even in the cold and wet, that he might, at least at a distance, pay his homage to his sacramental Consoler. When any affliction befell St. Francis of Assisi, he went immediately to communicate it to Jesus in the Blessed Sacrament. The Blessed Bertha of Oberried in Alsace, being one day asked by one of her sisters in religion how she could discharge so many distracting duties without prejudice to her piety, replied: "Whenever I am entrusted with an office, I go to Jesus Christ in the Blessed Sacrament. He is my Comforter, my Lord and best Counselor, and I do carefully what He inspires me to do. He governs me, and it is by Him that I govern those whom He has confided to me."

Do you, O Christian, understand this language? Do you understand how the blessing of Heaven is to be obtained upon your affairs and undertakings? Oh, were you to visit Jesus Christ in the Blessed Sacrament only for a quarter of an hour each day, from how many trials and hardships would you be delivered; from how many accidents, misfortunes, temptations and attacks of the devil would you be preserved; how few sins would you commit; and how much more consolation and peace of heart would you enjoy!

"How true it is," you would exclaim, "what Jesus Christ has said: 'Seek first the Kingdom of God, and the rest will be added unto you.'" "Ah," you would say, "since I have been in the habit of going to church every day, I labor only half as much as before, and yet I have more success than when I used to labor day and night by the sweat of my brow."

Instead then of spending your time in idle, useless talk, in games and amusements, go to church and pray there for a while, in order to draw down the blessing of Heaven upon you and your whole family.

Rest assured that you will experience what so many holy souls have experienced while before the Blessed Sacrament, namely, that you will feel a thousand times happier in the company of Jesus Christ than in the most delightful company of men. Men can only afford you vain consolations, but Jesus Christ has His hands full of lasting consolations and divine graces, which He is ready to pour out upon your soul, if you present yourself before Him.

One day as Frederic IV, King of Prussia, was passing through the Rhenish Province, a certain cow-herd approached the Royal carriage and commenced playing as artistically as he could on his rude horn. The King, admiring the simplicity and token of honor of the cow-herd, presented him with a piece of money to repay him for the loyalty he had exhibited towards his Sovereign. Now if this earthly prince so readily rewarded this slight act of honor, how much more readily will not Our Lord pour out His graces upon all those who come to honor Him in the Blessed Sacrament, for ever so short a time.

Our Lord manifested this readiness to Blessed Balthasar Alvarez when once kneeling before the altar. He showed Himself in the Sacred Host as a little child with His hands full of precious stones, saying: "If there were only some one to whom I might distribute them." Are you, then, in temporal want? Go to Jesus Christ in the Blessed Sacrament; He can and He will help you. St. Peter of Alcantara one day, seeing his brethren in religion destitute of bread and without the means of procuring it, ordered them to go and pray before the Blessed Sacrament.

No sooner had they done so, than the bell was rung at the door, and the janitor, on opening the door, instead of seeing some person there, as he expected, found a large basket of white bread, which Jesus Christ had sent them, probably by His angels. When the soldiers of the Emperor Frederic II were in the act of scaling the walls of Assisi, in order to sack the city, St. Clare went before the Blessed Sacrament and prayed there in the following manner: "O Lord, shall then Thy servants be delivered up into the hands of the infidels?" "No," said Jesus Christ to her, "I have always protected you and will continue to do so." At the same moment, some of the soldiers took to flight, being struck with an inward terror; others fell down from the walls, while others became suddenly blind.

Maximilian I, Emperor of Austria, having ascended the steep mountains in the neighborhood of Innsbruck to so great a height that he could neither venture to descend again nor could anyone come to his aid, cried out to the people below to bring the Blessed Sacrament as near to him as possible, in order (as in his great peril he was unable to receive It) that he might at least honor It as well as he could by adoring It and recommending himself to Jesus Christ from the rock above. Accordingly, the Blessed Sacrament is carried thither; the Emperor adores It with most profound respect and great devotion and implores Jesus Christ to help him. What happens? No sooner had the Emperor commenced to pray to Jesus in the Blessed Sacrament than he saw a beautiful youth behind him, probably his guardian angel, who led him safely down among the most frightfully steep rocks by a path hitherto unperceived, and when the Emperor was about to reward him, he suddenly disappeared. (Dauroltius, c. 3, tit. 37).

Many similar facts occur in Church history and in the lives of the Saints. Now if Jesus Christ is so ready to help us in our temporal wants, how much more readily will He bestow spiritual graces and favors upon our souls. Whence did St. Thomas Aquinas draw all that knowledge which enabled him to write so learnedly on every subject of our holy religion? Was it not from the fervent prayers which he used to pour out in the presence of the Blessed Sacrament whenever he had a difficulty in understanding or explaining a point? Whence have so many pious souls obtained strength to resist every kind of temptation? Was it not from the frequent visits which they paid to Jesus in the Most Holy Sacrament?

Father Thomas Sanchez, who was in the habit of visiting the church five times a day and eight times on Thursdays, used to exclaim whenever he was tempted: "Jesus in the Blessed Sacrament, help me"; and no sooner had he pronounced these words than his temptation ceased. One day a young man said to a priest of our Congregation: "When the devil assails me with bad thoughts and impure representations and I command him in the Name of Jesus Christ in the Blessed Sacrament to leave me, he instantly withdraws from me."

And again, when God sent forth missionaries to convert sinners, heretics, infidels, whither did they go to obtain their conversion? Certainly to that place where He resides who can change all hearts, how hardened soever they may be. We read in the life of St. Francis de Sales, that nine hundred heretics presented themselves to him to abjure their heresy after he had prayed with the faithful during the Forty Hours' Devotion. A few days after, having prayed with the people most humbly and fervently for the same object, a great many heretics of the suburbs of Focigni came to abjure their heresy. Their example was followed by three hundred more of the parish of Belevaux and three hundred of the parish of St. Sergues. Therefore, one of the best means to convert sinners is to recommend them to Jesus Christ in the Blessed Sacrament.

You have heard and read that there have been Saints who burned so ardently with the fire of divine love that they often trembled in their whole body and that the objects which they touched bore the impress of this fire of divine love. This we read in the lives of St. Philip Neri, St. Catherine of Genoa and St. Wenceslaus, King of Poland. The last loved Jesus in the Blessed Sacrament with so much fervor that, with his own hands, he gathered the wheat and the grapes and made the hosts and the wine which were to be used in the Mass. He often went at night, even in winter, to visit the church in which the Blessed Sacrament was kept. At such times the flames of divine love were burning so ardently in his soul that they communicated to his body a sensible warmth and melted the snow under his feet. He turned this gift on one occasion to a charitable account. His servant who accompanied him by night suffered much from the severity of the cold; whereupon, the holy man ordered him to follow closely and tread in his footsteps. He did so, and no longer felt the coldness of the snow.

Now, where did the Saints obtain this inestimable gift of the love of God? Do you think perhaps in conversation with men? Oh no; it was from conversing frequently with Jesus Christ in the Blessed

Sacrament. The oftener and the longer they conversed with Him, the more they felt their hearts inflamed with divine love. How were so many souls enlightened to see and to know the vanity of this world? How did they find strength and courage to leave all the comforts of their homes, and to lead a holy, mortified, poor and despised life?

Whence this great grace? It was derived from their frequent conversations with Jesus Christ in the Blessed Sacrament. Listen to what St. Alphonsus, Bishop of St. Agatha in Italy, that great lover of the Blessed Sacrament, says about this: "Nowhere have holy souls made more admirable resolutions than here at the feet of their hidden God. Out of gratitude to my Jesus, veiled in this great Sacrament, I must declare that it was through this devotion, visiting Him in His tabernacles, that I withdrew from the world where, to my misfortune, I had lived until the age of twenty-six. Happy will you be if you can separate yourself from it earlier than I did and give yourself wholly to that Lord who has given Himself wholly to you. I repeat it, you will be happy, not only in eternity, but even in this life. Believe me, all else is folly—banquets, plays, parties, amusements— these are enjoyments full of bitterness and remorse; trust one who has tried them and who weeps that he did so."

I assure you that the soul, by remaining with any degree of recollection before the Blessed Sacrament, receives more comfort from Jesus than the world with all its pleasures and pastimes can ever afford. What delight to be before the altar with faith—and with even a little tender love—and to speak familiarly to Jesus, who is there to hear and grant the prayers of those who visit Him, to implore pardon for our sins, to lay our wants before Him as one friend does before another whom he fully trusts, to beg for His grace, His love, His paradise. Above all, what a heaven to make acts of love to this Lord who remains on the altar, praying to His Eternal Father for us and burning with love toward us! In a word, you will find that the time you spend devoutly before this divine Sacrament will be the most useful of your life and that which will most console you in death and for eternity. You will gain more perhaps in a quarter of an hour's prayer before the Blessed Sacrament than in all the other spiritual exercises of the day. God does indeed grant, in every place, the petitions of those who pray to Him; He has promised to do so: "Ask, and it shall be given you." (*Matt.* 7:7). But in the Most Holy Sacrament, Jesus dispenses favors more abundantly to those who visit Him. But of what use are mere words? "Taste and see."

To this little exhortation I can add nothing more consoling, nothing more encouraging or more persuasive. I will but repeat once more His words: "Taste and see." Go often with devotion to visit Jesus in the Blessed Sacrament, and after a while you will experience the truth of what St. Alphonsus has said; nay, perhaps it may even be given to you to feel transports of joy and gladness such as the Saints have experienced in the presence of the Blessed Sacrament and to exclaim in the fullness of consolation with the blessed Gerard (a lay-brother of the Congregation of the Most Holy Redeemer): "Lord, let me go, let me go". . .or with St. Francis Xavier: "It is enough, Lord, it is enough". . .or with St. Aloysius Gonzaga: "Withdraw from me, O Lord, withdraw from me."

But, most assuredly, there is one hour when the remembrance of the visits you have paid to the Blessed Sacrament will give you indescribable pleasure—the hour of your death. And if you never, at any other time, feel remorse for neglecting this great duty, certainly you will feel it when your soul has left the body and you know how near you have been to Jesus Christ on earth. Oh, with what shame and confusion will you not be covered when Jesus will say to you: "I was a stranger and you received Me not." I was so near to you and you visited Me not. You have treated Me as an outcast; you have not conversed with Me nor asked graces of Me; you have left Me alone; you have thought of Me but seldom, or not at all. How confused, I say, will you feel at such a well-deserved reproach! Save yourself this shame and confusion; resolve from henceforth daily to spend some time, say half an hour or a quarter of an hour at least in church in the presence of Jesus Christ in the Most Holy Sacrament.

And at the hour of death He will say to you: "I was indeed a stranger to many lukewarm Christians, but not to you; you came to visit Me; you kept company with Me on earth; you shall, from henceforth, enjoy My Presence in Heaven forever and ever."

CHAPTER 5

On the Great Desire of Jesus Christ to Enter into Our Hearts in Holy Communion

IN a preceding chapter I treated of the great love which Jesus Christ has shown us in the institution of the Holy Eucharist, and because love demands love in return, I went on to prove how this condescension of His places us under the obligation of visiting Him frequently and of paying reverence to Him in this Sacrament of His love. Jesus Christ, however, is not satisfied with the visits and reverence which we pay to Him. He wishes especially that we should receive Him in Holy Communion; this is indeed His chief object in remaining among us under the Sacramental species.

Now, if you ask why it is that Jesus Christ wishes us to receive Him, I answer, it is because He so ardently desires to be united to us. Yes, strange as it may seem, Our Lord's heart yearns to be united to ours. He burns with the desire of being loved by us. Holy Scripture represents Him as standing at the door of our hearts, knocking until we open to Him. This great desire of Jesus Christ, to enter into our hearts in Holy Communion, will be the subject of our present consideration; but I must begin by acknowledging my entire inability to describe it as it really is. That indeed would simply be impossible. No tongue can express the longing of our Saviour to unite Himself to us. I will merely endeavor to point out some of the ways in which He manifests this desire, and I am sure that this effort of mine, as well as your devout attention, dear Reader, will cause great joy to the loving heart of Jesus, whose desire that we should know His love is as great as His love itself. The first proof, then, of Our Lord's great longing to enter into our hearts in Holy Communion is His own declaration.

When He was about to institute the Holy Eucharist, He said to His disciples: "With desire I have desired to eat this Pasch with you," thereby expressing, according to the commentary of St. Lawrence Justinian, His most ardent wish, His most earnest desire to unite Himself to us in Holy Communion. And what He expressed in so touching a manner at the Last Supper He as often declared in other ways.

One day, as St. Gertrude was meditating on the greatness of the love which made the Lord and King of Heaven find His delight in the society of the children of men, our Saviour illustrated what seemed to her so incomprehensible by the following comparison: The son of a king is surely much higher and greater than the children who run about the streets; he has in his father's palace everything that can delight and gratify him; yet, if you give him the choice either to go out and play with the children in the street or to stay at home amid the splendors of his father's court, he will certainly prefer the former.

"Thus, I too," said Our Lord, "find my pleasure in being with you; and having instituted the Blessed Sacrament for this end, anyone who prevents a soul

from receiving Me, deprives Me of a great pleasure."
He also said to St. Matilda: "Look at the bees and
see with what eagerness they seek the honey-flowers,
yet know that My desire to come to you in Holy
Communion is far greater." Nay, He declared to St.
Margaret of Cortona that He would even reward her
Confessor, and that richly, too, for having advised
her to receive Holy Communion frequently; and
Father Antonio Torres, as we read in his life,
appeared shortly after death in great splendor to a
certain person and revealed to him that God had
increased his glory in Heaven in a special manner
for [his] having allowed frequent Communion to his
penitents. Most remarkable is that promise of Jesus
Christ by which He induced the Blessed Prudentiana
Zagnoni (a nun of the order of St. Clare) to receive
the Blessed Sacrament frequently. "If thou wilt
receive Me often in Holy Communion," said He, "I
will forget all thy ingratitude towards Me."

Words and promises of Our Lord like these are
indeed powerful arguments to convince us of His
excessive desire to enter our hearts in Holy Communion, but the extraordinary miracles which He has
performed in order to enable His servants to receive
Him frequently in Holy Communion are still more
powerful arguments. St. Teresa at one period of her
life was afflicted with a severe sickness, attended with
vomiting, which occurred regularly every morning
and evening. What most distressed her was that this
illness prevented her from receiving Holy Communion. In this affliction she had recourse to Our Lord,
and He, whose desire to come into her heart was far
greater than hers to receive Him, was pleased to cure
her. But as if to show for what purpose the relief

was granted, He only delivered her from the attack to which she was subject in the morning, leaving her subject to that which usually came on in the evening.

A similar difficulty prevented St. Juliana Falconieri from receiving Our Lord when her last hour had come. After having thought of every possible means of satisfying her desire for Communion, she at last entreated her confessor to bring the Sacred Host near her, that she might at least humbly kiss It. This being refused her, she begged that It might be laid upon her breast, in order that her heart might feel some refreshment from being near to Jesus; and when the priest, in compliance with her request, spread the corporal on her breast and laid Our Lord upon it, she exclaimed with the greatest delight: "O my sweet Jesus!" As she drew her last breath, the Sacred Host disappeared, and as it was not to be found, the bystanders were sure that our Saviour, in the Blessed Sacrament, had united Himself to her heart, to strengthen her in her passage and accompany her to Heaven.

In the eighth chapter of the life of St. Lawrence Justinian, it is related that there lived in Venice a nun who was prevented from receiving Jesus Christ on the feast of Corpus Christi. Being much grieved thereat, she besought St. Lawrence at least to remember her at Mass. Our Lord could not allow her piety to go unrewarded. Accordingly, while the holy Patriarch was saying Mass in the crowded church, the nun saw him enter her cell with the Blessed Sacrament to give her Holy Communion.

At other times Our Lord has made the miracle still more remarkable by employing the ministry of an Angel or a Saint, instead of a priest, or by dispensing

altogether with a visible agent. The Blessed Gerard
Majella [now St. Gerard Majella], lay-brother of the
Congregation of the Most Holy Redeemer, when he
was but nine years old, approached one day the
communion-rail while the priest was distributing
Holy Communion, impelled by a strong desire to
receive his Saviour; but the priest, seeing his youth,
asked him whether he had made his First Communion, and finding that he had not, sent him away.
But the good heart of Jesus could not suffer the
child to hunger after Him in vain: That very night
Our Lord's Body was brought to him by the Arch-
angel St. Michael.

In like manner St. Stanislaus Kostka was sick in
the house of a Protestant relative; and debarred of
every opportunity of receiving his beloved Lord, he
made his appeal to the Queen of Heaven and
obtained through her intercession the grace to
receive the Blessed Sacrament at the hands of St.
Barbara. One day while St. Bonaventure was assisting at Mass, he felt an ardent desire to receive Holy
Communion, but abstained through fear of not
being sufficiently prepared. Our Lord, however,
could not refrain from gratifying His own desire;
when the priest had broken the Host, the Saint perceived that a small particle of it had come and
rested on his tongue.

I might multiply instances of such miraculous
Communions, but those which I have adduced are
sufficient to show how much Our Lord has done in
order to satisfy His wish to enter into our hearts
in Holy Communion. I will therefore proceed to
point out another way by which He has manifested
this desire, namely, the threats and the promises He

has made in order to induce us to receive the Blessed Sacrament.

When a lawgiver wishes to insure the observance of a law, he promises rewards to those who keep the law and threatens with punishment those who violate it. And the greatness of these rewards and punishments is the measure of the importance which he attaches to the law. Now consider what Our Lord has done to urge us to receive Him frequently in the Blessed Sacrament. Not content with giving us the bare precept, "Take and eat, for this is My Body," He has added thereto the strongest inducements. What more could He do to prevail upon us to receive Him than to promise us Heaven if we do so. "He who eats My Flesh and drinks My Blood," says He, "shall have life everlasting." On the other hand, He threatens us with Hell if we refuse. "Amen, Amen, I say unto you, unless you eat the Flesh of the Son of Man and drink His Blood, you shall not have life in you." Moreover, as He threatens with eternal torments those who never receive Him, or who do not receive Him when the precept of Communion requires it, so He also punishes, though less severely, those who from negligence and indifference refuse to receive Holy Communion as often as their state of life demands.

While St. Mary Magdalen de Pazzi was praying one day before the Blessed Sacrament, she saw one of her deceased sisters in the choir, completely enveloped in a robe of fire and reverently adoring the Blessed Sacrament. By this the Saint was given to understand that the deceased nun was in Purgatory and that in penance she was to wear that mantle of fire and to adore the Blessed Sacrament for one hour every day—because in her lifetime she had often, through negligence, omitted to receive Holy Communion. Now what do all these invitations, these promises, these rewards and punishments prove? What, but the unutterable desire of Jesus Christ to unite Himself to us in Holy Communion. He seems in a manner to force us to receive Him. He makes our temporal and eternal welfare depend on our receiving Him, and thus makes use of our natural desire for happiness to bring us to His Altar. He seems to say, "If you do not receive Me, you shall have no health, no strength or vigor, no comfort, peace or rest, no courage, zeal or devotion; you will be vehemently assailed by temptations, which you will not have strength to resist; you will commit mortal sin, lose My grace and friendship, and becoming a slave of the devil, you will finally fall into Hell and be unhappy forever."

I do not know that I can add any proof of our Saviour's desire to enter our hearts in Holy Communion more striking than those which I have already presented, but there yet remains one to be considered, which is certainly more affecting. I allude to the patience with which He has borne the insults which for eighteen hundred years [now nineteen hundred years] have been heaped upon Him in the Holy Eucharist. I will not offend you, dear Reader, with the relation of the indignities which have been offered to Our Dear Lord in the Sacrament of His love; it is too dark a page in the history of human depravity.

Suffice it to say that He has been loaded with almost every species of outrage which malice could suggest or impiety perpetrate. Infidels, Jews, heretics and sometimes even nominal Catholics have united together to insult Him. All the sorrows which Our Lord had to endure during His life on earth are repeated again and again in this Holy Mystery. Now why does Jesus Christ endure such affronts? Surely none of us would be willing to remain with those who continually maltreat and persecute us; a life in the desert, in the midst of extreme poverty and desolation, would be preferable to such a lot.

Why, then, is our Saviour so patient amid so many outrages? Is He not free to act as He pleases? Is He forced to remain with us in the Blessed Sacrament? Yes, He is forced. He does indeed sometimes vindicate His honor and visit irreverence with exemplary punishment, but there is one point to which His anger never goes: He will never take back the gift of His love. Men may do what they will, but the desire of Jesus Christ to be united with us will always force Him to remain in the Blessed Sacrament. This is the secret of Our Lord's endurance. He endures all things for the sake of the elect.

All the outrages which the wicked have heaped upon Him are compensated for by one devout Communion, and He is willing to remain in our churches, abandoned, alone for hours and hours, that He may be able to unite Himself with the first soul that comes hungering for the Bread of Life. Oh, how true are the words which Jesus Christ spoke to His disciples at the Last Supper! "With desire I have desired to eat this Pasch with you."

God desires that we should receive Him. He commands us to receive Him; He threatens us with Hell if we refuse; He punishes us in Purgatory if we are careless in receiving Him. He promises to forgive all our ingratitude, to remit the temporal punishment due to our sins, nay, to give us Heaven itself if only we receive Him. He promises a special reward to those of His priests who encourage others to receive Him; and as if all this were not enough, He employs His Angels and Saints, yea, His own Omnipotence, to convey the Blessed Sacrament to those who are prevented from receiving Him. Shall we not respond to this desire of Our Lord? Jesus, our King, the Creator of Heaven and earth, longs after us, and shall not we, His creatures and subjects, long after Him? Jesus Christ, the Good Shepherd, desires to feed His sheep, and shall not the sheep know His voice and follow Him?

Ah, if we knew that some great and rich prince had so set his heart on us as to find his happiness in dwelling with us, how impatiently would we expect his arrival; how eagerly would we count the days and hours until he had come! Now, Jesus Christ is far greater and richer than any earthly prince. What honor is so great as that of receiving our God and Saviour? And shall we say: "Delay, O Lord; come not now; wait a little longer!" Alas! That there should be any Christians who speak thus! Can we conceive anything more extraordinary than that a man who believes and knows that God desires to unite Himself to his soul should yet remain indifferent to so great a favor? Can anything show more clearly how the world and sin have usurped the place of God in the human heart, and blinded it to its true happiness? Let me warn you at least, dear Reader, against such folly and ingratitude. If your own desire does not impel you to receive Holy Communion, at least let the desire of Jesus Christ urge you. Do not stay away because your love is cold; go, and your love will grow warm. Begin by going to please Him, and you will keep on to please yourself.

This Sacrament is the great means of advancing in divine love. Those who taste a little honey desire to eat more; but those who know not its sweetness do not desire it at all. In like manner, this heavenly banquet continually satisfies and creates spiritual hunger. The Saints, by often receiving their Saviour, obtained such a longing desire to possess Him as even to cause them suffering until it was satisfied. St. Teresa's desire for Holy Communion was so great that she used to say that neither fire nor sword could deter her from receiving her Divine Lord.

St. Mary Magdalen de Pazzi used to go to that part of the Communion-rail where the priest came first to distribute the Blessed Sacrament in order to receive Our Lord as quickly as possible. St. Philip Neri was often unable to sleep at night on account of his great desire to receive Holy Communion. One night, as Father Antonio Gallonio was about to give him Holy Communion, he held the Sacred Host in his hand for some time; at last St. Philip, unable to endure the delay any longer, cried out: "Antonio, why do you hold my Lord in your hands so long? Why do you not give Him to me? Why? why? Give Him to me; give Him to me!" It is also related that this saint, when taking the Precious Blood at Mass, used to lick and suck the chalice with such affection that it seemed as if he could not tear himself away from it. He gradually wore off the gilding on the rim of the chalice and even left there the print of his teeth.

But still more remarkable is that which is related

of St. Alphonsus. Once, on Good Friday, being unable to receive Holy Communion, his affliction was so great that a violent fever came on him; his life was even in danger. The Doctor came and bled him, but there was no improvement until the next day, when the Saint learned that he could again receive his Saviour. On receiving these joyful tidings, the fever immediately left him. *Gustate et videte quoniam suavis est Dominus.* ("Taste and see how sweet is the Lord.") Come, then and taste this heavenly food for yourself. Let neither the example of others nor the pleasures of the world nor the coldness of your own heart deprive you of so rich a consolation.

How truly does the author of *The Imitation of Christ* remark: "If Jesus Christ were offered only in one city in the world, how cheerfully would men endure even hardships to go to that favored spot! How would they long for the time when they could receive their God. Many holy pilgrims have undertaken long and arduous journeys and have encountered dreadful perils by land and sea only that they might be able to weep in the places in which our Saviour suffered and to kiss the ground on which He trod.

What is there, then, that should prevent you from receiving your Saviour Himself? Should you not be willing to sacrifice everything—to sacrifice health and riches and life itself that you might be deemed worthy of so great a favor? So, at least, thought the Christians of other days. I need not refer you to the examples of the early Christians—there are instances even in later times. In the time of the penal laws in England under Queen Elizabeth a Catholic nobleman was fined four hundred crowns for having received Holy Communion; but, regardless of the iniquitous law, he continued to communicate, cheerfully paying the fine each time he was detected, although he was thereby obliged to sell two of his best estates. He declared that he never spent any money with greater joy than that which he was obliged to pay for the privilege of receiving his Lord. (Schmid's *Histor. Catech.*)

Still more affecting is the example which is related of a dying man in the time of St. Charles Borromeo, Archbishop of Milan. A dreadful pestilence had broken out in the city, and a certain man in the hospital of St. Gregory, having been attacked by it, was soon reduced to the last extremity. In this state, he was carried, more dead than alive, to a place where the dead bodies were thrown before being buried. Life, however, was not yet quite extinct, and after a night spent in this horrible situation, he heard in the morning the sound of the bell announcing the approach of the Blessed Sacrament. Seized with an ardent desire of receiving his Saviour, he extricated himself with great difficulty from the dead bodies that were piled upon him, and crawling to the feet of the priest who carried the Holy Viaticum, he conjured him to give him Holy Communion. The priest, touched with compassion, immediately communicated him, but the efforts the poor man had made were too much for his feeble strength, and while his lips were yet moving in prayer, and his eyes looking up to Heaven, he fell back cold and lifeless at the feet of the priest.

You, dear Reader, have no such efforts, no such sacrifices to make in order to receive your Lord; you need not undertake long journeys nor cross stormy seas and high mountains; Jesus Christ is at your door; you have but to go to the church and you will find Him. You have everything to gain and nothing to lose in receiving a good Communion. Avail yourself, then, of so great a privilege.

If hitherto you have communicated but seldom, for the future communicate oftener. Our Lord Himself solicits you; He repeats the cry He uttered on the Cross. *Sitio!* "I thirst." And for what does He thirst? He thirsts for your heart; He urges you as He did Zacheus: "Make haste, for today I must abide in thy house."

How exceedingly great is the reward of those who obey this loving invitation! Does not Jesus Christ declare that He will recompense those that receive Him and show mercy to Him in the person of the poor? How much more will He reward those who receive Him and show mercy to Him in person. To such He will say: "I was naked" in the Blessed Sacrament, stripped of My glory, and your faith, reverence and devotion supplied what was wanting to My Majesty; I was "imprisoned" in the form of bread and wine, and "sick" with love for you, and you did lovingly visit Me and refresh Me; I was a "stranger," unknown to the greater part of mankind, and you gave Me your heart for My abode; I was "hungry" and "thirsty," consumed with the desire of possessing your affections entirely, and you satisfied My desire to the utmost. Come, then, blessed of My Father, possess the kingdom prepared for you from the foundation of the world.

CHAPTER 6

On Preparation for Communion

IN order to receive the abundant fruits of the Holy Eucharist, a certain cooperation is required on the part of the receiver—not indeed that the efficacy of the Sacrament considered in itself depends at all on the recipient (this efficacy it has entirely from God)—but because its salutary effects in each particular case depend upon the disposition with which it is received. The cooperation which is required on our part consists in general in approaching it with a sincere desire to receive the graces which are imparted through it, and afterward, in turning them carefully to account. In order to obtain this disposition, it is advisable to devote some time before and after Communion to preparation and thanksgiving. Of these, then, I will proceed to speak. First, of the preparation before Communion.

When speaking of preparation for Communion, the previous qualification of being in the state of grace is always pre-supposed. It is related of the Emperor Frederic that, having on one occcasion gone to visit a nobleman at his own castle, he was received into an apartment which was thickly hung with cobwebs; whereupon, being transported with rage, he immediately left the house, exclaiming: "This room is better fitted for a dog-kennel than for the chamber of an emperor!"

How much more justly might Jesus Christ feel

indignant at being received into a soul defiled with mortal sin? "He Whose eyes are pure and cannot behold iniquity!" Accordingly, St. Paul teaches us that we must *prove ourselves* before we eat of the Body of the Lord, meaning thereby that, if upon examination we find ourselves guilty of any grievous sin, we should cleanse our conscience by a good Confession.

There are certain snakes, says St. Bernard, which spit out the poison that is in their mouths before they begin to drink; and we, before approaching the fountain of Life, must spit out the poison of sin. This preparation, as I have said, is always pre-supposed, and every Catholic knowing it to be an indispensable requisite, it will not, therefore, be necessary to dwell longer upon it, especially as occasion will be taken to speak of it hereafter. I have said we must be free from mortal sin, for it is this only which absolutely renders us incapable of receiving the fruits of Communion; but venial sins, especially those which are fully deliberate, and even voluntary imperfections, greatly hinder the efficacy of the Sacrament.

One who now and then speaks in disparagement of his neighbor or tells petty falsehoods, though he may not commit a mortal sin, yet deprives himself of many graces which he would otherwise have received.

The first step in our preparation for Communion, after we have been reconciled to God, is an habitual effort to please Him. It is, moreover, carefully to be noticed that, in order to receive the full extent of grace attached to this Sacrament, our hearts must be free from all inordinate affections. St. Gertrude on one occasion asked Our Lord how she ought to prepare for

Holy Communion, and He replied: "I ask nothing more than that you should come with an empty heart."

There is also another disposition which is always pre-supposed, pertaining to the body. No one can receive the Flesh of Christ unless he be fasting, that is to say, unless he has abstained from eating or drinking anything whatsoever from the preceding midnight, the only exception to this rule being when the Holy Communion is administered to the dying by way of Viaticum. [The current rules allow water anytime right up to Communion and prescribe fasting for one hour before. —*Editor*, 1994.] This law of the Church, which is intended to secure greater reverence for the Blessed Sacrament, is founded on the most evident reasons of propriety, so much so that St. Augustine takes it for granted that no Christian would be guilty of the indecency of taking anything into his mouth before the Body of the Lord has entered it. (*Epist.* 54). Besides this requisite, Christians generally employ a longer or a shorter time, according to their ability, in actual preparation; and of this, it will be useful to speak more particularly.

Having treated in a former chapter of the duty of reverence towards the Blessed Sacrament, I deem it useless to prove here at great length the propriety of making some actual preparation for Communion. Common sense is enough to teach every man that it is not becoming to receive his God into his heart without previous preparation. I suppose you have at some time witnessed the public reception of some great man whom the people wish to honor—some distinguished warrior or successful candidate or great orator. What a crowd in the streets! What anxiety to secure a place for seeing! What a cry and tumult on all sides! And when the hero of the day arrives, what eagerness to get a sight of him! How dense the crowd becomes behind him! How happy they on whom he smiles or to whom he speaks! How greatly envied is the favored citizen with whom he will take up his abode! What hurry and bustle and excitement in the house where he is to lodge! Now stop and ask yourself, for whom is all this? For a man—a poor, weak, mortal man. And I, alas, with unconcern, receive Him who is the "Splendor of His Father's Glory and the Figure of His Substance"!

When King David was asked why he had prepared such a vast quantity of gold, silver and precious stones for the temple he was about to erect, he answered: "The work is great, for a house is not prepared for man, but for God." And yet, in that Temple the Holy of Holies, the Ark of the Covenant and the manna were but shadows. We have the true Holy of Holies, the Living Manna, the Life-giving Bread that came down from Heaven! Should we not, then, exert all our care in arranging a dwelling place for this Divine Guest! "When thou shalt sit to eat with a prince," says the wise King Solomon, "consider diligently what is set before thy face."

How much more diligently ought we to consider what we are about to do when we appear at the table of the great King of Heaven and earth to feed on the Flesh of His beloved Son! This reflection, so natural and obvious, is sufficient to show us the *propriety* of some actual preparation for Communion. To this I will add another reflection to show its great *utility*. It is in the highest degree advantageous to prepare ourselves for Holy Communion because the fruit it produces depends on the disposition with which we receive it. Divines use the following figure in illustration: As wood that is not seasoned will not burn well because the moisture that is in it resists the action of the fire, so the heart which is full of earthly affections is not in a fit state to be enkindled with the living fire of Divine Love by means of this Holy Sacrament.

Father Lallemant says that many souls are almost as little benefitted by the Holy Eucharist as the walls of the church in which it is preserved because they are as hard and as cold as the very walls themselves. And St. Bernard concisely expresses the same truth by saying: *Sicut tu Deo apparueris, ita tibi Deus apparebit.* "God will exhibit Himself to you just as you show yourself disposed towards Him." When, therefore, people complain of receiving but little fruit from their Communions, they but betray their own negligence. As the light of the sun far exceeds the light of the moon, so do the effects of the Holy Eucharist in a loving heart greatly surpass those which it produces in a tepid, slothful soul.

The well-known story of Widikend, Duke of Saxony, illustrates this. This prince, while yet a pagan, was at war with Charlemagne; having a great curiosity to see what took place among the Christians, he disguised himself as a pilgrim and stole into their camp. It happened to be the Paschal time, and the whole army were making their Easter Communion. The stranger watched the ceremonies of Mass with interest and admiration, but how much was he surprised when the priest administered the Sacrament to see in the Host an Infant of shining beauty! He gazed at the sight with amazement, but his astonishment became yet greater when he saw that this wonderful Child entered the mouths of some of the communicants with joy, while only with great reluctance It allowed Itself to be received by others. This vision was the means of the conversion of Widikend and the submission of his subjects to the Faith, for having sought instruction from the Christians, he understood that Our Lord meant to show him, not only the truth of the Real Presence, but that He comes into our hearts with willingness or unwillingness, as we are well or ill prepared for receiving Him. (*Timal. Arende* I., 1 Collat.).

Something similar is related in the life of the venerable Margaret Mary Alacoque. One day she saw Our Lord in the Host as the priest was giving Communion, and she noticed that when the priest came to some of the communicants, Our Lord stretched out His arms and seemed eager to unite Himself to them, while there were others toward whom He showed the greatest repugnance and only suffered Himself to be dragged into their mouths by certain cords and bands with which He was bound.

He explained to her afterwards that the souls which He entered willingly were those who were careful to please Him, and those to whom He showed so much aversion were tepid Christians, who received Him into hearts full of hateful faults and imperfections. He told her, moreover, that He entered into such hearts merely on account of His promises and the law which He had laid upon Himself in the institution of the Blessed Sacrament and that this was the meaning of the bands and cords which she had seen. "How, then," you ask, "am I to prepare for Holy Communion?"

The Church sufficiently indicates the dispositions for Holy Communion in the following words: *Domine, non sum dignus, ut intres sub tectum meum, sed tantum dic verbo, et sanabitur anima mea.* "Lord, I am not worthy that Thou shouldst enter under my roof, but only say the word and my soul shall be healed." These words were spoken by the Centurion, who came to our Saviour asking Him to heal his servant. Our Lord at once offered to go with him to his house to perform the cure, but the good Centurion replied: "Lord, I am not worthy that Thou shouldst enter under my roof, but only say the word and my servant shall be healed." This answer pleased Our Lord so much that He not only instantly healed the servant, but greatly commended the Centurion's faith. These words express a great esteem for Jesus Christ, a great sense of unworthiness on the part of the supplicant, and a great confidence that he would obtain what he asked.

These are precisely the dispositions which the Church requires for the reception of Holy Communion. Hence she repeats the words of the Centurion in a loud voice each time she distributes the Bread of Life, in order to remind the communicants of the duty of approaching the Sacred Banquet with a deep sense of their own utter nothingness and with a great desire of being united to their Divine Saviour. To excite these affections when about to communicate, you have but to ask yourself the following questions: "Who is it that is coming?" " To whom does He come, and why is He coming?" "*Who* is coming in this Holy Sacrament?" "It is my Creator, who has given me everything I possess, in whom I live, and move, and am. It is God all Powerful, all Wise, all

Holy, all Beautiful! Jesus Christ is coming, the Eternal Son of the Father, who moved by love unspeakable, came down from Heaven into the pure womb of the Virgin, was born into this world and lived as man among sinners. The Good Shepherd is coming to seek His lost sheep; My Redeemer is coming who died on the Cross for sinners. To whom is He coming? To a miserable sinner who has not fulfilled the end of his creation, to a steward who has wasted his master's goods, to a servant who has disobeyed his lord, to a subject who has rebelled against his prince, to a redeemed captive who has been unthankful to his deliverer, to a soldier who has deserted his commander, to a prodigal child who has turned his back upon his father, to a spouse who has been unfaithful to her bridegroom." Oh! what a mingling of sentiments, exalting and depressing, must arise in the heart when about to approach Holy Communion! How great the distance between Him who is received and the sinner who receives!

Who can think of this and not feel himself completely unworthy of such a grace! Eusebius relates of St. Jerome that, when the Holy Viaticum was brought to him at the hour of his death, he exclaimed: "Lord, why dost Thou lower Thyself so much as to come to a publican and a sinner, not only to eat with him, but even to be eaten by him!" And then, casting himself upon the earth, he received his Saviour with many tears.

If a saint who had spent a long life in penitential works for the love of Christ felt so penetrated with a sense of his unworthiness before God, how much more should we humble ourselves when we draw nigh to Him! Should we not, with a true sorrow for our past unfaithfulness, accuse ourselves before Him and resolve by the help of His grace to amend all that is displeasing in His sight? The Publican of whom we read in the Gospel stood far back in the temple and smote his breast, saying: "Lord, be merciful to me a sinner!" And should not we, when going to the altar, hesitate and smite our breasts, saying, in the depths of our hearts, "I am not worthy! I am not worthy!"

But now the soul, having perceived the depth of her own unworthiness, must once more lift up her eyes to Heaven and ask: "Why does this Holy God come to visit a sinner like me?" And here she finds immensity of goodness which fills her again with courage and joy. Why does He come? Surely not for Himself, for He has no need of us. We cannot make Him richer or happier; we cannot give Him anything that He has not first given us. He sees in us nothing of our own but misery and sin. He is perfectly happy. The Angels serve Him day and night. There is not one of them that would not willingly be annihilated if He were to will it.

What, then, is it that induces Him to come to us? It is love, pure undeserved love. He comes to apply to our souls the fruits of His Redemption which He accomplished on Calvary, for in this Sacrament He becomes to each one of us a Saviour in a special sense. He comes to accomplish the work for which He created us, to prepare us for the place in Heaven which He has destined for us. It is He that works in this Sacrament, not we. He created us; He redeemed us; now He comes to pour out upon us all the riches of His love; He comes to give us light to know and strength to do His will; He comes to repair what is decayed and to restore what is wasted; to forgive rebellion and unthankfulness; in a word, to receive us as children; to clothe us with the first robe; to put a ring on our hands and shoes on our feet; to eat and make merry with us. What, then, should be our sentiments when we approach Our Lord in this mystery but those of the returning prodigal: "I will arise and will go to my Father." And when at this wonderful banquet our good Father, Jesus Christ, falls upon our necks and gives us the kiss of peace, when He feeds us, not with the fatted calf, but with His own most precious Flesh, what has the soul to do but yield to His loving embrace and to say, with humble gratitude: "O Lord, I am not worthy! I am not worthy to be called Thy son!" Our mistake is this: we think we have much to do, and we have but little to do.

I have already said that habitual fidelity, even in the smallest matters, is a condition for our receiving special graces in this Sacrament, but at the moment of Communion what is chiefly necessary is a great *confidence* arising from a deep conviction of our own nothingness and from a sense of God's exceedingly great goodness. He comes to us with His hands full of graces; we should meet Him with an affectionate *desire* to be united to Him and with a *hunger* and *thirst* for His justice.

But perhaps you will say: "I see the truth of what you have said; I am sure that a great desire to receive Jesus Christ is the best disposition for approaching Him, but this is precisely my difficulty. I have not this desire; I am cold and dry; my heart is dull and sluggish. I go to Communion, not indeed without the wish to please Our Lord, but with little fervor or affection for Him. Our Lord Himself has given the reply to this difficulty. He said one day to St. Matilda: "When thou art about to receive My Body and Blood, desire for the greater glory of My name to have all the ardor of love which the most fervent heart ever had for Me, and then thou mayest receive Me with confidence, for I will attribute to thee, as if thou really hadst it, all that fervor that thou desirest to have."

What can be more consoling than this? You have no devotion, but you can wish to have it. You do not feel all the respect and confidence you would like to feel, but your wish to have more supplies what is wanting; you have no humility, but you can humble yourself for your pride; you have no love, but you can offer your desire to love. From the poor, small presents are accepted. Offer what you have, and if you have nothing, then do what the Saints recommend: say, "Lord, if a great king were to lodge with a poor man, he would not expect the poor man to make a suitable preparation, but would send his own servants to make ready for him; do Thou so, O Lord, now that Thou art coming to dwell in my poor heart!" This alone will be an excellent disposition for receiving and one very pleasing to Jesus Christ.

One day St. Gertrude went to receive Holy Communion without being sufficiently prepared. Being greatly afflicted at this, she begged the Blessed Virgin Mary and all the Saints to offer up to God in her behalf all their merits, that they might in some way supply her own deficiency; whereupon, our Saviour appeared to her and said: "Now, before the whole heavenly court, thou appearest adorned for Communion as thou wouldst wish to be."

Comply, then, O Christian, with that which Jesus Christ requires of you. Communicate, but communicate as He desires that you should. Do not be content with keeping yourself free from mortal sin; make war against venial sin also, at least those which are fully deliberate; for though venial sins do not extinguish love, they greatly weaken its force and fervor. Strive also to wean your heart from creatures; endeavor to mortify your attachment to honors, riches and pleasures; spare no trouble for the sake of the Kingdom of Heaven; practice little but frequent acts of self-denial; keep yourself always in the fear of God, and strive to adorn your soul with the virtues which Jesus Christ especially loves—humility, meekness, patience, prayer, charity, faith, peace and recollection.

On the eve of your Communion, renew your good resolutions; spend some little time in prayer; go to rest with the thought, "Tomorrow I shall receive my Saviour"; and if you awake in the night, think of the great action you are about to perform. In the morning make again acts of love, humility, contrition and confidence, and then go forward to the altar with a sincere desire to love and honor Jesus Christ more and more. Do what you can, and however imperfect that may be, it will be acceptable to Jesus Christ, provided He sees in you a true desire to do more. By such Communions you will gain the precious graces which are imparted by this Holy Sacrament, for they will not be merely Communions, but real unions of Jesus Christ with your soul.

I will conclude this chapter with the following story: Father Hunolt, of the Society of Jesus, relates that two students were once discoursing together about the hour of their death. They agreed that if God would allow it, he who should die first should appear to the other to tell him how he fared in the other world. Shortly afterwards, one of them died and appeared soon after his death to his fellow-student, all shining with heavenly brightness and glory, and in answer to his inquiries, told him that by the mercy of God he was saved and was in possession of the bliss of Heaven. The other congratulated him on his felicity and asked him how he merited such unspeakable glory and bliss. "Chiefly," said the happy soul, "by the care with which I endeavored to receive Holy Communion with a pure heart." At these words the spirit disappeared, leaving in his surviving friend feelings of great consolation and an ardent zeal to imitate his devotion. "You have heard these things; blessed shall you be if you do them." (*John* 13:17).

CHAPTER 7

On Thanksgiving after Communion

IF a good preparation before Communion is so important, a good thanksgiving after Communion is of even greater importance. St. John Chrysostom says that when a person has eaten some delicious food at a banquet, he is careful not to take anything bitter in his mouth immediately after, lest he should lose the sweet flavor of those delicate viands. In like manner, when we have received the precious Body of Jesus Christ, we should take care not to lose its heavenly flavor by turning too soon to the cares and business of the world.

St. Francis de Sales expresses the same idea. "When the merchants of India," he says, "have brought home their precious porcelain, they are very careful in conveying it to their storehouses lest they should stumble and break their costly wares. In like manner should the Christian, when he carries the priceless treasure of Our Lord's Body, walk with great care and circumspection in order not to lose the costly gift committed to his keeping." The meaning of both Saints is that after Communion we should spend some time in devout recollection and prayer. This is the general practice of good Catholics. And indeed, reason itself tells us that a good thanksgiving after Communion is of even more importance than a good preparation before it. If we are required to pause and consider what we are about to do when we approach Our Lord, what should be our devotion when He is actually in our hearts?

When the Blessed Virgin Mary visited St. Elizabeth, the aged Saint was astonished at the condescension of the glorious Mother of God, and said: "Whence is this to me, that the Mother of my God should come to me?" Now, in Holy Communion, it is the Lord Himself that comes to us, the Eternal "Wisdom which proceeded from the mouth of the Most High," the "Lord and Prince of the House of Israel, Who appeared to Moses in the burning bush," the "King of nations," "Emmanuel," "our King and Law-giver." To remain indifferent after having received the Blessed Eucharist is to evince either a total want of faith or a levity and stupidity unworthy of a reasonable being.

What a spectacle for the Angels, to see a creature approach that Sacred Host before which they bow in lowliest adoration and, when he has had the unutterable happiness of receiving his Redeemer, leave the church with as much unconcern as if he had but partaken of ordinary bread! If indeed this should be done by one who has had no opportunity for receiving instruction on this subject, no doubt the Angels will have compassion on his ignorance, but should a well-instructed Catholic be guilty of such ungrateful behavior towards Jesus Christ after Communion, I think that nothing but the mercy of Our Lord would prevent them from avenging the impiety.

St. Alphonsus relates that a priest, seeing a man leave the church immediately after Communion, sent the servers of Mass with lighted candles to accompany him home. "What is the matter?" asked the man. "Oh," said the boys, "we are come to accompany Our Lord, who is still present in your heart.'' If everyone who follows the example of this indevout communicant received the same reproof, the scandal of going directly from the altar to the world would soon cease.

Although the greatness of Our Lord is a sufficient reason why we should not leave Him alone in our hearts after Communion, it is not the argument which He Himself employs. There is in this Sacrament nothing that breathes of majesty. Our Lord is silent, whether we leave the church immediately or kneel and reverently converse with Him. The stones do not cry out against our ingratitude if, after eating the Bread of Angels, we do not give thanks to God. Jesus Christ might send twelve legions of angels to stand around us after we have left His table, to remind us that He is present in our hearts, but He does not do this.

Now it is from this very fact of *not* surrounding Himself with anything calculated to inspire fear that we ought to draw the most powerful incentive to gratitude. This Sacrament is a Sacrament of love. In it God is pleased to treat with His creatures in all familiarity. Jesus Christ, having accomplished the work of our Redemption, draws nigh to converse with us, as He did to the two disciples on their way to Emmaus. He wishes to speak with us as one friend speaks to another. Oh then, what an affront it is to leave Him the moment that He comes to us! Scarcely to say one word to Him! Would you not consider it great unkindness if a loving friend had travelled far to see you, and when he has but a little time to stay, to leave him as soon as he had entered your house and go to attend to your business or to seek your pleasure?

Would you not rather give him the best welcome you could and prepare the best room in your house and adorn it with your richest furniture; would you not sacrifice something of your time to keep him company and exchange some tokens of love before you allowed him to depart? Now, should you not do as much for Jesus Christ, who has come so far to visit you, who has suffered so many sorrows for your sake, who is thinking of you always and has given you so many tokens of His love? It is by this argument that Jesus Christ Himself prefers to incite us to make a due thanksgiving after Communion, and it is one which must have irresistible weight with every faithful heart. I feel that this point needs no further proof. I will therefore pass on to consider the *manner* in which we ought to make our thanksgiving. What has been said in regard to preparation is, of course, equally true here, *viz.,* that each one is free to use such prayers as he shall find most suited to his devotion. My object is only to show in what a good thanksgiving essentially consists.

Now it consists first in completing the union with Our Lord, which He has come to effect, by a sincere oblation of ourselves to Him. The moment of Communion is different from any other moment of our lives. Then we can truly exclaim, "My God and my All!" When we communicate, God Himself is present in our little hearts as our Friend and Bridegroom. Nothing can be more intimate than the union that then takes place between the Creator and His creatures. It is more like the Incarnation of the Eternal Son of God in the womb of the Blessed Virgin Mary than anything else. To her it was said, "The Holy Ghost shall come upon thee, and the power of the

Most High shall overshadow thee. And therefore also, the Holy One which shall be born of thee shall be called the Son of God.''

And the same Son of God, the Holy One, that was born of the spotless Virgin, comes into our hearts in the Sacred Host. Think of all that is most beautiful and most precious in the world, of all the riches of the whole universe, of all the glory of Heaven, and you have as yet but a faint idea of the wealth of a soul that has received Holy Communion. Such a soul possesses not only earth and Heaven, but the Lord and Maker of Heaven and earth.

It is a mystery which almost baffles thought. Certainly God can never cease to be what He is; He can never cease to be awful in His Greatness and Infinite in His Wisdom—our Ruler, our King and our Judge—but in this Sacrament, as if He had nothing to think of but the soul which He comes to visit, He lavishes upon her all the riches of His bounty and reveals Himself to her in no other but the most amiable and most *humble* manner. Perhaps it is for this reason that He has been pleased so often to manifest Himself as an *Infant* in the Sacred Host, in order to show us how small He has become for love of us and to take away from us all fear.

Of old it was said, *Magnus Dominus et laudabilis nimis.* ''Great is the Lord and exceedingly to be praised.'' But now we may rather say: *Parvus Dominus et amabilis nimis.* ''Small is the Lord and exceedingly to be loved.'' Accordingly, we find from the expressions of the Saints that the thought which possessed their souls after Communion was admiration at the unutterable love of God. St. Mary Magdalen de Pazzi once asked a pious person after Communion what she was thinking of. "Of love," was her reply. "Yes," rejoined the Saint, "when we think of the immense love of Jesus Christ for us, we cannot think of anything else." It is related of Artaxerxes, King of Persia, that when he saw Themistocles, his dearest friend, he exclaimed, in a transport of joy: "I have Themistocles, Themistocles I have!"

With how much greater joy should not the soul exclaim after Communion: "I have my Jesus, my Jesus I have! I have found Him whom my soul loves! I will keep Him, and not leave Him!" It is not, however, enough to wonder at our Saviour's love. Love must be mutual to produce union; and we must return Him love for love. Now is the time to repay Him for the trials and tears, the shame and sorrow, the contradiction and reproach which He underwent for the ransom of our souls.

They were already His by the title of creation, and now they belong to Him by the title of Redemption. We must make to Him a childlike, generous, sincere, and complete oblation. "But what," you say, "have I to offer? I am poor and indigent; I stand in need of everything. What can I give to the Lord, who made Heaven and earth?" I will tell you.

Imitate Aeschines, a disciple of Socrates, of whom Seneca relates that, not being able on account of his poverty to make such rich presents to his master as his fellow disciples did, he went out and said to him: "Master, my extreme poverty leaves me nothing to give you as a token of my gratitude; I offer you, then, myself, to be yours forever." "Truly," said Socrates, "you have given me more than all the rest." Act thus with Jesus Christ. You have no treasure to offer Him; you have no station to renounce for Him; you have no occasion to die for Him; you cannot do for Him what He has done for you, but you can give Him that which He values more than anything else—your heart.

There is nothing that gives so much pleasure to Jesus Christ as a heart truly resolved to serve Him. Give Him, then, this pleasure; offer yourself to Him to be disposed of as He pleases; to receive indifferently at His hand bitter and sweet; to serve Him with all the fervor that you can; to avoid sin and to lead a Christian life. Do this, and then your Communion will really be a Communion, that is to say, a union with God.

To receive the Body of Christ is common to the good and the bad, but it is the good alone who are truly united to Him. Are you perhaps afraid to make such promises? "It is easy," I hear you say, "to make an offering of ourselves to Jesus Christ, but it is not so easy to carry it into effect." Oh, Christian soul, thou dost not yet understand the generosity of love! Did not Our Lord ask St. James and St. John whether they were ready to drink of the chalice that He would drink of, before He actually gave them the grace of martyrdom? Did He not make us promise to renounce the devil and his works and his pomps and to live in obedience to the Christian law before He adopted us as His children in Baptism? We must first promise much, and then God will help us to do much. He comes into our hearts, not only to claim them as His own, but to give us grace whereby we may truly make them His. After we have made an oblation of ourselves to Him, then we must immediately proceed to beg of Him the grace to fulfill that which we have promised—and this is the second part of a good thanksgiving.

There is no doubt that *petitioning* Our Lord for special graces should be our principal occupation after Communion. "The time after Communion," says St. Teresa, is the best time for negotiating with Jesus Christ, for then He is in the soul, seated, as it were, on a throne of grace and saying as He said to the blind man: "What wilt thou that I should do to thee?" And another great servant of God says that in the beginning of his conversion he was accustomed to employ the time after Communion chiefly in making devout aspirations, but that afterwards he devoted almost the whole time to petition, which he found more profitable to his soul.

When a prince goes for a short time to visit his subjects in a distant province, his whole time is taken up in hearing their complaints, in redressing their grievances, in consoling them in their miseries and in relieving their wants. So Jesus Christ, our Heavenly King, comes in this Sacrament on a short visit to inquire into our wants and to relieve them. I say "to inquire into our wants," not as if He needed to be informed of them, but because, as St. Alphonsus says, He wishes that we should lay them before Him. When the storm was raging on the sea of Tiberias, Our Lord continued to sleep in the ship, although He knew well the danger of His disciples. Why did He do this? It was because He wished that they should awaken Him and implore His aid. Lay then before Him all your troubles, your weaknesses, your fears and your desires. Are you in temporal difficulties? Hear what He has said: "What man is there among you, of whom if his son ask bread, will he reach him a stone? Or if he ask a fish will he reach him a serpent? If you, then, being evil, know how to give good gifts to your children, how much more will your Father who is in heaven, give good things to them that ask Him?'' (*Matt.* 7:9-11).

Do you wish to subdue your passions and disorderly affections? Hear what He has said: "As the division of waters, so the heart of the king is in My hands.'' (*Prov.* 21:1). If the hearts of kings are like wax in His hands, is He not able to change your heart also? Is He not able to convert you as He converted the prophet David, St. Mary Magdalene, St. Paul, St. Margaret of Cortona and a host of others? Ask Him then to destroy in you what is bad and to make you what you wish to be, to change your wavering purposes into a firm resolution to follow His example, your fear of self-discipline into an earnest desire to advance in virtue and holiness. Ask Him to change your dissipated heart into a recollected one, your unmortified heart into a mortified one, your ambitious heart into an humble one, your faint and timid heart into a brave and courageous one, your irritable and peevish heart into a mild and patient one, your sinful heart into a holy one.

In the life of St. Catherine of Siena, we read of a wonderful grace that she received from Our Lord. He took out her heart and gave her *His* in its place. Each one of us has it in his power to receive a grace somewhat similar. Let us only ask of Jesus Christ, and He will transform us, as it were, into Himself. Pray to Him for humility, for patience, for meekness, for contempt of the world, for a lively faith, a firm hope, ardent charity; for brotherly love, for love of your enemies, for the prosperity of the Church, for the conversion of sinners, heretics and infidels; for the souls in Purgatory; for devotion to His Passion, to the Blessed Sacrament, to His Immaculate Mother; for the crowning grace of perseverance—and He will give you all, for His Arm is not shortened nor His Love diminished.

The Sacrament of the Eucharist never grows old; it is as efficient now as it was at the time of the Apostles. There is nothing necessary to your true sanctity that your Lord is unwilling to impart to you. If you are diligent in asking graces of Him after Communion, if you persevere in asking, with a real desire to obtain, you will infallibly become a Saint— yea, a great Saint!

There is another exercise of devotion which should form part of your thanksgiving after Communion: I mean *Praise*. It is good sometimes to rejoice; it enlarges the heart and gives it courage. "Rejoice in the Lord always," says St. Paul, "and again I say— rejoice!" The life of men would be much happier than it is were they with a lively faith to receive Holy Communion often. How sorrowful soever you may be when about to receive, afterward you will not be without consolation. When Our Divine Saviour entered the Temple, the little children cried out, "Hosanna to the Son of David!" and shall not you sing a song of praise when He comes into the temple of your heart? Oh, how much should you rejoice! How great a thing it is to be a Christian! Where is the nation that has its gods so nigh as our God is with us? What king or emperor is so honored as the faithful Catholic? What Angel of Heaven so favored as the good communicant? "Do you not know," says St. Paul, "that you are temples of God?" Yes, indeed, each good Catholic is a true Christopher, that is to say, a carrier of Christ! After Communion, he carries in his heart Jesus Christ, the Incarnate Son of God.

"All things are yours," says St. Paul; "all are yours and you are Christ's." "Exult ye who live in Sion!" Why should you take life so hard and complain of your crosses and trials and be so impatient in every difficulty? Why should you envy the rich of this world, the great and the honored? Why should you vex yourself at injuries and groan in adversity? Why should you faint at the thought of self-denial and conflict? Are you not a Catholic? Have you not the sweet services of the Church to soothe you and her Sacraments to nourish you, her benedictions to strengthen you and her absolution to cleanse you? Have you not Mary for your Mother and the Angels and Saints for your patrons and protectors, and above all, in the Blessed Sacrament, Jesus for your Father?

O my soul, rejoice and sing a song unto the Lord! Alleluia! Praise the Lord, ye servants of God; praise ye the name of the Lord from henceforth, now and forever. From the rising of the sun unto the going down of the same, the name of the Lord is worthy of praise. Who is as the Lord our God who dwelleth on high and looketh down on the low things in heaven and on earth, raising up the needy from the earth and lifting up the poor out of the dunghill, that He may place them with princes, with the princes of His people! Alleluia! Bless the Lord, my soul, and let all that is within me bless His holy name! Bless the Lord, O my soul, and never forget all He has done for thee: who forgiveth all thy

iniquities; who healeth all thy diseases; who redeem-
eth thy life from destruction; who crowneth thee with
mercy and compassion; who satisfieth all thy desires
with good things. He hath not dealt with thee
according to thy sins, nor rewarded thee according
to thy iniquities; for according to the height of
Heaven above the earth, He has strengthened His
mercy towards them that fear Him; and as far as the
West is from the East, so far hath He removed our
iniquities from us. As a father hath compassion on
his children, so hath the Lord compassion on them
that fear Him. Bless the Lord, all ye Angels, you that
are mighty in strength and execute His word, heark-
ening to the voice of His orders. O my Soul, bless
thou the Lord! My soul doth magnify the Lord, and
my spirit hath rejoiced in God my Saviour. For He
that is mighty hath done great things to me, and
Holy is His name. And His mercy is from generation
to generation to them that fear Him. He hath shown
might in His Arm; He hath scattered the proud in
the conceit of their hearts; He hath put down the
mighty from their seat and hath exalted the humble;
He hath filled the hungry with good things and the
rich He hath sent away empty; He hath received
Israel His servant, being mindful of His mercy—as
He spoke to our fathers, to Abraham and his seed
forever.

Having spoken of the *necessity* of making a
thanksgiving after Communion and shown the *manner* in which it may profitably be made, I must say
a few words about *the length of time* which you
should devote to it. Above all I must remark that I
have no intention of putting your conscience under

any law; in this point you are altogether free to consult the duties of your state of life, or even your inclinations. I know that the Saints desired to spend their lifetime in thanksgiving after Communion and felt a kind of reluctance to attend to temporal affairs after having received the Body and Blood of Jesus Christ in the Holy Eucharist.

Hence, in *The Imitation of Christ*, the blessed Thomas à Kempis complains of the necessity of eating, drinking, sleeping and attending to temporal affairs because they interrupted his converse with the Lord and Master of his heart. But at the same time, I know that the Saints never allowed their prayers to interfere with the faithful performance of the duties of their state of life. It is very important to know that true devotion does not consist in sacrificing work to prayer, but in making prayer a preparation for work and work a continuation of prayer. Hence, then, your thanksgiving should not be longer than the duties of your state of life will permit.

Father Avila used to spend two hours in thanksgiving after Mass, even when he was very busy. St. Alphonsus advises everyone to devote at least half an hour to it, if it is at all possible. But whatever time you fix upon, do not imagine that your thanksgiving is at an end when you leave the church. The best thanksgiving is to cease from sin and to remain united with God; your half hour's prayer is only to help you to do this. You cannot remain always in the church, but you can go to your business with a recollected mind. You cannot always keep your prayerbook and beads in your hands, but you can make ejaculatory prayer to God at every time and in every place.

It is said of St. Aloysius Gonzaga that he used to

receive Communion once a week and that he was accustomed to spend three days in preparation before it and three days in thanksgiving after it. How did he manage to do this? Was he all the time prostrated before the Altar or reading a spiritual book? Not at all; he went wherever obedience called him, quietly performing his duties and keeping his heart lifted up to God. He offered up all his actions to Jesus Christ by way of thanksgiving, and he made now and then some short acts of faith, hope and charity, some acts of self-oblation or admiration or supplication. By this means, the angelic youth was enabled to walk continually with God; one Communion was the preparation for another; thus, he constantly advanced in purity of heart and in love for Jesus Christ.

Now, everyone who has but little time at his disposal can make such a thanksgiving as this, if not with all the perfection of St. Aloysius, at least with great fruit and consolation to his soul. Everyone can offer to Jesus Christ the crosses he may meet with during the day and bear them patiently for the sake of Him whom he wishes to thank. He can crush the movements of impatience, the thought of vanity, the immodest glance, the word of bitterness, the laugh of folly, the look of pride. He can, for the love of the good Jesus, be just and true, pure and obedient, pious and humble.

This is the way to honor and please Jesus Christ. He did not institute this adorable Sacrament to give us a little excitement of devotion, but to make us *holy*. "I have chosen you," said Our Lord, "that you should bring forth fruits, and that your fruit should remain." "In this is My Father glorified that you bring forth very much fruit." Make then, Christian

Soul, a good use of the precious moments after Communion. You will never fully understand how precious they are. Nothing will cause you more confusion after death than the little account you have made of the Blessed Sacrament.

It is related in the Book of Esther, that one night when King Assuerus could not sleep, he ordered the chronicles of his reign to be read to him. When the reader came to the place where it was related that Mardochai, the Jew, had once crushed a wicked plot against the King's life, Assuerus asked, "What reward has Mardochai received for this fidelity?" "None at all," they answered him. Whereupon, in all haste, the King ordered the long delayed acknowledgment to be made to his deliverer, that Mardochai should be carried in procession through the streets clothed in royal apparel and crowned with the King's crown and seated upon the King's horse, and that it should be proclaimed before all: "This is the honor he is worthy of whom the King hath a mind to honor."

To you also, my dear Reader, there will come a sleepless night when mortal sickness shall tell you that death is near, and then you will look back upon your life and see many benefits for which you have made no acknowledgment. When you think of your Communions, you will say, "What acknowledgment have I made to my Deliverer who has so often saved my life?" When the two disciples at Emmaus understood that it was Jesus who had been with them by the way, they remembered how their hearts had burned as He conversed with them; so at the hour of death, you will see how precious were the graces you received when Jesus in the Holy Sacrament came into your heart. Your Communions will then seem to have

been the greatest blessings of your life. The world will
have disappeared, friends will have deserted you, all
your past life will seem to have been a dream; but the
moments when you received your Saviour will appear
to you in their true bearing in eternity.

What regret will you not then feel for your unfaithfulness! How earnestly will you desire to live your life
over again to repair your indevout thanksgivings! A
holy nun who had suffered very much in this life
appeared after her death to one of her sisters in religion. She told her that she would willingly return to the
world and undergo once more all the pains she had
suffered here on earth, provided she could say but *one
Hail Mary,* because by that one prayer, her glory and
joy would be increased by one degree for all eternity.
(P. Michael a St. Catherine, Lib. III, Tract. 16).

If the blessed in Heaven are willing to do so much
for *one Hail Mary,* what would they not do for one
Communion? And yet they cannot have it. It is the
privilege of mortals alone to feed on the Flesh of
Jesus Christ in the Holy Eucharist. I repeat, then:
make great account of your Communions. Do now
what you will wish to have done at the hour of death.
Make the most of every moment of your thanksgiving. Pay to Jesus Christ all the honor that you possibly can. You cannot do as Assuerus did. Jesus Christ
is great and you are poor and miserable; you cannot
give Him royal honor—you can but give Him the tribute of an humble loving heart. But this He is pleased
to accept. Offer it to Him, then, in all sincerity. Converse with Him reverently and familiarly while you
have Him in your heart; try to obtain some grace
from Him which may remain after He has ceased to
be sacramentally present with you and which may

enable you to make your next Communion better. Thus you will live always united with Jesus Christ, and by your example and conversation you will edify your neighbor.

St. Veronica Juliana had, even at the age of three years, a great devotion to the Blessed Sacrament, and it is related of her that, not being permitted to receive Communion, she used to come very close to her mother after she had communicated and cling to her dress. One day her mother noticed the child and asked her why she thus hung around her, and she replied: "Mother, you taste of Jesus and you smell of Jesus!" If you too, my Reader, are careful to make a good thanksgiving, you will carry with you a sweet odor of sanctity, and Angels and good Christians will love to keep you company. You will advance in virtue and happiness here and, what is more, hereafter. When the tepid and indifferent will be lamenting in a bitter Purgatory their negligent thanksgivings, or will be cursing them in Hell as the first steps to mortal sin, you will be blessing the retired and mortified life which left you time to love and honor your Saviour. Nay, even this is not all, for your most bountiful Saviour will reward the little honor you have paid Him by a great and royal recompense. He will do far more for you than Assuerus did for Mardochai. He will cause you to be honored by all the Angels and Saints in Heaven, clothe you in royal attire and "confess your name before His Father," as He promised when He said: "Whosoever shall glorify Me, him will I glorify!" (*1 Kings* 2:30).

CHAPTER 8

On the Effects of Holy Communion

I AM sure, dear Reader, that if you would once begin the practice of frequent Communion in order to please Our Lord, you would continue it in order to please yourself. I will now proceed to make good this assertion by showing the great and admirable effects which this Bread of the Strong produces in the soul. First, it confers an increase of Sanctifying Grace. The life of the soul consists in its being in a state of acceptance or friendship with God, and that which renders it acceptable to God is Sanctifying Grace.

This grace, which was merited for us by Our Lord Jesus Christ, is infused into the soul by the Holy Ghost through the Sacraments; but each Sacrament does not confer it in the same manner. Baptism and Penance bestow it upon those who are entirely out of the grace of God, or in other words, who are spiritually dead; Baptism being the means appointed for those who have never been in the grace of God, and Penance for those who have lost it.

These Sacraments are therefore called *Sacraments of the Dead*, as being instituted for the benefit of those who are in mortal sin or dead to grace. When these Sacraments are received with the right dispositions, they truly reconcile the sinner with God, so that from being an enemy of God, he becomes His friend and an object of His complacency. But this acceptance, though true and real, is not in the highest degree; it admits of an increase, as the Holy Scripture says: "Let him that is just be justified still; and let him that is holy be sanctified still"; and therefore God appointed the other Sacraments, *the Sacraments of the Living*, not only to convey special graces peculiar to each, but to impart an *increase of Sanctifying Grace* to those who are already in His favor.

A rich man, when he has taken possession of a field which he wishes to convert into a garden, is not content with putting a wall around it and clearing it of the most noxious weeds and setting it in good order, but he continues to cultivate it assiduously, to fill it with the most beautiful plants and to embellish it with new and choice ornaments. Thus Almighty God, in His love and goodness, has multiplied means by which the soul may be enriched with the graces and merits of Jesus Christ and become more and more agreeable and beautiful in His eyes.

Now among all these means, there is none greater or more powerful than the Blessed Eucharist. Each time that we receive our Saviour in Holy Communion, we participate anew in all the merits of His Redemption, of His poverty, His hidden life, His scourging and His crowning with thorns. The Holy Eucharist, then, differs from the other Sacraments in this, that while the other Sacraments bestow upon us one or another of the fruits of Christ's merits, this gives us the grace and merits of our Saviour in their source.

The soul, therefore, receives an immense increase of Sanctifying Grace at each Communion. Dear Christian, let us reflect upon this for a moment. It is no slight thing for a soul to be beautiful in the sight of God. That must needs be something great and precious which can render us—sinful creatures as we are—truly amiable before God. What must be the value of Sanctifying Grace, which can work such a transformation? What is it and who can declare its price?

St. Thomas tells us that the lowest degree of Sanctifying Grace is worth more than all the riches of the world. Think, then, of all the riches of this world! The mines of gold, of precious stones, the forests of costly wood, and all the hidden stores of wealth, for the least of which treasures the children of this world are willing to toil and struggle and sin for a whole lifetime.

Again, consider that the lowest grace which a humble Catholic Christian receives at the rails of the sanctuary at dawn of day, before the great world is astir, outweighs all those riches. But why do I draw my comparison from the things of this world? St. Teresa, after her death, appeared to one of her sisters in religion and told her that all the Saints in Heaven, without exception, would be willing to come back to this world and to remain here till the End of Time, suffering all the miseries to which our mortal state is subject, only to gain one more degree of Sanctifying Grace and the eternal glory corresponding to it.

Nay, I even assert that all the devils in Hell would consider all the torments of their dark abode, endured for millions upon millions of ages, largely recompensed by the least degree of that grace which they had once rejected. These thoughts give us a grand and sublime idea of the value of grace; but there is another consideration that ought to raise our estimate of it still higher, namely, that God Himself, the Eternal Son of the Father, came down upon earth, was made man, suffered and died the death of the cross in order to purchase it for us. His life is in some way the measure of its value.

Now in Holy Communion, this Sanctifying Grace is poured upon us in floods! The King of Heaven is then present in our souls, scattering profusely His benedictions and making us taste of the powers of the world to come. Oh, if any one of us were to see his own soul immediately after Communion, how amazed and confounded would he not be at the sight of it. He would take it for an Angel.

St. Catherine of Siena having been asked by her confessor to describe to him the beauty of a soul in the state of grace—as it had been revealed to her—replied: "The beauty and lustre of such a soul is so great that if you were to behold it, you would be willing to endure all possible pains and sufferings for its sake." Need we wonder, then, that the Angels loved to keep company with those saints on earth who every day with great devotion received Holy Communion, and that even the *faces* of those who have been ardent lovers of the Blessed Sacrament have sometimes shone with the glory with which they were filled? Does not Christ say of such a soul: "How beautiful art thou, My beloved! How beautiful art thou."

What great value should we then not set on this Divine Sacrament? At each Communion, we gain more and more upon what is bad in our hearts; we bring God more and more into them, and we come nearer to that heavenly state in which they shall be altogether "without spot or wrinkle," holy and without blemish. Should we not, then, esteem this wonder-working Sacrament more than anything else in this world? Ought we not continually to give thanks to God for so great a blessing and, above all, show our thankfulness by receiving it frequently and devoutly? I leave it to you, O Christian soul, to answer what I have said. I will not dwell longer on this point; reflect and act accordingly. I must pass on to explain some of the other wonderful effects of this precious Sacrament.

The benefit to be derived from Holy Communion which I will notice in the second place consists in this, that we are thereby preserved from mortal sin. In like manner as the body is continually in danger of death by reason of the law of decay which works unceasingly within us, so in like manner the life of the soul is constantly in jeopardy from that fearful proneness to sin which belongs to our fallen nature.

Accordingly, as Almighty God, in His Wisdom, has ordained natural food as the means of repairing the decay of the body and of warding off death, so has He seen fit to give us a ´spiritual and heavenly food to keep us from falling into mortal sin, which causes the death of the soul. This food is the Holy Eucharist, as the Council of Trent teaches us, saying that the Sacrament of the Eucharist is "the antidote by which we are freed from daily faults and preserved from mortal sins." And hence St. Francis de Sales compares Holy Communion to the Tree of Life which grew in the midst of the garden of Paradise, saying that "as our first parents by eating of that tree might have avoided the death of the body, so we, by feeding on this Sacrament of Life, may avoid the death of the soul."

Do you ask how the Blessed Sacrament preserves us from mortal sin? I reply: in two ways, by weakening our passions and by protecting us against the assaults of the devil. Everyone has some besetting sin, some passion which is excited in his heart more easily and more frequently than any other and which is the cause of the greater part of his faults. In some it is anger; in others, envy; in others, pride; in others, sensuality and impurity.

Now, however weak one may be, and by whatsoever passion he may be agitated, let him frequently receive the Body of Christ, and his soul will become tranquil and strong. The saints would express this by saying that, as the waters of the Jordan stood back when the Ark of the Covenant came into the river, so our passions and evil inclinations are repelled when Jesus Christ enters into our hearts in Holy Communion.

St. Bernard says: "If we do not experience so frequent and violent attacks of anger, envy and concupiscence as formerly, let us give thanks to Jesus Christ in the Blessed Sacrament, who has produced these effects in us." Accordingly, in the thanksgiving which the Church has provided to be used by the priest after the celebration of Mass, there is a prayer for imploring God that in like manner as the holy martyr St. Lawrence overcame the torments of fire, the soul, which has been fed with this Bread of Heaven, may be enabled to extinguish the flames of sin. There are thousands of cases which attest the efficacy of the Blessed Sacrament in this respect.

In Ferrara there lived a man who in his youth was very much molested with temptations of the flesh, to which he too often gave consent, and thus committed many mortal sins. To free himself from this miserable state, he determined to marry; but his wife died very soon, and he was again in danger. He was not disposed to marry again; but to remain a widower was, he thought, to expose himself anew to his former temptations. In this emergency he consulted a good friend and received the advice to go frequently to Confession and Holy Communion. He followed this advice and experienced in himself such extraordinary effects of the Sacrament that he could not help exclaiming: "Oh, why did I not sooner meet with such a friend! Most certainly I would not have committed so many abominable sins of impurity had I more frequently received this Sacrament which *maketh virgins*." (Baldesanus in *Stim. Virt.* I, c. 8).

In the life of St. Philip Neri, we read that one day a young man who was leading a very impure life came to the saint to Confession. St. Philip, knowing that there was no better remedy against concupiscence than the most sacred Body of Jesus Christ, counselled him to frequent the Sacraments. By this means he was in a short time entirely freed from his vicious habits and became pure like an angel. Oh, how many souls have made the same experience! Ask any Christian who has once lived in sin and afterwards truly amended, from what moment he began to get the better of his passions, and he will answer, from the moment that he began to frequent the Sacraments. How should it be otherwise? Jesus calms the winds and seas by a single word. What storm will be able to resist His power? What gust of passion will not subside when, on entering the soul, He says: "Peace be with thee; be not afraid; it is *I*!" The danger of mortal sin, however, arises not only from the strength of our passions, but also from the violence of the temptations with which the devil assails us; and against these, too, the Blessed Sacrament protects us.

When Ramirus, King of Spain, had been fighting a long time against the Saracens, he retired with his soldiers to a mountain to implore the assistance of Almighty God. While he was at prayer, St. James the Apostle appeared to him and commanded him to make all his soldiers go to Confession and Communion the day following and then to lead them out against their enemies. After all had been done that the Saint commanded, they again had an engagement with the Saracens and gained a complete and brilliant victory. (*Chron. Gen. Alphon. Reg.*).

In our conflict with the devil, how much more shall we not be enabled, by means of Holy Communion, to put him to flight and cover him with shame and confusion! St. Thomas says: "Hell was subdued by the death of our Saviour, and the Blessed Sacrament of the Altar being a mystical renewal of the death of Jesus Christ, the devils no sooner behold His Body and Blood in us, than they immediately take to flight, giving place to the Angels, who draw nigh and assist us." St. John Chrysostom says: "As the angel of destruction passed by all the houses of the Israelites without doing them any harm, because he found them sprinkled with the blood of the lamb, so the devil passes by us when he beholds within us the Blood of Jesus Christ, the Lamb of God."

And St. Ambrose says: "When thy adversary shall see thy habitation taken up with the brightness of the presence of God in thy soul, he departs and flies away, perceiving that no room is left for his temptations. Oh, how often has it happened that souls were so dreadfully tormented by the evil representations, suggestions and temptations of the devil as not to know what to do! But no sooner had they received Holy Communion, than they became at once quite calm and peaceful! Read the life of any of the Saints, and you will find instances of this; or ask any devout Catholic, and he will tell you that what I have asserted is but reality.

Nay, the devil himself must confess, and has often confessed, this truth. If he were forced to say why it is that he cannot tempt such and such a soul oftener and more violently, why it is that, to his own shame and confusion, he is forced to withdraw so often from a soul which once he held in his power, what do you think he would answer? Hear what he once answered. A person whom by a special permission of God he was allowed to harass very much and even drag about on the ground was exorcised by a priest of our Congregation, and the devil was commanded to say whether or not Holy Communion was very useful and profitable to the soul.

At the first and second interrogatory he would not answer, but the third time, being commanded in the name of the blessed Trinity, he replied with a howl: "Profitable! Know that if this person had not received Holy Communion so many times, we should have had her completely in our power." Behold, then, our great weapon against the devil! "Yes," says the great St. John Chrysostom, "after receiving the Body and Blood of Jesus Christ in the Holy Eucharist, we become as terrible to the devil as a furious lion is to man."

When the King of Syria went out to take the

prophet Eliseus captive, the servant of the man of God was very much afraid at seeing the great army and the horses and chariots, and he said: "Alas! alas! alas! my Lord; what shall we do?" But the prophet said: "Fear not, for there are more with us than with them." And then he showed the trembling servant how the whole mountain was full of angels ready to defend them.

So, however weak we may be and however powerful our enemies, fortified with the Bread of Heaven, we have no reason to fear; we are stronger than Hell, for God is with us. "The Lord ruleth me, I shall want nothing. Though I should walk in the midst of the shadow of death, I fear no evils, for Thou art with me. Thou hast prepared a *table* before me against them that afflict me."

In concluding this point, let me then once more address to you, dear Christian, the words of exhortation. With what justice does not St. Francis de Sales appear to you, saying: "O Philothea, what reply shall reprobate Christians be able to make to the reproaches of the just Judge for having lost His grace when it was so easy to have preserved it?" If the means of avoiding sin had been very difficult, the case of the reprobate might seem hard, but who can pity him who has but to obey the easy command: "Take and eat; if any man shall eat of this bread he shall live forever." For a Catholic to fall into mortal sin is as if one should starve at a splendid banquet, and for a Christian to die in the power of the devil is to be in love with death.

But there are other riches in this Blessed Sacrament which remain to be unfolded. It not only increases in us sanctifying grace and preserves us from mortal sin, but it truly unites us to God, and this is the third effect of this Holy Sacrament. The most obvious sense in which this Sacrament is said to unite us to God is that which is suggested by the doctrine of the Real Presence itself. In the Holy Eucharist we receive the very Body and Blood of Jesus Christ; and as members of the same family are united together by the ties of the common blood which flows in their veins, so we become truly kinsmen of Christ by participation of the Blood which He received from His most Holy Mother and shed on the Cross for us.

Hence, St. Alphonsus says that as the food we take is changed into our blood, so in Holy Communion God becomes one with us—with this difference, however: that whereas earthly food is changed into *our* substance, we assume, as it were, the nature of Jesus Christ, as He Himself declared to St. Augustine, saying, "It is not I that shall be changed into you, but you shall be changed into Me."

"Yes," says St. Cyril of Alexandria, "he who communicates unites himself as closely to Jesus Christ as two pieces of wax, when melted, become one." And the Saints have always been so penetrated with this belief that after Holy Communion they would exclaim: "O Jesus, now Thou art mine and I am Thine! Thou art in me, and I am in Thee! Now Thou belongest entirely to me, and I belong entirely to Thee. Thy soul is mine, and my soul is Thine! Thy life is mine, and my life is Thine!" But this is not all.

We are united to Our Lord's sacred humanity in order that we may be made conformable to His image in will and affections; accordingly, in the

Eucharist we receive from Him infused virtues, especially Faith, Hope and Charity, the three distinguishing characteristics of the children of God. As to Faith, it is so much increased by Communion that this Sacrament might be called *the Sacrament of Faith*, not only because it makes the largest demand on our faith of any mystery of our Holy Religion, but also because it more than any other increases and confirms it. It seems as if God, in reward of the generous faith with which we believe this doctrine, often gives an inward light which enables the soul in some way to comprehend it, and with it the other truths of faith.

So, the Council of Trent says that "the mode of Christ's presence in the Eucharist can hardly be expressed in words, but the pious mind, illuminated by faith, can conceive of it." The reception of this Sacrament is the best explanation of the difficulties which sense opposes to it. It was in the *breaking of bread* at Emmaus that the two disciples recognized Jesus. He Himself gives us evidence of the reality of the Divine Presence in this heavenly food and makes us *taste* what we do not understand. One day a holy soul said to Father Surin of the Society of Jesus: "I would not exchange a single one of the divine communications which I receive in Holy Communion for anything whatever that men or angels might present to me."

Sometimes God adds to these favors the gift of a spiritual joy and delight, intense and indescribable. St. Thomas says that "Holy Communion is a spiritual eating which communicates an actual delight to such souls as receive it devoutly and with due preparation." And the effect of this delight, according to St. Cyprian, is that it detaches the heart from all worldly pleasures and makes it die to everything perishable.

Nay, this joy is sometimes even communicated to the exterior senses, penetrating them with a sweetness so great that nothing in the world can be compared to it. St. Francis, St. Monica, St. Agnes and many others are witnesses of this, who, intoxicated with celestial sweetness in Holy Communion, exulted for joy and exclaimed with the psalmist: "My heart and my flesh have rejoiced in the living God. For what have I in Heaven? and besides Thee what do I desire upon earth? Thou art the God of my heart and the God that is my portion forever. My Jesus, my Love, my God, my All."

Oh what a firm faith men would have in this mystery did they communicate often and devoutly! One single Communion is better than all the arguments of the schools. We have not a lively faith, we think little of Heaven, of Hell, of the evil of sin, of the goodness of Our Lord and the duty of loving Him, because we stay away from Communion; let us eat and our eyes shall be opened. "Taste and see that the Lord is sweet."

Hope also receives a great increase from this Sacrament, for it is the pledge of our inheritance and has the promise of eternal life attached to it. "He who eateth of this Bread shall live forever. He who eateth My Flesh and drinketh My Blood abideth in Me and I in him. As the Father Who liveth sent Me, and I live by the Father, so he that eateth Me, the same also shall live by Me. He shall never hunger or thirst. He shall not die, but have life everlasting, and I will raise him up on the last day." (Cf. *John* 6).

St. Paul argues that "if we are sons, then we are heirs, heirs indeed of God, and joint heirs with Christ." And elsewhere he says that "we glory in hope of the glory of God." It is true that in this life we can never have an infallible assurance of our salvation, but Holy Communion most powerfully confirms and strengthens our hope of obtaining Heaven and the graces necessary for living and dying holily. However great the fear and diffidence may be with which our sins inspire us, what soul is not comforted when our Saviour Himself enters the heart and seems to say: "Ask whatever you will, and it shall be done unto you." "Can I refuse the less Who have given the greater? Can I withhold any necessary graces Who have given Myself? Shall I refuse to bring you to reign with Me in Heaven, Who am come down on earth to dwell with you?"

Charity, however, is the virtue which is more especially nourished by the Holy Eucharist. This may be called, by eminence, the proper effect of this Sacrament, as indeed it is of the Incarnation itself. "I am come to cast fire on the earth, and what will I but that it be kindled!" (*Luke* 12:49). And St. Dionysius the Areopagite says that "Jesus Christ in the most Holy Eucharist is a fire of charity." It could not be otherwise. As a burning house sets the adjacent ones on fire, so the Heart of Jesus Christ, which is always burning with love, communicates the flames of charity to those who receive Him in Holy Communion. Accordingly, St. Mary Magdalen de Pazzi, St. Catherine of Siena, St. Teresa, St. Philip Neri, St. Francis Xavier and thousands of others, by their frequent Communions, became, as it were, furnaces of divine love. "Do you not feel," said St. Vincent de

Paul to his brothers in religion, "do you not become sensible of the divine fire in your hearts after having received the adorable Body of Jesus Christ in the Holy Eucharist?"

In proof of the strength of love which souls derive from Holy Communion, I might appeal to the ecstasies and raptures which so many souls have experienced at the reception of the most Holy Eucharist. What were all these favors but flames of Divine love enkindled by this heavenly fire which, as it were, destroyed in them themselves and conformed them to the image of their Saviour.

Or, I might take my proof from those sweet tears which flow from the eyes of so many servants of God when at the Communion rail they receive the Bread of Heaven. But I have a better proof than these transports of devotion: I mean suffering. This is the true test of love. St. Paul says that the Christian glories in tribulation because the charity of God is poured out into his heart, and so the Holy Eucharist, by infusing love into our hearts, gives us strength to suffer for Christ.

In the life of St. Lydwine, who was sick for thirty-eight years uninterruptedly, we read that, in the beginning of her sickness, she shrank from suffering. By a particular disposition of Providence, however, a celebrated servant of God, John Por, went to see her, and perceiving that she was not quite resigned to the will of God, he exhorted her to meditate frequently on the sufferings of Jesus Christ, that by the remembrance of His Passion she might gain courage to suffer more willingly. She promised to do so and fulfilled her promise, but she could not find any relief for her soul. Every meditation was disgusting and unpleasant, and she began again to break out into her usual complaints. After a while, her director returned to her and asked her how she had succeeded in meditating upon Our Lord's Passion and what profit she had derived from it. "O my Father," she answered, "your counsel was very good indeed, but the greatness of my suffering does not allow me to find any consolation in meditating on my Saviour's sorrows."

He exhorted her for some time to continue this exercise, no matter how insipid soever it might be to her; but perceiving at last that she drew no fruit from it, his zeal suggested another means. He gave her Holy Communion and afterwards whispered in her ear: "Till now *I* have exhorted you to the continual remembrance of Christ's sufferings as a remedy for your pains, but now let Jesus Christ Himself exhort you." Behold! No sooner had she swallowed the Sacred Host than she felt such a great love for Jesus and such an ardent desire to become like unto Him in His sufferings, that she broke out into sobs and sighs, and for two weeks was hardly able to stop her tears.

From that moment the pains and sufferings of her Saviour remained so deeply impressed upon her mind that she thought of them all the time and thus was enabled patiently to suffer for Him, who for the love of her had endured so many and so great pains and torments. Her disease at last grew so violent that her flesh began to corrupt and to be filled with worms, and the putrefaction extended even internally, so that she had to suffer the most excruciating pains. But comforted by the example of Jesus Christ, she not only praised God and gave thanks to Him for all her sufferings, but even vehemently desired to suffer still more; nay, by meditating on the Passion of Jesus Christ, she was so much inflamed with love that she used to say, "It was not she who suffered, but her Lord Jesus Christ Who suffered in her." (Surius 14 April in *Vita S. Ludwinae,* Part I. C. 14).

Thus, by Holy Communion this Saint received a grace by which she has merited to be numbered among the most patient of Saints. Nor is this a single case. Animated by this heavenly food, St. Lawrence braved the flames, St. Vincent the rack, St. Sebastian the shower of arrows, St. Ignatius of Antioch the fury of lions, and many other martyrs every kind of torture which the malice of the devil could invent, content if they could but return their Saviour love for love, life for life, death for death.

They embraced the very instruments of their tortures; yea, they even exulted and gloried in them. Now this was the effect of the Holy Eucharist; this life-giving Bread imparted to them courage and joy in every pain and trial. For this very reason, in the early times of the persecutions, all Christians, in order to be prepared for martyrdom, received the Blessed Sacrament every day, and when the danger was too pressing for them to assemble together, they even carried the Sacred Host to their own homes, that they might communicate themselves early in the morning. The same was done by Mary, Queen of Scots, during her captivity in England when she was deprived of the ministry of a priest.

It was for the same reason that Christ instituted the Holy Eucharist just before His Passion, that He might thereby fortify His Apostles for the trials that were coming on them. It is true we have not so fierce a conflict to endure as the early Christians had, nor has anyone such a dreadful sickness as St. Lydwine had; but in our lighter trials, we have also need of this fortitude of love; nor is it refused to us.

Multitudes of pious souls confess that it is the Holy Communion alone which keeps them steady in the practice of virtue and cheerful amid all the vicissitudes of life. How often do we hear such souls declaring that on the days they do not receive Communion they seem to themselves lame and miserable; everything goes wrong with them, and all their crosses seem tenfold heavier than usual. But when in the morning they have had the happiness of partaking of the Body of Christ, everything seems to go well; the daily annoyances of their state seem to disappear; they are happy and joyous; words of kindness seem to come naturally in their mouths; and life is no longer the burden which once it seemed to be.

O truly wonder-working Sacrament! Marvelous invention of Divine Love, surpassing all power of speech to describe or thought to fathom! When the children of Israel found in the fields the bread from Heaven which God gave them in the wilderness, they called it *Manhu*, "What is it?" because they did not know what it was. So, after all that we have said of the true Manna, the Sacrament of the Holy Eucharist, we must confess that we are unable to comprehend it. "Man does not live on bread alone." He has a higher life than that which is nourished by the fruits of the ground, a spiritual and divine life, and this life is nourished by the Body of Christ.

Hidden under the Sacramental form, our Divine Saviour comes down to make us more and more acceptable to Him, to preserve us in this dangerous world from mortal sin, to make us true children of God, to console us in our exile, to give us a pledge of our eternal happiness, to shed abroad in our hearts the love of God.

And as if this were not enough and as if to set the seal on the rest, He is sometimes pleased to make His own most Sacred Body supply the place of all other nourishment and miraculously to sustain even the natural life of His servants by this Sacramental food. St. Catherine of Siena, from Ash Wednesday to Ascension Day, took no other food than Holy Communion. (Surius 29 April). A certain holy virgin of Rome spent five whole Lents without tasting anything else but the Bread of Angels. (Cacciaguerra).

St. Nicholas of Flüe, of whom I have spoken, for fifteen successive years lived without other nourishment than the Sacred Body of Our Lord. (Simon Majolus *Canicular*, Collet IV). And St. Liberalis, Bishop of Athens, fasted every day in the week, taking nothing whatever, not even the Blessed Sacrament, and on Sunday his only nourishment consisted of this heavenly food, yet he was always strong and vigorous. (P. Nat. L. IV., Collat. Sanct. c. xciii).

We can but repeat: O wonder-working Sacrament!! We are at a loss what to say. We are silenced by the greatness of God's bounty. What can we do but humbly thank God in the depths of our hearts for so great a blessing, so rich a consolation in this valley of tears. There is nothing short of the vision of God in Heaven which the mind of man can conceive so precious as one Communion. "Thou hast given us, O Lord, Bread from Heaven, having in it all manner of delights!" "O sacred banquet in which Christ is received, the memory of His Passion is celebrated, the mind is filled with grace, and the pledge of future glory is given to us! Alleluia!"

CHAPTER 9

The Excuses of Those Who Do Not Communicate Frequently

AFTER having heard of the great desire of Jesus Christ to unite Himself to us in Holy Communion and the great benefit which we reap from such a union, we might naturally expect to find men eager to avail themselves of a means of grace so rich and so powerful. But our greatest misery is that we are blind to our true happiness. Such is the deceitfulness of sin and the subtlety of the devil that almost everyone has some reason to give why he at least should not receive Communion frequently, and thus all the arguments I have presented in favor of frequent Communion are frequently set aside under the most silly and frivolous pretexts. It will not be without utility to consider in detail the reasons which are alleged for such strange conduct, and I will therefore, Dear Reader, call up before you the various classes of Catholics who do not often approach Holy Communion, and I will examine the excuses which they give, that you may judge of their validity. I will make the examination class by class.

Why do you not go often to Communion?

1st Excuse. Because I do not receive the great graces you spoke of in the preceding chapter.

Answer. How do you know that you do not receive

them? Is it because you do not *feel* them? But this is no certain proof that you do not really receive them. If you were sick and had no relish for food, would the food on that account cease to nourish you? Now it is the same with regard to the Blessed Sacrament, the spiritual food of your soul. Consolations and delights are graces which God bestows when and upon whom He thinks fit; and if He often deprives His servants of them, it is to try them, to keep them humble and to give them an opportunity of meriting greater graces. As corporeal food nourishes you and makes you strong without your perceiving it, so also does this heavenly food silently and imperceptibly enrich your soul with grace. You cannot see a plant grow, but you can see very well that it has grown; in like manner you do not see your soul grow in the spiritual life by receiving Holy Communion, yet experience shows you that it really does grow. You now live in the fear of God; you have not committed a mortal sin for years, perhaps not even in your whole life. You do not grow lukewarm in the practice of virtue; you fulfill your duties faithfully. Are not all *these* great graces and favors? And are they not all the admirable effects of Holy Communion? Is not the remedy that protects us from disease better than one that restores us to health? But let us suppose the truth of what you allege. I ask you why do you not receive great fruit from this Sacrament? Do you prepare yourself sufficiently? Do you not approach the altar negligently? Do you consider beforehand what you are about to do; and afterwards, do you reflect sufficiently on what you have done? Or do you commit venial sins willfully and with full deliberation? Are not these the reasons why you fail to derive from the reception of this Sacrament that profit which others draw from it? If so, you must ascribe the fault to yourself that Holy Communion does not produce in you all the fruit it should.

Why do you not receive Holy Communion frequently?

2nd Excuse. I fear to lose my reverence for it: the proverb says: "Familiarity begets contempt."

Answer. I admit the proverb is true in regard to men, but not in regard to God. The more familiar you become with men, the more faults and defects you discover in them, and on this account you will feel less respect for them; but this is not the case in regard to God. The more intimate you become with Him and the oftener you approach Him, the better you become acquainted with Him, the more perfections you will discover in Him, and the more you will love Him. Is it not a blasphemy to say that conversing with God makes man worse and more wicked and that, in order to be a Saint, one must withdraw from Him? Can the most perfect exercise of religion derogate from the respect which we owe to this Sacrament? When do you make acts of faith, hope, love, adoration and humility if not after Communion? The Church *prescribed* daily Communion in the first ages of Christianity, and she now strongly *recommends* it by the Council of Trent. Can the Holy Church recommend or advise anything sinful?

Why do you communicate so seldom?

3rd Excuse. Because I fear to receive Holy Communion unworthily.

Answer. I suppose you mean by this that you do not know for certain that you are in the state of grace. It is true we are required to be in the state of grace, but we are not required to have any greater certainty of it than that which is ordinarily given to good Christians. Will you wait till an Angel comes down from Heaven to tell you that you are in the state of grace? Do you not know that you can place far more reliance on the assurance of your confessor than in that of an Angel? If an Angel should appear to you, you might have some reason to fear that it was the devil come to deceive you; but you know that in listening to your confessor you have the promise of Christ that you shall not be led astray. Hence, St. Alphonsus says: "Place more confidence in the minister of God than in the revelations of all the Angels of Paradise." He adds, moreover, that there is no species of disobedience more hurtful than to omit a Communion prescribed by one's confessor, because such disobedience proceeds from a want of humility. Therefore, when you have the permission of your director, go forward with confidence. No one goes tremblingly to a feast, but cheerfully and joyfully. The Son of God does not appear on our altars under the appearance of bread in order to be regarded with fear, but to be approached with love and desire. Besides, if you fear to approach this Sacrament, do you not also fear to stay away from it? The Son of God declares in the parable of the great supper that the guests who declined their lord's invitation were entirely excluded from his friendship, even though their excuses for staying away had some plausibility. Should not this example cause you to fear?

Why do you not communicate often?

4th Excuse. I wish indeed to do so and trust that I am in the state of grace, but I am so much afraid of committing a sacrilege.

Answer. One never commits a sacrilege without intending it. This is but a deceit of the devil. Oh execrable malice! He seduced our first parents by the promise of a happy life to eat of that fruit which brought death into the world, and now he makes every effort to prevent Christians from eating the true Bread of Life by inspiring the fear that it may prove the cause of eternal death!

Why do you not communicate often?

5th Excuse. Because I commit so many faults, that it would seem like presumption to receive Holy Communion often.

Answer. It is no presumption for one who has many imperfections and defects to go often to Communion. Nay, it is not presumptuous to go, even though one commits many faults, provided they are not altogether willful and deliberate. Do you think you will commit fewer faults by staying away from Communion? Can you avoid sin without God's grace? And how will you obtain His grace if not from this Sacrament? I would rather advise you to go often *because* you are so imperfect, for the longer you stay away, the more imperfect you will become. The Church teaches that the Holy Eucharist is food and medicine at the same time; food for the healthy and medicine for the sick. Hence a holy Dominican nun used to say: "For my part, being sensible of my unworthiness, I would wish to communicate three times a day, for by more frequent Communion I should hope to render myself more worthy." Did not the Son of God answer to the Pharisees who were scandalized at seeing Him eat with sinners: "They who are in health need not a physician, but they that are sick." You say, "I am not worthy," thinking perhaps that such a sentiment proceeds from humility; but you ought to know that generally it shows greater humility to receive frequently than to receive seldom, because one who receives frequently, by applying so often a remedy to his sickness, acknowledges his infirmities. If indeed your abstaining from Holy Communion really proceeds from humility, it is not displeasing to God, but it would be a thousand times more acceptable to Him if you would join confidence to your humility. Fear is good, but love is far better. One day when St. Frances of Rome was going to receive Communion, the devil said to her: "How can you, who are so full of venial sins, dare to receive the Immaculate Lamb!" She instantly perceived that the enemy intended to deprive her of so great a joy, and silenced him by spitting in his face. After this the Blessed Virgin appeared to her, and having praised her conduct, she said that our defects, instead of being an obstacle, should be an incentive to Communion, since in Communion we find the remedy for all our miseries.

Why do you communicate so seldom?

6th Excuse. Because I am not holy enough to receive Holy Communion worthily.

Answer. If you mean that, in order to receive Holy Communion worthily, it is required to have a holiness equal to His whom you receive, then not even the Blessed Virgin was worthy. If you mean that it is necessary to have a purity without spot, then the Apostles were unworthy, because even they had imperfections and defects; and much more so were the first Christians, and yet they communicated daily. If you mean only that it is required to make a suitable preparation, the Church declares that the necessary preparation consists in not having knowingly a mortal sin on your conscience which you have not confessed, although indeed she *advises* and *exhorts* her children to a better and more perfect preparation, namely, to endeavor to avoid venial sins and strive earnestly to correct their faults. What is it, then, that keeps you back from Holy Communion? Do not fancy that the Son of God requires as a preparation for the reception of a Sacrament what is properly its fruit, effect and end, any more than a physician requires a sick person to be healthy as a preparation for taking medicine. Holiness and purity of soul are the effects of this Sacrament, according to the declaration of the Council of Trent; is it not then folly and injustice to demand them as a necessary preparation for its reception? Tell me, if those virtues were required, who could ever communicate, even at Easter?

Why do you stay away from Holy Communion?

7th Excuse. Alas! I have offended God so often and grievously in my past life that I dare not go often to communicate.

Answer. Have you offended Him more deeply than St. Augustine? Have you committed more sins than St. Margaret of Cortona did before her conversion? And do you not remember that Our Lord one day told this Saint that He would give her confessor a great reward for having advised her to go often to Communion? Or have you forgotten that He said to the venerable Prudentiana Zagnoni: "If you receive Me frequently in Holy Communion, I will forget all your ingratitude"? Remember that it was for the sake of sinners that the Son of God came down from Heaven. If you are truly sorry for your sins, if you have sincerely confessed them all, if you are firmly resolved not to sin anymore, then you have even a special *right* and *claim* to go to Communion. Our Lord said: "I am not come to call the just, but sinners to penance."

Why do you not go oftener to Communion?

8th Excuse. I fear that it may come to be a mere custom.

Answer. A good custom is a good thing. Ought you to give up hearing Mass daily from fear of becoming used to it? Or omit your daily prayers from an apprehension of praying through custom?

Why do you not go often to Communion?

9th Excuse. Because when I do go, I am so cold, distracted and indevout.

Answer. There is a great difference between devotion and the *feeling* of devotion. One may have much devotion without feeling it at all. Sensible devotion is not always the best, for it is liable to many illusions. Besides this, it does not always depend upon us. God grants it to whom He pleases. If sensible devotion were required, most undoubtedly those who have it not would not be allowed to receive Holy Communion even at Easter. If you feel no devotion, humble yourself before God, but do not stay away from Him. The devotion which is necessary for receiving Holy Communion consists in approaching your Lord with humility, confidence and love; with a desire to honor Jesus Christ, to unite yourself to Him and to obey Him. You say: "I am so cold," but tell me, will you become warm by staying away from the fire? Would it not be wiser to go to Communion in order to become devout? Do you not know that Holy Communion is a fire which enkindles love, devotion and spiritual joy in the heart? Is it not true that the less frequently you receive, the less desire you have to receive, and that the oftener you receive, the more you will wish to receive?

Why do you not receive Communion more frequently?

10th Excuse. Because it seems to me that I feel more devotion when I receive but seldom.

Answer. That may be true, although it is not the general experience; however, it will always be true that if you communicate seldom, your soul will lack grace and fervor. One who kept a continual fast would become very weak and attenuated, although he might take his scanty food with the keenest relish.

Why do you not receive Holy Communion frequently?

11th Excuse. My confessor does not allow me.

Answer. If this is really the case, you must obey—and supply as well as you can the want of the Holy Sacrament by multiplying spiritual Communions. Say to Jesus Christ: "Lord, I would receive Thee more frequently if I were not prevented by obedience," and He will be pleased with your obedience and your desire for Holy Communion. But are you certain that your confessor is not inclined to allow you frequent Communion? Do you often *ask leave* to communicate more frequently? This, at least, is in your power, and it is very useful and by no means opposed to the perfection of obedience. Your confessor knows that, to produce great fruit, this divine food must be eaten with hunger, and as long as you show but little eagerness for the Holy Sacrament, he will not advise or permit you to communicate often. But perhaps you *have* asked for it several times, and he has not granted your request. Well, and *how* did you ask? Did you imitate St. Catherine of Siena, who when deprived of Communion by her confessor, exclaimed: "Father, give my soul its food!" Had you, like her, manifested with humility and resignation this holy hunger, your confessor would have treated you very differently; but because you appear cold and not unwilling to be repulsed from Communion, he prudently abstains from advising you to receive it very often.

Why do you receive Holy Communion so infrequently?

12th Excuse. I have not time to prepare myself as I ought.

Answer. How much time do you need for preparation? Must you spend the whole morning in prayer or in reading pious books? St. Teresa received Communion every day for twenty-three years; do you think she had nothing else to attend to? I think she was more busy than you will ever be. The first Christians went daily to Communion; do you imagine their occupations were of less consequence than yours, or their family affairs less troublesome? Shall I tell you the reason why the Saints and first Christians were able to prepare themselves for daily Communion? They were more fervent than the Christians of the present day and had a greater love for Jesus Christ. If you foresee that you will not have time in the morning to prepare for Communion, endeavor the preceding evening to make some preparation by reading some pious book and making the acts which ought to be made in the morning; or rise a little before the usual time, and spend whatever time may be at your disposal in preparing yourself as well as you can; or endeavor to perform the duties of your state with a view to please God, and you may rest assured that this will be an excellent preparation for your Communion. St. Mary Magdalen de Pazzi used to say to her sisters in religion: "Offer to God all your actions as a preparation for Communion; perform them with the intention of pleasing Him, and communicate."

Why do you not communicate often?

13th Excuse. I abstain in order to avoid the remarks of others.

Answer. If you communicate by the advice of your confessor and through a desire of correcting your faults and advancing in divine love, you need not be disturbed at what others may say about you. Father Avila used to say that they who censured their neighbors for receiving Communion frequently perform the office of the devil. Why, then, should you pay attention to such people? If it be wrong to listen to the devil, is it right to listen to his agents? Do you not know that everything good must meet with contradiction? Let people say what they please; at the Day of Judgment they will find out their mistake, and then they will despise you for having listened to them.

Why do you communicate so seldom?

14th Excuse. Because the Church does not command me to receive oftener than once a year, and in obeying her I cannot go astray.

Answer. If the Church commanded you to eat meat or drink wine only once in the year, would you be so exact in keeping to the letter of the law? The Church requires us to abstain from flesh-meat on Fridays and to fast during Lent and at certain other seasons; do you never, for a slight cause, seek exemption from this precept? How is it that for the most part those who are such literal interpreters of the law of Easter Communion are so lax in the observance of the law of fasting? How is it that they who find one Communion a year just enough generally complain of one Lent a year as a great deal too much? Ah! I fear that faith and reverence for the Church have but little share in this excuse and that the real reason of your urging this precept is the earthliness and sordidness of your affections. Your desires are low and groveling; you have more relish for the food of the body than for the food of the soul. With the Israelites in the desert, you prefer the good things of Egypt to the Manna that comes from Heaven; and your taste is so corrupted by the impure pleasures of the world, that you can find no delight in the sweet fountains that flow from the Saviour's side. Believe me, this is no good sign; it is a sign of great danger; for as the Royal Prophet has said, "Behold, they that go far from God shall perish." But I have another remark to make on your excuse.

You have not represented the precept of the Church quite exactly. You have left out an important word. The Church says that her children must receive Holy Communion "*at least* once a year." I will tell you: In former times Christians were accustomed to communicate every day, and then their lives were holy and edifying and chaste and humble; and infidels and heretics, struck by the purity of their manners, were converted in crowds to the Faith. But in after ages, luxury crept in, and the world and the flesh had sway, and too many grew cold in love and lost their relish for this heavenly food.

And now what can the Church do to cure the evil? If she were to make it *obligatory* to receive Holy Communion frequently, she would run the risk of multiplying mortal sins and of plunging her imperfect members more deeply into guilt. She uses, therefore, a wise and loving moderation, and as a tender mother, when every other expedient fails, speaks sternly to her sick child and forces it to take the food or medicine which is absolutely necessary to life— she enjoins, under pain of mortal sin, a single Communion in the year, *as the least which can be required of a Christian!*

But is this all that she wishes us to do? Oh no! She desires that we should continually nourish ourselves with the Bread of Life. In the Council of Trent she bewails the disuse of daily Communion and earnestly exhorts all the faithful to a frequent use of this sanctifying food. Since then you insist so much on obedience to the Church, show the spirit of an obedient child, and fulfill her ardent wish. It is true you will not fall under her censures if you receive but once a year, but you will be a much better Christian if you receive more frequently.

Why do you communicate so seldom?

15th Excuse. I do not see any necessity for it! There are many others who do not receive oftener than I do—that is, once or twice a year—and yet they are good Christians; yea, as good as those who receive very often.

Answer. I will not dispute your assertion. No one knows the heart of another, and I rather wish that you should form as charitable a judgment as you can of your neighbors who do not receive often. Neither will I say of all those who go often to Communion that they are exactly what they ought to be. But scarcely anyone will affirm that persons who communicate but once or twice a year are, generally speaking, as exemplary in their conduct as those who communicate frequently.

Point out to me those whom you consider the most pious; who live in the world without following its manners or adopting its principles; who, when adversity overtakes them, are calm and resigned to the will of God, and when it overtakes their neighbor, are ready for every act of charity; who are meek and kind, rich in good works and fond of prayer; who are constant in their attendance at Mass, diligent in seeking spiritual instruction, faithful in their duties and edifying in their conversation—and I will show you these same persons regularly at the altar every month, fortnight, or week; yes, even oftener. Grant that among these frequent communicants there is but one who lives a truly devout life, still you have sufficient evidence of the fruit of this Sacrament, for you know that no one can live holily without the grace of God and that this Sacrament was instituted to impart grace to us in an abundant measure. "I am come that they may have life, and may have it more abundantly." (*John* 10:10).

But after all, is this the proper way to reason? Do not ask whether others are good Christians, but whether you yourself are. You know a *good Christian* means something more than one who does not rob or commit murder or such like crimes. A good Christian means a person who endeavors to keep his heart pure in the sight of God and to overcome pride, envy, avarice, unchasteness and gluttony, to which his lower nature is so prone. Now, do *you* find *within* you no sting of the flesh, no movements of hatred or desires of revenge, no rebellion of pride? Palladius tells the story of a young man who, after endeavoring for a long time to corrupt a virtuous married woman, and finding her chastity proof against all his assaults, sought to revenge himself upon her through the intervention of the devil. By the permission of God, the evil one caused her to assume the appearance of a wild beast, and her husband, greatly distressed at so horrible a transformation, took her to St. Macarius, that by his prayers and blessing she might be delivered from the malice of the devil. The Saint easily effected this by his power with God; and after the good woman was restored to her natural appearance, he gave her this advice: "In future go more often to Communion than you have hitherto done, for know that the reason why God permitted you to appear in such a form is your negligence in not having received Communion for five successive weeks. So it has been revealed to me from on high. Remember it and take it to heart."

Five weeks! And you stay away for five months; yea, for an entire year, and find no necessity for receiving more often? And do you think the devil has been idle and that no hideous transformation has taken place in your soul in the eyes of the Angels? Has not your soul become a sow in impurity, or a tiger in rage, or a viper in treachery, or a filthy creeping worm in its low and groveling affections?

I leave it to yourself to answer. God grant that it may not be so. I know that it is the testimony and experience of the Saints that with all their efforts and continual use of the Sacraments they found it a hard thing to keep their hearts clean; and if for a short time they were prevented from receiving the Bread of Heaven, their hearts became withered and dry, and they exclaimed: "I am smitten as grass, and my heart is withered because I forgot to eat my Bread." (*Ps.* 101:5). I also know that Holy Scripture says: "They that go far from Thee shall perish." (*Ps.* 72:27).

And now, Dear Reader, I think you have come to the same conclusion, that there is no valid excuse for not communicating frequently and that, for the most part, they who give these excuses are influenced by a secret unwillingness to lead a Christian life in good earnest. They are unwilling to practice retirement, detachment from creatures and self-denial. They stay away from Communion as long as they can in order to avoid the rebuke of Jesus Christ for their sensuality, pride, vanity, uncharitableness and sloth. Miserable are the consequences of such a course of conduct. Not being able to find true peace of heart in religion, such men seek their consolation in exterior things and multiply faults and imperfections in proportion as they withdraw from God. And what is most lamentable is that not infrequently their venial sins lead them into mortal sins and they live in such a state for months, remaining in constant danger of being overtaken by a sudden and unprovided death, the just punishment of their ingratitude and indifference towards Jesus Christ.

I have said *"for the most part,"* for I know there are cases in which reluctance to receive this Sacrament proceeds from a vain fear of irreverence, inspired by the teaching of misguided men. I have said enough already to show the groundlessness of such a fear and its injuriousness to God; would that I could sufficiently express its hurtfulness to souls.

St. Vincent de Paul, when speaking of this subject, used to relate the following story: A noble and pious lady who had long been in the habit of communicating several times a week, was so unhappy as to choose for her confessor a priest who was imbued with the principles of the Jansenistic heresy. Her new director at first allowed her to go to Holy Communion once a week; but, after a while, he would not permit her to go oftener than once a fortnight; and at last he limited her to once a month. The lady went on in this way for eight months, when wishing to know the state of her soul, she made a careful self-examination; but, alas! she found her heart so full of irregular appetites, passions and imperfections that she was actually afraid of herself. Horror-struck at her deterioration, she exclaimed: "Miserable creature that I am! How deeply have I fallen! How wretchedly am I living! Where will all this end? What is the cause of this lamentable state of mine? I see! I see! It is for no other reason than for my having followed these new teachers and for having abandoned the practice of frequent Communion." Then, giving thanks to God, who had enlightened her to see her error, she renounced her false guide and resumed her former practice. Soon after, she was enabled to get the better of her faults and passions, and to regain tranquility of heart. Oh how effectually do such men perform the work of the devil! The great adversary of mankind has nothing so much at heart as to keep men back from the means of grace, especially the Blessed Eucharist. In his warfare against the faithful, he acts as the nations bordering upon Abyssinia are said to do in their conflicts with the inhabitants of that country. The Abyssinians are known to observe a strict fast of forty days at a certain period of the year, and it is the cruel custom of their enemies to wait until they are weakened by this long abstinence, and then to rush upon them and gain an easy victory.

Thus I say it is with the devil: a forty days' fast from the Blessed Sacrament is a rich conquest for him. It is his greatest delight to keep men away from the altar. Every excuse for staying away from Holy Communion is legitimate in his eyes; every doctrine which teaches that it is useless or hurtful to frequent the Holy Eucharist is stamped with his approval; every taunt with which a tepid Catholic upbraids his more fervent brother for nourishing his soul often with the Bread of Life is music in his ears. And he is in the right, for let men but once be persuaded to deprive themselves of the strengthening Body of Jesus Christ, and the work of Satan is no longer difficult. When the soul is weak in grace, by reason of long abstinence from the Flesh of Jesus Christ, then the evil one comes down upon it with his strong temptations and almost without resistance makes it his slave.

Once more, those who discountenance frequent Communion do the devil's work. They give Hell much pleasure and deprive Our Lord of great delight. It is on this account that Our Lord so often visits with severe punishments those who dissuade others from receiving Him. A woman who mocked St. Catherine of Siena for going so often to Holy Communion, on her return home, fell down to the ground and died instantly without being able to receive the last Sacraments. Another woman, who had committed the same offense, became crazy all at once. Nay, even where the fault was much slighter, God has shown His displeasure. St. Lutgaard was in the habit of receiving Holy Communion very often, but her superioress, disapproving, forbade her doing so in the future. The Saint obeyed, but at that very moment her superioress fell sick and had to suffer the most acute pains. At last, suspecting that her sickness was a punishment for having interdicted frequent Communion to Lutgaard, she withdrew the prohibition, when lo, her pains immediately left her, and she began to feel better!

Come then, O Christian, to the heavenly Banquet which your Divine Saviour has prepared for you. "All things are ready." Jesus Christ desires to unite Himself to you. "Behold," He says, "I stand at the door and knock. Open to Me, My Sister, My beloved, My dove, My undefiled; for My head is full of dew, and My locks of the drops of the night." He has waited for you through a long night of sin, and now that He has restored you to the state of grace by the Sacrament of Penance, He wishes to take up His abode in your heart and to enrich you with His graces. Let no temptation whatever keep you from so great a Good.

With St. Mary Magdalen de Pazzi say, "I would rather die than omit a Communion permitted by obedience." As often as your director advises you, go forward to receive your Lord with confidence and simplicity of heart, and reply to those who blame you for communicating so often as St. Francis de Sales advises you to do: "If," says he, "they ask you why you communicate so often, tell them that two classes of persons should communicate frequently: the perfect to persevere in perfection, and the imperfect to attain perfection; the strong not to become weak, and the weak to grow strong; the sick to be cured, and the healthy to prevent sickness.

"And as to yourself, tell them that because you are imperfect, weak and infirm, you stand in need of Communion." (*Introduction to the Devout Life,* c. 21). Tell them you wish to become patient, and therefore you must receive your patient Saviour; that you wish to become meek, and therefore you must receive your meek Saviour; that you wish to love contempt, and therefore you must receive your despised Saviour; that you wish to love crosses, and therefore you must receive your suffering Saviour; that you wish to love poverty, and therefore you must receive your poor Saviour; that you wish to become strong against the temptations of the world, the flesh and the devil, and therefore you stand in need of your comforting and strengthening Saviour. Tell them He has said: "He that eateth My Flesh shall live by Me." I wish to live, and therefore I receive Jesus, my life, "that He may live in me and I in Him!"

He in whose words you put your trust, will justify you; your soul will continually grow stronger in virtue; your heart will become more and more pure; your passions will become weaker; your faith more lively; your hope more firm; your charity more ardent; you will receive grace to live in the world as an heir of Heaven; and when at your last hour, the priest comes to administer the Holy Viaticum, you will be able to say with St. Teresa: "My Lord and my Bridegroom, so then the hour is come at last for which my heart has longed so much. Now is the time that we shall see each other face to face. Blessed be this hour! Thy will be done! O happy hour in which my exile has an end and my soul takes its flight to Thee for Whom it has longed so much!"

[NOTE: This chapter expresses the traditional and profoundly Catholic approach to frequent Holy Communion, with the constant understanding that the author is referring to *worthy* Communion, or Communion received in the State of Grace. This stands in absolute contrast to the currently prevalent abomination of Holy Communion being received by *everyone* at Mass, without regard to whether the recipient is in the State of Grace, whether he believes in the Real Presence (and all other Catholic doctrines), or whether he is even a Catholic. To receive Holy Communion under any of these conditions is a mortal sin of sacrilege. To receive Holy Communion worthily, a Catholic in the state of mortal sin must first confess all his mortal sins to a priest in Confession and be absolved of them, after which Our Lord will be pleased to come once again into his heart in Holy Communion. The following chapter treats the mortal sin of sacrilegious Communion in detail and with great power. —*Publisher*, 1994.]

CHAPTER 10

On Unworthy Communion

THERE remains, Dear Reader, one more subject to treat of before my task is ended: It is unworthy Communion. It is not so agreeable a subject as those with which we have been hitherto engaged; but reverence for our Divine Saviour, as well as zeal for the salvation of souls, require that the truth should be told. There is nothing that gives more honor to God and contributes more to our own welfare than the devout reception of the Holy Eucharist; and there is, on the contrary, nothing more injurious to God and more hurtful to our souls than an unworthy Communion.

You will perhaps ask in astonishment: "Are there, then, really people so wicked as knowingly and willfully to make an unworthy Communion?" Alas that I must say it, there are but too many! I do not mean to say that there are many who receive the Sacrament unworthily *out of pure malice,* with the express purpose of dishonoring God—though as we have seen, even that has happened—but I do say that there are many who wish to enjoy the privileges of a Christian while leading an immoral life and who dare receive the Author of all purity into a heart that is defiled by mortal sin.

This crime is committed by three classes of persons: First, by all those who are in mortal sin and who go to Communion after having been refused absolution; secondly, by all those who have willfully concealed a mortal sin in confession; and finally, by all those who, though they have confessed all their mortal sins, have nevertheless no true sorrow for them or no firm purpose of amendment. To the latter class belong all those that do not intend to keep the promises they made in Confession; who are not willing to be reconciled to those who have offended them; those who will not restore the property or good name of their neighbor; those who are not fully determined to keep away from taverns, grog-shops, and the like, that have proved occasions of sin to them; and finally, all those that will not break off sinful and dangerous company.

Now, if we consider the actual state of the world, we cannot help fearing that there are many Christians who make bad Communions. The Catholic priest, therefore, is in duty bound to warn the faithful against this grievous crime. Even in the very first ages of Christianity, in those days of primitive fervor, St. Paul was compelled to warn the Christians of Corinth against this heinous crime, and the few energetic words he addressed to them on that occasion comprehend all that may be said on the subject.

"Whosoever," he says, "shall eat this bread or drink the chalice of the Lord unworthily, shall be guilty of the Body and Blood of the Lord." And again: "He that eateth and drinketh unworthily, eateth and drinketh judgment to himself." We will follow the Apostle, both in the choice of arguments and the order of presenting them. We will consider in the first place the heinousness of the *crime* which they commit who receive Communion sacrilegiously, and in the second place, the terrible chastisement that awaits them.

St. Paul paints this crime in the most fearful colors: "Whosoever," he says, "shall eat this bread or drink the chalice of the Lord unworthily, *shall be guilty of the body and blood of the Lord.*" By this he evidently asserts that whoever receives the Blessed Eucharist unworthily is, in a certain sense, guilty of the murder of Our Lord. This may, at first sight, appear extravagant. It may seem harsh to class the sacrilegious communicant with the enemies of Our Lord, with those wicked men who put Him to death; but a little reflection will show how closely he resembles them.

While our Blessed Lord was yet living on earth, He had many cruel enemies. There were, however, *three* that persecuted Him with special malice. They were Herod, Judas, and the Jewish priests and people. In Herod we see cruel violence towards an innocent and unoffending babe; in Judas we see base treachery and ingratitude to a friend and benefactor; and in the Jewish priests we behold outrage, insolence and contempt of the Anointed Messias, the true Son of God.

Now we shall find all these crimes united in a sacrilegious Communion. "Go," said Herod to the Wise Men; "go and search diligently after the Child, and when you have found Him, bring me word that I also may come and adore Him." These words seem full of faith and reverence, but under this outward show of reverence, Herod concealed a wicked and cruel design. He was determined to destroy the new-born King of the Jews, and when he found that he had been disappointed, in his fury he slew all the children of Bethlehem and the neighborhood thereof.

He did not, however, succeed in destroying the Divine Infant. St. Joseph, in obedience to the command of God, carried Him into Egypt. There he remained until the Angel of the Lord appeared again to St. Joseph and said: "Take the Child and His Mother, and return to thy country, for those that sought the life of the Child are dead." O Angel of God! What dost thou say? They are dead who sought the life of the Child? Ah! Would that it were true!

Are not those wicked Christians who outrage their Saviour in the true Bethlehem, *the house of bread,* that is to say, at the very foot of the Sacred Altar, are they not so many Herods? They present themselves at the table of the Lord in the attitude of adoration; they strike their breasts as if in sorrow for their sins; they fold their hands as if in deep devotion, and they open those lips defiled by sin; they receive the innocent Lamb of God and make Him a prisoner in a sinful and polluted heart. Mortal sin is so opposed to God that, if He could die, sin would destroy Him.

To receive Our Lord into a heart that is defiled by mortal sin is to bring Him into the power of His greatest enemy; it is to treat Him with even greater cruelty than Herod. Herod was an unbelieving Jew, but those who receive Him unworthily are Christians and Catholics. They know whom they maltreat; Herod did not know Him. Our Lord does not work a miracle to deliver Himself out of their hands, as He did to free Himself from the hands of Herod; He does not send an Angel to inform the priest who, among the throng that presses to the altar, are in the state of mortal sin; and even if He were to do so, the priest is not at liberty to make use of this knowledge—at least not unless the criminal should be a notorious sinner—so tender is Jesus of the reputation of those very men who are heaping outrages upon Him. He does *not* desert the consecrated species the moment He is laid upon the tongue of the sacrilegious communicant. No, true to His own Institution, He remains and enters unresistingly even the basest heart! Oh what must be His feelings at such a moment? When Jesus was struck by that infamous servant in the judgment hall, in presence of Annas, He said: "If I have spoken ill, give testimony of the evil; but if well, why strikest thou Me?" It is thus too that Jesus seems to address the unworthy communicant: He says, "What have I done, O Christian soul, that thou shouldst treat Me so cruelly? Was it not enough that I had to flee from the rage of tyrants when I was on earth? Wilt thou too lift up thy hand against Me? Ah! From them I fled, but from thee I cannot flee. Strike then, I will not avoid the blow. Strike! It shall fall upon My heart, for My love has bound My hands. I do not resist."

In the early ages of the Church, distorted accounts of the Eucharistic Sacrifice having reached the ears of the heathens, they accused the Christians of the horrid custom of murdering, in their assemblies, an infant whom they adored as their God. This was a base calumny, but alas, the accusation is but too true of those wicked monsters who are guilty of an unworthy Communion!

Yes, the unworthy communicant is another Herod, but he is even worse; he is a second *Judas*. All men abhor Judas Iscariot; his very name is held in execration. No Christian would bear the name of Judas.

The Church seems unwilling to pronounce it, even when belonging to another Apostle. In the canon of the Mass, when the names of the twelve Apostles occur, she designates the Apostle who was named *Judas Thaddeus* simply as *Thaddeus*, omitting the title which he shared in common with the apostate traitor.

Now, whence comes this deep, universal detestation of Judas? What crime has he committed, thus to make an object of horror to all men? Ah, you know it already! Judas was a traitor! He was guilty of the blackest ingratitude, the basest treachery. He professed to be the friend of Jesus; he had received innumerable benefits from Him; he had been treated as an intimate friend, and he used the knowledge which this intimacy gave him to betray his Master into the hands of His enemies. He came into the garden where Our Lord was praying with His disciples; he gave Him a kiss, the usual salutation between Our Lord and His Apostles, and said: "Hail Rabbi!" Immediately, the armed multitude he had brought with him seized upon Our Lord, bound Him and carried Him captive to the palace of the High Priest.

How touching is the reproach which Christ then made to Judas: "Ah, Judas! Dost thou betray the Son of Man with a kiss?" Our Lord seems to feel the circumstances of His betrayal even more than the betrayal itself. If it had been anyone but Judas, who was one of the Apostles, one whom Jesus had chosen to be a priest and prince of His Church, one whom He had admitted to His most unreserved intimacy; or if it had been done in any other way; if the wretched man had thrown off the mask; if he had openly joined the Jews and Roman soldiers; if he had come out like the rest, sword in hand—it would have been less bitter. But to come as a friend, to come as a cherished disciple, to come with a kiss—Oh, this was too much! This was that deep and cruel pang that pierced our Saviour to the heart! It is of this that Our Lord complains by the mouth of the Psalmist: "If my enemy had reviled me, I would indeed have borne it; and if he that hated me had spoken grievous things against me, I would perhaps have hidden myself from him. But thou, a man of my own mind, my guide and my familiar! In the house of God we walked with consent."

But oh how much more justly may Jesus make the same complaint of the sacrilegious communicant? The Holy Eucharist is a pledge of love. In Holy Communion, God lovingly caresses the soul. When St. John reposed in Our Lord's bosom, he did not enjoy so much familiarity with Him as does the soul that receives Him in Holy Communion. We call it "Communion" because it is a union between the soul and God. How horrible then must it be to abuse this Holy Sacrament, to receive it with a traitorous heart! How painful must it be to Our Lord to receive a false caress, to be folded in a sinful embrace, to be brought into the loathsome prison of a sinful heart!

O loving Saviour, how great is the wrong that is done to Thy love! Well has the prophet predicted of Thee: "The wicked have fought against me without a cause. Instead of making me a return for my love, they have only repaid me with evil and hate. They spoke indeed peaceably to me, but they devised guile. Their words were smoother than oil, but they are cruel darts." From the tabernacle I hear Thy outraged heart complain: "Behold, all ye that pass by the way, come and see the wounds with which I have been wounded in the house of my friends; attend and see if there be any sorrow like unto my sorrow!"

The base treachery of Judas, however, was but the prelude to the many outrages that were heaped upon Our Lord by the Jewish priests and people. These too find a parallel in an unworthy Communion. When David had cut off a piece of the mantle of Saul, his royal enemy, his heart smote him because he had "lifted his hand against the anointed of the Lord." Indeed, this feeling was quite natural, for the greatness of an injury depends always on the dignity of the person offended.

Who would not feel more indignant at seeing a parent dishonored than at seeing a stranger? It is related in the life of St. Joseph Calasanctius, that in his old age he was summoned before court on some frivolous charge. He was rudely dragged from the altar; he was hurried through the public streets bareheaded, under a burning sun, amid the shouts and jeers of the populace. Who could have looked upon the serene face of that hoary-headed old man as he was thus ignominiously dragged along without being moved to tears? How horrible a crime would it be in the eyes of the Catholic world to kill a bishop at the altar, or the Pope upon his throne! Justice would require that such a criminal should be punished with much greater severity than an ordinary murderer. How grievous, then, must have been the crime of those who persecuted Our Lord Himself. Let us read the simple words of Holy Scripture:

"He was despised and the most abject of men, a man of sorrows and acquainted with infirmity; He was led as a sheep to the slaughter; He was mute as a lamb before His shearers, and He opened not His mouth; He gave His cheek to the striker, and He was filled with reproaches; He was made a derision to the people and their song all the day long; He was cut off from the land of the living."

We feel the deep meaning of those words only when we ask, as did the Eunuch of St. Philip: "Of whom doth the prophet speak?" That face, bruised with blows and defiled with spittle, is the face of God—that face which is the everlasting brightness of Heaven; those hands, transfixed with nails, are the hands of the Almighty, who in His wisdom laid the foundations of the universe; He who hangs between two malefactors on the accursed tree is the Immaculate Lamb of God, the Eternal Son of the Father.

"Ah!" you exclaim, "here human wickedness has reached its height!" Can there be a greater proof of God's patience than His forbearance at the perpetration of a crime like this? Yes, I will assert that almost every instance of unworthy Communion is even a stronger proof of God's patient endurance. In some respects, the dishonor which is shown Our Lord in an unworthy Communion is far greater than that which was shown Him at His death.

Then indeed He died a death of shame, but it was for the salvation of the world. He offered His soul because *He willed* it. He was satisfied because He saw the abundant fruit of His labors. But when He is received unworthily in Holy Communion, He is crucified anew, without any compensation and against His will. He is brought as a prisoner into the horrid and filthy dungeon of a sinful heart. He is chained there to passions which He loathes; He is forced to become, as it were, *one* with the sinner.

Can anything be conceived more horrible than this? Would it not be far better that the Sacred Host should be thrown upon a dunghill, that it should be devoured by an unclean beast than that it should be received into a heart defiled with mortal sin? Most certainly, for in that case Our Lord would suffer no real dishonor. He fills all things and is essentially everywhere. He cannot be sullied except in the heart of the sinner, where He is brought into contact with that which alone is hateful to Him—*sin*.

It is related in the annals of the Society of Jesus that a young man who through shame had concealed a mortal sin in Confession had the rashness to receive Holy Communion, but on attempting to swallow the Host, he was seized with such excruciating pains that he was compelled to rush out of the church and to cast forth the Sacred Particle into the filth of the street. After this he felt instantly relieved. Our Lord gave him thereby to understand that the very filth of the street was more acceptable to Him than a heart that is defiled by sin.

Should any amongst us be still unmoved, still callous, grant, O Lord, that we may at least be touched by Thy chastisements! The impious Abiron placed his sacrilegious hand upon the censer, and immediately the earth opened and swallowed him up. The neglectful sons of the high priest Aaron filled their censers with unhallowed fire, and in an instant fire from Heaven killed them. Ophni and Phinees profaned the sacrifice offered to the Lord, and shortly after they fell under the sword of the enemy. Thus did God punish the disobedience of Israel. How then will He punish him who attacks His own Divine Person, in whose name altars are erected and sacrifices offered? How will He punish him who is guilty of the Body and Blood of Jesus Christ? It does not admit of a doubt that severer punishment awaits one who tramples upon the Son of God, profanes the Blood of the Covenant and insults the Spirit of Grace.

The Bethsamites cast a curious glance at the Ark of the Covenant, and immediately the ground was strewn with their dead bodies. Balthasar laid his profane hands upon the sacred vessels, and there suddenly appeared upon the opposite wall the fingers of a man's hand, tracing a few words, in which the sacrilegious monarch read his own sentence of death. Antiochus plundered the Temple of Jerusalem, and the avenging hand of God stretched him upon a bed of agonizing pain, where he died of a loathsome disease. Such were the chastisements of the Almighty in the Old Law.

What then will be the punishment of him who dishonors, not the Ark of the Covenant, but the Body of Jesus; who not merely raises to his polluted lips the holy vessels, but receives into his sinful heart the thrice Holy God Himself; who draws the Lord of Hosts from His sanctuary to place Him side by side with Satan in his heart; who becomes guilty of the Body and Blood of Jesus Christ! What punishment is there for such a one? Listen once more to the words of St. Paul and tremble: "He who eats of this bread and drinks of this chalice unworthily, eats and drinks judgment to himself!" What an expression! Eats and drinks judgment to himself! His own condemnation! That is to say, his condemnation penetrates his innermost being. It incorporates itself with him; it flows in his veins; it becomes one flesh, one blood, one being with him.

O frightful punishment! He eats and drinks his own judgment! What kind of judgment does he eat and drink? A sentence of eternal damnation, a sentence of never-ending misfortune, a sentence sealed with the Blood of Christ Himself, a sentence which is often carried into execution even in this world! You see, continues St. Paul, your houses daily falling into ruin; you behold the daily ravages of war and pestilence; you see how unexpectedly death everywhere seizes upon its victims; you see how many among you are dragging along weak bodies, never enjoying an hour's health. (See *1 Cor.* 11:30.)

Why, think you, do these troubles press upon you? Because many among you partake unworthily of the Body and Blood of Christ. The miserable end of King Lothaire and his vassals is but too evident an illustration of this. Lothaire, king of Loiraine, conceived a great dislike for his lawful queen. His eyes fell upon a beautiful young maid of honor of his court named Waldrada, and his heart followed his eyes. The Pope was informed of this scandal, and he commanded Lothaire to quit his paramour and to take back his lawful wife. He threatened to excommunicate the wicked king in case of refusal.

Lothaire made a thousand false promises; he even went to Rome in order to be absolved from the ban he had incurred. He requested the Pope to reconcile him solemnly during Mass, and he wished to receive Holy Communion from the hands of the Pope himself. The Pope took the most prudent measures to find out the sincerity of the king's intentions, but all to no purpose. He then celebrated Mass. The king, with many of the nobles of his court, was present. The time of Communion came, and the king, with his nobles, went to the altar-rail to receive. The Pope then turned to the monarch and, holding the Sacred Host in his hand, said in a loud and distinct voice: "O king, if you are sincerely resolved to quit Waldrada and to take back your lawful wife, then receive this Holy Sacrament unto life everlasting; but if you are not sincerely resolved, then do not dare to profane the sacred Body of Jesus Christ and eat your own damnation."

Lothaire turned pale and trembled, but he had already made a sacrilegious Confession, and now he sealed his doom by adding a sacrilegious Communion. The Pope turned then to the noblemen who were kneeling beside their king and said to them: "If you have taken no part in the crime of your king, then may the Body of Our Lord Jesus Christ be to you a pledge of eternal salvation." Some of the noblemen were terrified and left the altar-rail without receiving, but the greater part of them followed the example of their king. They had committed a fearful crime, and the punishment of God was swift and terrible. The king and his suite quitted Rome. They had no sooner arrived at the city of Lucca than they were attacked by a most malignant fever, in consequence of which they lost their speech; they were tormented by an inward fire, and their nails, hair and skin fell off, while on the other hand, the lives of those of the king's suite who had left the Communion-rail before receiving were spared, so that the vengeance of Heaven was quite evident.

Again, "He eats and drinks judgment to himself!" What kind of judgment does he eat and drink? A sentence involving darkness of the understanding and hardness of heart to a most frightful degree, possession of the devil, despair, an impenitent death and everlasting malediction. These punishments are in a particular manner indicated by the words of St. Paul: "He eateth and drinketh judgment to himself." Nothing makes any impression upon him; he is no longer edified at praiseworthy actions; he scoffs at those who practice virtue; all admonition is lost on him; he does not understand the heinousness of his sin. What is here said of an unworthy Communion he does not believe; he is perfectly indifferent to the affair of his salvation; his thoughts no longer rise above the narrow and impure circle of earthly interests; he is like a worm which day and night sucks in nourishment from the earth, its native element, groveling all the while in the mire; he cares little for spiritual things; eternal punishment has no terror for him. In such a condition, what is there that he would shrink from undertaking? We might indeed say to this wretch when he is leaving the sacred table what Jesus said to His betrayer: "What thou wilt do, do quickly; go now and accomplish thy criminal designs; let loose thy passions, for since thou hast dared to dishonor the Body of Christ, nothing will appear horrible or abominable to thee; nothing will be able henceforth to restrain thee. Unhappy wretch! hitherto thou hast been preserved from certain abominations by an innate feeling of horror; but now, go bravely forward, wallow in sin, for thy conscience has no longer a reproach for thee! Go on in the road to Sodom and

Gomorrha! Give thyself up to the base desires of thy heart!''

No, nothing makes an impression upon such a heart. I here speak of what usually happens. Our Lord might indeed mournfully exclaim in his presence: ''Verily, verily, one of you is about to betray Me!'' It would affect him but little. Should he even hear from Jesus' own lips the terrible words, ''Woe to him by whom the Son of Man will be betrayed,'' he would remain cold and unmoved. In vain would Jesus call such a sinner ''friend'' and give him the kiss of peace! In vain would He work miracles before him! His eyes would remain closed; or if they opened, it would be only to cast him into despair; to urge him, like Judas, to execute the sentence of his damnation; in a word, the spirit of darkness, Satan, has taken complete possession of him.

Is not Judas a most terrible example of this? He received unworthily; immediately the devil entered into him! St. Cyprian tells us of a certain young woman who, after an unworthy Communion, was instantly possessed by the devil. She became quite furious and in her rage bit her tongue to pieces and endeavored to kill herself. At last she died in horrible agony. Behold the judgment of God! But what is even worse than all, this sin dries up the fountain of hope in the breast and plunges the unhappy sinner into despair. Judas is also but too sad an illustration of this. After his sacrilege, *''He went out and hanged himself.''*

The following example was witnessed by a priest of my acquaintance. He was called to the deathbed of a young man. No sooner had the dying youth perceived the Blessed Sacrament, than he exclaimed:

"Behold Him whom I received unworthily at my First Communion!" And turning his face towards the wall, he expired. Here, then, you see again a verification of the Divine Justice, which is the most terrible of all that could be inflicted in this life! I say in this life, for in the life to come, there is another scourge still more dreadful, namely, that remorse which will fill the soul of the sacrilegious communicant for all eternity.

Here, however, description is baffled. Words are inadequate to express or describe it. The story of the wanderer mentioned in the "Spiritual Meadows" furnishes but a feeble illustration of it. There was a certain convent of most austere discipline presided over by an abbot of strict and holy life. One day a stranger came to this convent asking admission. He was received and lived there for nine years in the practice of the most rigorous penance. At the end of that time, he came to the abbot and told him that an infant whom he had slain when he followed the life of a highwayman had appeared to him and said in the most heartrending tone of voice: "Why didst thou kill me?" The abbot treated the poor man as if he were the victim of a diseased imagination and bade him go work in the garden. He did so, but the voice still rang in his ears: "Why didst thou kill me?" He went to the church to pray, but the voice followed him thither. At last, no longer able to endure his sufferings, he threw off the religious habit, went to the civil magistrate, confessed his crime and begged to be condemned to death. His request was granted and he was executed. Oh, if remorse can inflict so terrible a sting in this life, what will it be to hear the eternal cry of conscience in the caverns of Hell, the eternal malediction of Jesus Christ against those who have outraged Him in the Most Holy Sacrament!

Such then is the life and death of the sacrilegious communicant. Such is the vengeance of God. Having committed deicide, he must be punished as such. Yes, the Bread of Life becomes in his mouth the bread of malediction for body and soul, for time and eternity, unless he has recourse to the Mother of God, that by her powerful intercession she may prevail upon the heart of her Divine Son to forgive the crime with its punishment and obtain for the unworthy communicant courage to confess his sin and the gift of tears to weep over it, in order that thus, through the merits of the same Blood which condemned him, he may receive again by the sacramental absolution the grace of justification.

CHAPTER 11

On Spiritual Communion

WHEN a soul has once begun to practice frequent Communion, she can no longer live without it. Even if she were to communicate every day, it would seem too little. She would desire, if possible, to receive Our Lord every moment. It is the Blessed Sacrament itself which produces this effect, for such is the sweetness of that Divine Food that they that eat it hunger still and they that drink it thirst again. It is Our Lord Himself who excites this desire in the hearts of the faithful, and He also has provided a means of satisfying it. While He was yet on earth, He not only imparted many graces to those who were near Him, but He also wrought many miracles in behalf of those who were at a distance.

In like manner, He now not only bestows many graces upon us when He actually enters our hearts in Holy Communion, but He also imparts many to us by means of Spiritual Communion. St. Catherine of Siena, while on one occasion assisting at the Mass of her confessor, St. Raymund, felt the most ardent desire to be united to Jesus Christ; but as she had been forbidden to communicate, she did not dare to receive. Our Lord, however, was so moved by the fervor of her love that He worked a miracle in her favor. At that part of the Mass in which the priest breaks the Sacred Host into three pieces, the smallest portion disappeared from the altar, flew through the air and rested upon the tongue of St. Catherine. St. Raymund was much disturbed at the disappearance of the particle, but the Saint relieved his anxiety by telling him that Our Lord Himself had been pleased to communicate her in reward for her great desire for Holy Communion.

He displays a similar love towards everyone who has a true desire to be united to Him. As soon as a soul ardently desires to receive Our Lord in the Blessed Sacrament, He comes to satisfy her desire, not indeed as He did to St. Catherine under the Sacramental species, but by the way of *Spiritual Communion*. This devotion is so full of grace and consolation that it is of the greatest importance that everyone should know how to practice it. I will therefore say a word in explanation of it.

Spiritual Communion, according to St. Thomas, consists in an ardent desire to receive our Lord Jesus Christ in the Most Holy Sacrament. It is performed by making an act of faith in the presence of Jesus Christ in the Blessed Sacrament, and then an act of love, and an act of contrition for having offended Him. The soul then invites Him to come and unite Himself to her and make her entirely His own; and lastly, she thanks Him as if she had really received Him sacramentally.

The Spiritual Communion may be made in the following manner: "O my Jesus, I firmly believe that Thou art truly and really present in the Most Holy Sacrament. I love Thee with my whole heart, and because I love Thee, I am sorry for having offended Thee. I long to possess Thee within my soul, but as I cannot now receive Thee sacramentally, come at least in spirit into my heart. I unite myself to Thee as if Thou wert already there; never let me be separated from Thee." The graces which are bestowed in this way are so great that they may be likened to those which are imparted by an actual reception of the Sacrament.

One day Our Lord Himself told St. Jane of the Cross that as often as she communicated spiritually she received a grace similar to that which she received from her Sacramental Communions. He also appeared to Sister Paula Maresca, foundress of the Convent of St. Catherine of Siena at Naples, with two vessels, one of gold and the other of silver, and told her that in the golden vessel He preserved her Sacramental Communions and in the silver vessel her spiritual Communions. The Fathers of the Church go so far as to say that one who has a very great desire for Communion, accompanied with great reverence and humility, may sometimes receive even more graces than another who, without these dispositions, should actually receive Our Lord in the Sacramental species; for as the Psalmist says: "The Lord hears the desire of the poor, and fills their hearts with good things."

The advantages of this mode of Communion are very great. To practice it, you will not need to go to church or make a long preparation or remain fasting; you will not need to ask the permission of your confessor, or to seek a priest to give it to you as in Holy Communion. Hence, the venerable Jane of the Cross used to say: "O my Lord, what an excellent mode of receiving without being seen or remarked, without giving trouble to my spiritual father, or depending on anyone but Thee, who in solitude dost nourish my soul and speak to my heart."

But the chief advantage of Spiritual Communion is that it may be so often repeated. You can receive Sacramental Communion at most but once a day, but

Spiritual Communion you may receive as often as you please. St. Alphonsus advises one who wishes to lead a devout life to make Spiritual Communions at his meditations, at his visits to the Blessed Sacrament and whenever he hears Mass. But especially he should endeavor to multiply them on the eve of his Communions because, as Father Faber of the Society of Jesus remarks, they are most powerful means to attain the dispositions necessary for a good Communion. The Saints were much addicted to this devotion.

The Blessed Angela of the Cross, a Dominican nun, was accustomed to make a hundred Spiritual Communions every day and a hundred more every night, and she used to say: "If my confessor had not taught me this method of communicating, I could scarcely live." If you ask how she could make so many, I answer with St. Augustine: "Give me a *lover*, and he will understand; give me a soul that loves nothing but Jesus Christ, and she will know how to do it."

CHAPTER 12

Considerations on the Virtues that Jesus Christ Teaches Us in the Most Holy Sacrament of the Altar

Altered from Crasset

I. POVERTY

JESUS in the Most Holy Sacrament of the altar is a Master who teaches us every virtue. On earth He led a life of poverty. On the altar, too, we behold Him stripped of everything. It is the same to Him whether He be in a city or in a village; and He dwells as cheerfully in a ciborium of copper as in one of gold or of silver. In Heaven He has a royal retinue, but on earth, who keeps Him company? "I am a man," He says, "who sees His poverty."

We too see the poverty of Jesus, but oh how slow are we to imitate it! Our affections are fixed on fine dwellings, good food, good clothing, good attendance! We dislike feeling the want of anything or suffering the slightest inconvenience, just as though the Son of God had said: "Blessed are the rich, but not the poor; blessed are those that laugh, but not those that weep."

II. HUMILITY

A humble soul debases herself before God and acknowledges her absolute dependence upon Him.

175

Mean and despicable in her own eyes, she accepts humiliations and contempt with cheerfulness. She is obedient to everyone and regards herself as the lowest, the vilest of creatures. She carefully conceals the graces with which God enriches her; she always seeks the last place and flies the praises of men, content to be praised by God alone. In the Most Holy Sacrament, Jesus offers Himself to honor His heavenly Father. Concealing His divinity and humanity under the appearances of bread and wine, He assumes a condition far more humiliating than that to which He reduced Himself in the crib, on the Cross or in the grave. Nay, He exposes Himself to the contempt, to the insults of idolaters, heretics and bad Catholics. And what is worse, He even submits to the horrible outrage of sacrilegious Communion. "In truth, Thou art a hidden God, my God and my Lord!" Thou art a humble God, and I am a proud creature! Thou fleest honors, and I seek them! Thou seekest humiliations, and I fly them!

III. PATIENCE

The body of the Son of God under the sacramental veils is indeed incapable of suffering, yet the love for sufferings which ever consumed the heart of Jesus is in nowise diminished. It was to leave us an eternal memorial of His Passion that Our Lord instituted this divine Sacrament. He commemorates His sufferings, and He is desirous that we too should preserve the recollection of them. But though His Sacred Body is now incapable of suffering, His divine Person is still sensible to every insult that is offered to Him! Oh, who can enumerate the outrages heaped upon Jesus in this Sacrament of His love? Consider the affronts He daily receives from atheists, heretics, superstitious persons and particularly from bad Catholics. Think of the crimes, the sins of irreverence that are committed in His churches, in His own Divine Presence! Think of all the bad and sacrilegious Communions that are made! O Jesus! What admirable lessons of patience dost Thou not daily give us in this Divine Sacrament! But alas, I profit so little by them! I am so passionate, so impatient! I am unwilling to suffer anything from God or man. I cannot bear anything from my superiors, equals or inferiors. I am a burden to myself, and yet I wish that everyone should bear with me. How unreasonable!

IV. OBEDIENCE

It was in obedience to His heavenly Father that the Son of God became man; it was in obedience that His Blessed Mother conceived Him. He was born while obeying an earthly emperor. He lived under obedience to His parents and died out of obedience to His heavenly Father and to His unjust judges. Although He now reigns in Heaven, yet He is ever ready to obey man. He obeys all His priests, the bad as well as the good. He obeys at all hours, by day and by night. He obeys instantly. No sooner are the words of Consecration pronounced by the priest than Jesus is instantly present. He obeys in all places wherever the Holy Sacrifice of the Mass is offered, whether it be on land or at sea, in a village or in a city, in a stately church or in a humble chapel. He submits to every sort of treatment. He suffers Himself to be preserved, to be consumed, to be given to all kinds of persons. He obeys without resistance, without complaint, without showing the least unwillingness. Christian soul, dost thou obey in this manner? Dost thou obey all thy superiors without exception? Dost thou obey blindly? Dost thou obey at all times, in all things, always showing that thou art a humble servant of the Lord, ready to follow the commands of thy superiors?

V. MORTIFICATION

The whole life of Jesus was one of continual mortification. He is now forever happy in Heaven; nevertheless, He has found a means to teach us by His own example, even to the end of the world, how to mortify our senses, our will and our judgment. He mortifies His judgment by suffering Himself to be disposed of according to the good pleasure of His priests, to be carried whithersoever they will, to be used for good or bad purposes, just as if He were entirely blind and helpless. He mortifies His will in bearing the numberless indignities that are offered to His Holiness, to His Majesty and to His other divine Perfections. He mortifies His senses by remaining present in the Sacred Host as if He were dead. He mortifies His tongue by keeping continually a profound silence. He mortifies His whole body, uniting Himself to mere lifeless appearances and remaining day and night in the tabernacle as in a prison of love. O my soul! addicted as thou art to sensual pleasures, what union can there be between thee and the mortified and crucified body of Jesus Christ? The Holy Sacrament continually reminds thee of His Passion, and thou holdest suffering in horror! His life under the sacramental veils is entirely spiritual, and thine is entirely sensual!

VI. LOVE OF GOD

Jesus teaches us also in this Sacrament how we ought to love God. If we love God truly, we will perform His will in all things, we will keep His commandments, we will suffer much for Him and sacrifice ourselves to His honor. This is what Jesus teaches us on our altars. He sacrifices Himself daily—nay, hourly—for the honor of His Father and for the good of men. He has thus found out a means to renew His death in a mystical manner, at all times and in all places. All men should offer themselves to God in order to acknowledge their dependence upon Him, to thank Him for His numberless benefits, to ask new blessings from Him and to atone for their sins. Jesus Christ, as the head of the human race, has taken upon Himself this obligation and daily offers Himself to pay homage to God for all men, to give thanks to God for all the graces they have received from Him, to make satisfaction to His Justice so often offended by their grievous crimes and to obtain for them all the graces necessary for soul and body.

O wretch that I am! God takes upon Himself my sins, He lays down His life to deliver me from death, He bears for love of me a thousand insults, and I in return despise and offend Him, I only provoke His anger more and more. I am unwilling to suffer the least thing for Him, and thus I render His passion and death fruitless to me. What ingratitude! What hardness of heart! What cruelty and injustice!

VII. LOVE OF OUR NEIGHBOR

One of the objects of the Incarnation was to reunite men in the bonds of charity which had been severed by sin. Jesus Christ made this charity an express commandment. He calls it His only commandment. He declares that it is the true mark of His religion. To preserve this charity, He has left us His Body and His Blood under the appearances of bread and wine, in order that, partaking of one Bread, we may also be one body and one soul. And the more to ensure the practice of charity among men, He has made our natural desire for happiness the motive for loving one another. He has commanded us to partake of His Body and Blood under pain of eternal damnation, and the indispensable condition to our receiving this heavenly food is charity.

But, not content with all this, He continually gives us in the Blessed Sacrament most persuasive lessons of charity. While other shepherds clothe themselves with the wool of their flocks and feed on their flesh, Jesus Christ, the Good Shepherd, strips Himself in order to clothe us; He even gives us His Flesh and Blood for our food; and when a devout soul, transported at a favor so divine, asks how she may repay so great a benefit, He replies: "Do good to your fellowmen, and I will hold you discharged of all your debts to Me. Whatsoever you do to them I will count it as done to Me." "Does it seem hard to you," He says, "to love your neighbor? Consider, then, how I have loved you. Does it seem hard to you *to give and to forgive?* Then think whether you are ever required to give anything as precious as the food which I give to you. Think whether you have ever to suffer as many affronts as I have suffered for your sake in this Sacrament of love! Is the disciple greater than his master, or the servant above his lord? Go, then, and do to others what I have done to you."

O Jesus, Thou hast conquered! We give our hearts to Thee that Thou maycst make them humble and gentle. O Thou, the Well-Beloved of the Father, who comest on earth and dwelleth in our tabernacles in order to impart to men Thy Divine Spirit of Charity, take from us all selfishness and hardness of heart and teach us how to love one another.

CHAPTER 13

The Most Holy Festival of Corpus Christi and its Origin

MANY a century had passed over the Church of Christ before there was any distinct feast of the Blessed Sacrament, and when in the thirteenth century Our Lord chose that it should be instituted, He had recourse to a holy nun in a vision to be the instrument of this devotion in His Church. St. Thomas was living then and so was St. Louis, but God chose neither the learning of the one nor the royal power of the other to be the means of executing His desire.

From the age of sixteen, for many years, a vision perpetually haunted a young Belgian nun, Juliana of Retinne, whenever she knelt in prayer. A brilliant moon continually appeared before her with one small portion obscured and invisible. She tried in vain to chase the vision away; at last Our Lord Himself came to explain it to her. He said it was to show that the ritual year of the Church would remain incomplete until the Blessed Sacrament had a feast of its own, and He wished it to be instituted for the following reasons:

First, in order that the Catholic doctrine might receive aid from the institution of this festival at a time when the faith of the world was growing cold and heresies were rife.

Secondly, that the faithful who love and seek truth and piety may be enabled to draw from this source of life new strength and vigor to walk continually in the way of virtue.

Thirdly, that irreverence and sacrilegious behavior towards the Divine Majesty in this adorable Sacrament may, by sincere and profound adoration, be extirpated and repaired.

Lastly, He bade her announce to the Christian world His will that this feast should be observed.

Tremblingly the maiden received the command, and heartily did she pray to be released from the charge. Our Lord answered her that the solemn devotion which He ordered to be observed was to be begun by her and to be propagated by the poor and lowly. Twenty long years had passed away and the secret still lay hidden in Juliana's breast; she dared not reveal it to anyone, and yet an interior impulse urged her on. So terrible was her repugnance that she shed tears of blood over it! At length she imparted it to her confessor, and with her leave he consulted others, especially James de Threzis, Archdeacon at the Cathedral of Liege. This priest was afterwards, for his piety and learning, elected Bishop of Verdun, then Patriarch of Jerusalem and at last Pope of Rome, being called Urban IV. From that time it became a public question, and sorely were men divided upon it. Canons and monks protested against the new devotion and urged that the Daily Sacrifice was sufficient to commemorate the love of Jesus in the Blessed Sacrament—without a special day being particularly assigned for that purpose. But the faithful nun prayed on; civil discord raged around her; the city where she lived was lost and won, sacked by a lawless army, and retaken; three successive convents were either burned or otherwise destroyed over her head, yet no earthly troubles could make her forget the task which her Lord had assigned her.

She died before it was accomplished, yet she had done enough in her lifetime to provide for its execution. In her wanderings, she had met with a few men with devotion to feel and learning to defend the feast of the Blessed Sacrament. When she was in her grave, the Sovereign Pontiff, Urban IV, wrote to inform one of her companions that he himself had celebrated the feast with the Cardinals in the Holy City. The triumph of the Blessed Sacrament was complete; St. Thomas Aquinas composed its office; the devotion spread throughout the length and breadth of Europe. From that time to this, every church in a Catholic country, from the cathedral of a royal city to the village chapel, keeps the festival. The procession issues into the streets followed by the authorities of the realm; it is the public recognition by the Catholic world of Jesus in the Blessed Sacrament.

The prophetic eye of Our Lord saw in the futurity this very doctrine attacked and the Faith in sore danger. In the full career of the victory of His Church, in the zenith of its medieval splendor, He foresaw our times. Surely no omen was ever better fulfilled than that which promised the Church good service by the institution of the feast of Corpus Christi! In France it has survived every revolution; its re-establishment has ever been the measure of the Church's power and the proof of her return. It is the dove with the olive branch which proclaims the passing away of the mighty deluge.

The memory of the procession in which, when a child, he scattered flowers before the Blessed Sacrament as it passed through the streets, is a hold on the very libertine and the pledge of his final conversion. The civil and military pomp displayed is a proof that the country is still Catholic, and the very infidel compelled to pass the Blessed Sacrament head uncovered or to remain within his house bears witness to the fact that public opinion is Christian and to the triumph of the Blessed Sacrament. (John Bern Dalgairns, priest of the Oratory of St. Philip Neri).

I believe, Dear Reader, that for your edification and instruction concerning the Most Holy Feast of our divine Redeemer's Sacred Body, I can place nothing better before you than the Brief of Urban IV, which runs thus:

"URBAN, BISHOP, Servant of the Servants of God, to our Venerable Brethren, the Patriarchs, Archbishops, and other Prelates of the Church:

"When Our Lord and Saviour Jesus Christ, ere He left the world and returned to His Father, ate on the eve of His passion the Last Supper with His disciples, He instituted the Most Holy and precious Sacrament of His Body and Blood, in which He gave us the former for our food and the latter for our drink; 'for as often as we eat of this bread and drink of this chalice, we show the death of our Lord.' At the institution of this mystery, He said to His Apostles: 'Do this in commemoration of Me'—giving them to understand that the great and adorable Sacrament, which He then instituted, was the greatest and most excellent remembrance of His infinite love towards us—an admirable, agreeable, sweet, secure, and supremely excellent remembrance—in which all the benefits of God are renewed, above all comprehension, in which we can find every pleasure, every sweetness and the most secure pledge of eternal life.

"It is the sweetest, holiest and most salutary remembrance, which recalls to our mind the great grace of our Redemption, which keeps us from evil and strengthens us in good, which promotes our advancement in virtue and grace, our divine Saviour producing in us all these effects by His real presence.

"The other mysteries which the Church reveres we adore in spirit and in truth, but in none of them do we enjoy the real presence thereof. It is only in the commemoration of the Last Supper that Jesus Christ is truly present and truly with us. When He ascended into Heaven, He said to His apostles and disciples: 'Behold I will be with you until the end of the world.' He said this in order to console them for His absence and to assure them that He would always remain, even corporally, in their midst. O Worthy and Ever Adorable Remembrance, which reminds us that death has lost its sting and that we are saved from ruin, since the living Body of the Lord, which was raised upon the wood of the Cross, has restored life to us! It is a most glorious remembrance, which fills the faithful with salutary joy and causes them, in the effusion of their joy, to weep tears of thanksgiving. We exult at the remembrance of our Redemption, and because it reminds us of the death of Jesus who purchased us, we cannot restrain our tears.

"Over this mystery, which prepares joy for us and elicits our tears, we rejoice weepingly and weep joyfully because our hearts are entranced with joy at the remembrance of so great a benefit, and in the sense of the most just gratitude which we owe it, we cannot refrain from tears. O infinite, divine love! O exceedingly great condescension of our God! O astounding miracle of His liberality! Not enough to make us masters of the goods of this world, He even places all creatures at our command. This was not even enough for His goodness to us. He raised man to so great a dignity as to give him Angels to guard him and celestial spirits to serve him and to guide the elect to the possession of the inheritance which is prepared for them in Heaven. After so many brilliant proofs of His munificence, He has given us a still greater pledge of His unspeakable charity by bestowing Himself on us. Exceeding the very fullness of His gifts and the very measure of His love, He offers Himself for our food and drink.

"O sublime and admirable liberality, in which the Giver is the Gift, and the Gift is the very One Who gives! O unexampled liberality by which He gives Himself! Our God has given Himself to be our food because man, condemned to death as he is, can be restored to life by this means only. By eating the forbidden fruit he incurred death, and by partaking of the tree of life, he has been redeemed. In the former was the sting of death; in the latter the food of life. By eating the former he inflicted a wound upon himself; by eating of the latter he recovered health. Thus the partaking of the one food wounded him; the partaking of the other healed him. Wound and cure proceed from the same source, and what entailed death upon us, has restored us to life. Of the former it is said: 'On the day on which you shall eat thereof, you shall die the death'; and of the latter, 'He that eats of this bread shall live for ever.'

"O Substantial Food which perfectly satisfies and truly nourishes, not the body, but the heart; not the flesh, but the soul! Our compassionate Redeemer, who knew that man needed spiritual nourishment, has in this institution of charity and mercy prepared for his soul the most precious and most nourishing food that His wisdom could devise. Neither could any work have been better befitting the Divine liberality and charity than that the Eternal Word of God, who is the real food and the real repast of the reasonable creature, should, after He was made flesh, give Himself to flesh and blood, that is to say, to man, for his nourishment.

"Man has eaten the bread of Angels, and therefore Our Lord said: 'My flesh is meat indeed!' This Divine Bread is eaten, but it is not changed, because it assumes no other form in him who eats it. It transforms the worthy receiver into Him whom it contains. O most excellent, most adorable and most venerable Sacrament, to which we can never give adequate praise, honor and glory and whose benefits we can never justly extol! O Sacrament, which is worthy of being revered from the bottom of the heart, loved with the most tender and fervent affection and of being deeply engraved upon our memory in indelible characters! O most precious remembrance, which ought to be made known and exalted in all places, which all Christians ought ever to remember with feelings of the deepest gratitude, which we can never sufficiently meditate upon or ever sufficiently worship. We are therefore bound to cherish a perpetual remembrance of it, so that we may constantly have Him before our eyes who offers this inestimable benefit to us. For the more we consider the Gift, the more we prize Him who bestows it.

"Although we daily commemorate this benefit in

the Holy Sacrifice of the Mass, yet we think it just that, in order to confound the infidelity and madness of heretics, we should at least once in the year solemnize and celebrate a feast in Its honor with the greatest pomp and magnificence possible. On the day on which Jesus Christ instituted this Sacrament, the Church is occupied with the reconciliation of sinners, the blessing of the holy oils, the washing of the feet and other mysteries. Wherefore, sufficient time is not left to honor this most sublime Sacrament, and thus it becomes necessary to appoint another day for this end.

"Finally, it is the custom of the Church to devote particular days for the veneration of her saints, although she daily honors them by prayers, litanies, in the Mass, etc., as also on other occasions. But since on these days Christians often do not comply with their duties towards the Saints, either through negligence or press of domestic affairs, or from human weakness, our Mother the Holy Church has appointed a certain day for the general commemoration of all the Saints, so that by this solemnity, the omissions which may, perchance, have occurred may be repaired.

"Now, if this has already been introduced into the Church, how much more are we not bound to do the same with regard to the life-giving Sacrament of the Body and Blood of Jesus Christ, who is the glory and the crown of all the Saints. We shall then be enabled to repair and make up for our want of devotion and other defects which we may have had in hearing Mass and ask Our Lord's pardon for the same. And indeed, at the time when our dignity was not so elevated as it now is, we learned how the Lord revealed to some few Catholics that the feast of Corpus Christi was to be celebrated throughout the whole Church. Therefore, in order to strengthen and exalt the True Faith, we have thought it just and reasonable to ordain that, besides the commemoration which the Church daily makes of this Holy Sacrament, a particular festival shall be celebrated every year on a certain day, namely, on the fifth day of the week after the octave of Pentecost, on which day pious people will vie with each other to hasten in great crowds to our churches, where the clergy and laity will send forth their holy hymns of joy and praise. On this memorable day, faith shall triumph, hope be enhanced, charity shall shine, piety shall exult, our temples shall re-echo with hymns of exultation and pure souls shall tremble with holy joy.

"On this day of devotion, all the faithful shall hasten to our churches with joyful hearts to discharge their obligations with unlimited obedience and thus, in a worthy manner, celebrate this great feast. May the Lord vouchsafe to inflame them with so holy a zeal that, by the exercise of their piety towards Him who has redeemed them, they may increase in merit and that He may also give Himself to them in this life for their food. May this God likewise be their reward in the other world.

"We therefore inform and exhort you in the name of the Lord, and through these apostolic letters we command you in virtue of holy obedience, and enjoin upon you, to have every year on the above-named fifth day of the week this so glorious and praiseworthy feast celebrated in all the churches and places of your diocese. Moreover, we command you to exhort, yourself and through others, those under your charge so to prepare themselves the Sunday before by a perfect and sincere confession, by alms, prayers and other good works, which are suitable to this day of the Most Blessed Sacrament, that they may reverently partake of the same and by this means receive an increase of grace. And as We also desire to stimulate by spiritual gifts the faithful to the celebration and veneration of this feast, We grant to him or her who, truly penitent, confessing his or her sins, attends the morning service or Vespers of the day, one hundred days' Indulgence, and to him or her who is present at Prime, Tierce, Sext, None and Complin, forty days for each of these hours.

"Finally, relying upon the merciful omnipotence of God and trusting in the authority of the Holy Apostles Peter and Paul, We remit to him or her who, during this octave, shall be present at the morning service, Vespers and Mass, one hundred days of penance imposed upon them."

CHAPTER 14

Additional Examples Relating
To the Real Presence

1. Padbert relates that a certain priest named Plegile asked of our Saviour the favor to be permitted to see Him with his bodily eyes in the Holy Eucharist. As this request did not proceed from unbelief, but rather from an ardent love, it was granted. One day during Mass this pious priest knelt down after the Consecration and besought Our Lord anew to grant his request. An Angel then appeared to him and bade him arise. He raised his head and saw our Divine Saviour in the form of an infant. Full of joy and reverence, he begged Our Lord to conceal Himself again under the Sacramental species, and immediately the Holy Eucharist assumed its usual appearance. This miracle was also witnessed by many other persons. (P. Favre).

2. The Abbé Favre also relates a miracle which took place at Turin in the year 1453 during the pontificate of Nicholas V. One night a thief entered one of the churches of the city and stole the sacred vessels. He then loaded his horse with the sacred burden and attempted to leave the city at daybreak, but his horse fell on its knees, and with all his efforts the thief could not make it rise. The people at length began to suspect something, so they took off the burden from the horse and found, to their horror, the

sacred vessels. A consecrated Host which had remained in the ciborium rose into the air to the height of about sixty feet.

The Bishop, hearing of this fact, went in procession to the place, accompanied by a great multitude. As soon as he arrived there, the holy Host descended into the chalice which he held in his hand and was carried to St. John's Cathedral. A splendid church was erected on the spot in which this great miracle happened, and on the balustrade the following inscription is still to be seen: *Hic stetit equus.* ("Here the horse stopped"). This miracle is still annually commemorated by a festival kept throughout the whole diocese and by a solemn procession in the city of Turin. God was pleased to work this miracle to confirm the faith of the people against the errors of the Hussites and Albigenses, who were then ravaging that part of Italy.

A few years ago, during one of these annual processions, another miracle took place which is too remarkable to be omitted. An impious barber had the impertinence to ridicule a person, whom he was shaving, for wishing to assist at this procession. He then went into the street in order to insult the Catholics and to ridicule the Blessed Sacrament. He kept his hat on and would not take it off, though repeatedly ordered to do so. But behold! The moment that the Blessed Sacrament passed by him, he was struck by the Divine Justice and fell to the ground a corpse. This event made such an impression on the whole city that the commissary caused the body of the impious man to be exposed before the courthouse for thirty-six hours. A great many of the eyewitnesses of this fact are still living, among others, M. Raet, formerly Rector of Plancherine in the diocese of Chauberg, who was staying at Turin when this melancholy occurrence took place.

3. In 1369, the following incident occurred in the Netherlands. A Jew of Enghien named Jonathas, prefect of the synagogue, persuaded a Jew of Brussels named John de Louvain, who was apparently converted to Christianity, to bring him some consecrated Hosts. The latter, urged on by the promise of a large sum of money, entered one night the church of St. John the Baptist at Malembeck, which was situated without the city, took the ciborium containing fifteen Hosts and gave it to Jonathas.

This wicked Jew now began to offer every imaginable indignity and outrage to our Blessed Lord in the mystery of His love. A few days after this occurrence, Jonathas was murdered. His wife, considering his death to be a just chastisement of God and fearing lest she might be punished in a similar manner, went to Brussels and gave the ciborium, with the Hosts, to some Jews, who preserved them till Good Friday of the year 1370. On this day they treated the sacred Hosts with every kind of indignity. At last they pierced them, and immediately miraculous blood began to flow from them. These impious wretches were so terrified at this sight that they fell to the ground. On recovering from their terror, they resolved to send the Hosts to the Jews of Cologne. A woman named Catherine was charged with this commission. She, however, full of fear and remorse of conscience, carried the Hosts to her parish priest at Aix-la-Chapelle and gave him an account of all that had happened. The priest then informed the duke and duchess of the whole affair. The impious

Jews were arrested and tried, and having been fully convicted of the crime, they suffered the punishment they so justly deserved. This happened on the eve of Ascension Day, 1370. This history is recorded in the archives of the city of Brussels. The sacred Hosts are still preserved in the church of St. Gudule in the same city. There are also several pictures in this church representing this event.

4. The following miracle is related by St. Francis de Sales: In a certain church in the town of Favernay in France, the Blessed Sacrament was once exposed on a side altar to the adoration of the faithful. During the exposition, a spark happening to fall from one of the lighted tapers set the altar on fire. In a short time everything was destroyed—even the repository in which the Blessed Sacrament was kept was consumed. The Blessed Sacrament itself, however, remained in its place, and when the priest endeavored to carry it to the high altar, he found that he could not move it. He then began to celebrate Mass, and when he came to the Consecration, the Host came of its own accord to the high altar and remained there till after the Communion, when it returned to its former place and remained suspended in the air as before. This miracle was repeated for several years in succession. St. Francis de Sales says that he himself made a pilgrimage to the place in order to witness this miracle.

5. In the year 1563, a Lutheran nobleman in the city of Erford ridiculed the Blessed Sacrament as it was carried in procession by the Rev. Father Th. Baumeier. "Behold," said he, "what a ridiculous thing that old man is carrying!" No sooner had he uttered these words than he fell speechless to the ground. Dr.

J. Hebenstreit was instantly called in, but pronounced him beyond recovery. A few days after, the nobleman was a corpse. (William of Gent).

6. Many facts of the kind have occurred even in our own day. The three following are related on the authority of ecclesiastics who were inhabitants of the places in which they occurred: There lived at Wittem, near Aix-la-Chapelle, a pious person who was accustomed to see Jesus Christ in the Blessed Sacrament whenever she assisted at Mass. Now, one day she did not behold Our Lord as usual. She went, therefore, to the priest after Mass and said: "Rev. Father, you have committed such and such a fault, and this is why I did not as usual see Jesus Christ during your Mass." The priest was filled with surprise at these words, as he knew that what she said was true.

7. In Holland, a church was set on fire. Among those present was an old man who rushed boldly into the flames in order to take away the Blessed Sacrament. Immediately the flames divided before him and left him a passage to the high altar. He then took down the Blessed Sacrament and carried it away without receiving the slightest injury. A painting representing this miraculous occurrence is still to be seen in the church in which it took place.

8. About thirty years ago, on the feast of Corpus Christi, several of the citizens of Duren, near Aix-la-Chapelle, were sitting together in an inn fronting on the great marketplace, when the solemn procession of the Most Holy Sacrament passed by. Among those present was the son of the burgomaster. Now, as the priest gave the benediction with the Blessed Sacrament at the altar that had been erected in the square,

this young man held up a silver dollar in his hand
and mimicked the sacred ceremony. In a few days the
very arm with which he had committed this crime
began to mortify; the mortification soon extended to
the shoulder; and after a short time, the unhappy
man died. Moreover, from this moment the blessing
of God forsook his house; several of his family died,
and the rest sunk into poverty and disgrace.

9. The three following instances will be of special
interest, as they have happened in this country. In
the year 1824, Mrs. Ann Mattingly, of Washington,
D.C., was miraculously cured of a severe illness in
the following manner: She had been suffering from
a dangerous cancer for seven years. Every remedy
was tried, but in vain; the disease was incurable. She
lost the use of her left arm; her back and shoulders
became ulcerated in consequence of her long con-
finement to her bed; and the symptoms of approaching dissolution began to appear. In this state, finding
that all natural means were unavailing, she had
recourse to God. In concert with Prince Hohenlohe
and her pastor, the Rev. Stephen L. Dubuisson, she
began a novena in honor of the Most Holy Name
of Jesus, and at the end of the novena she received
the Blessed Sacrament. When she was about to
receive Holy Communion, believing that the time
had come when she must either die or be restored
to health, she uttered these words: "Lord Jesus! Thy
holy will be glorified." Her tongue was so rough and
parched from fever that she was unable to swallow
the Host for five or six minutes, but the moment she
swallowed it, all pain instantly left her; her body was
entirely healed, and she found herself in perfect
health. She immediately arose and dressed herself,

and after having knelt down to give thanks to God, she received hundreds of visitors who came to congratulate her and to witness the miracle. These facts are all attested by a number of competent witnesses, and anyone who desires to examine the evidence can find a full statement of the case in the works of Bishop England.

10. At the burning of the Ursuline Convent near Charlestown, Massachusetts, when the nuns were driven from their cloister at the hour of midnight by a fanatical mob, one of the ruffians had the hardihood to open the tabernacle, and seizing the sacred vessels, he poured into the pocket of a companion the consecrated Hosts which they contained. The latter, on his way back to Charlestown, treated the sacred particles with the most atrocious irreverence, and even jestingly offered them to a tavern-keeper in payment for the liquor he had drunk. He then returned home and related to his wife an account of the night's proceedings. Shortly afterwards he went into the yard, but as he did not return, the family became uneasy and sought for him everywhere. After searching for sometime they found him a ghastly corpse. He had died the death of Arius. This fact was related by the late Bishop Fenwick of Boston.

11. The Rev. Anthony Urbanek, who in the years 1847 and 1848 exercised the functions of the holy ministry in the city of Milwaukee in the State of Wisconsin, gave the following account of a wonderful conversion wrought by the recital of the "Hail Mary": He frequently visited a Protestant family by the name of Pollworth, natives of Hanover, but then residing a few hours drive from Milwaukee. After a short time Mrs. Pollworth joined the Catholic

Church, but her husband remained obstinate and would often say that he would never become a Catholic. He would not even allow his children to be baptized, although his wife resorted to every possible means to obtain his consent. All who knew him used to say it would require nothing less than a miracle to make a Catholic of Pollworth.

The priest continued his visits, and their conversation generally fell upon the truths of Catholicity. But every effort to convince Mr. Pollworth was in vain; he had always a thousand objections to present. On one of these visits, after having long and uselessly endeavored to open the eyes of his headstrong friend to the truth of the Catholic Faith, Rev. Mr. Urbanek at last said to him: "I see well, Mr. Pollworth, that I can do nothing with you." At that moment the good priest was suddenly inspired with a feeling of extraordinary confidence in the intercession of the Blessed Virgin, and continuing to address Mr. Pollworth, he added: "But you must, at least, promise me one thing." "What may that be?" asked his friend in the low German dialect. "I will tell you after you will have promised it," answered Rev. Mr. Urbanek. "It is not difficult, and you can conscientiously do it." After a good deal of argument, Mr. Pollworth finally promised to do what might be asked of him. "Then," said the priest, "say on every Sunday henceforth one 'Hail Mary' for my intention, and you will in a short time experience a great change in your feelings." Mr. Pollworth laughed at these words, but he kept his promise faithfully. About fourteen days after the promise was made, he suddenly accosted his wife thus: "I am going to Milwaukee now to buy some new clothes for the children." The astonished wife asked: "But why at this time so particularly?" "Well, I have at last made up my mind to let the children be baptized," was his reply. The news spread like wild-fire through the entire neighborhood. "Pollworth has, at length, consented to have his children baptized," was in everyone's mouth.

Moreover, he begged the Rev. Mr. Urbanek to have the ceremony performed with the greatest solemnity. His request was granted. The Rev. Pastor invited another priest and two clerics to assist at the Baptism, which took place before High Mass. After Mass, the Most Blessed Sacrament was exposed and the hymn *Pange Lingua* sung by the choir. The newly baptized children stood close to the altar steps and their father immediately behind them. During the singing of the hymn, it suddenly occurred to Mr. Pollworth to look at the Blessed Sacrament, but being forced by the immense crowd that was pressing towards the sanctuary to stand if he would not kneel upon his children, he feared lest a free glance at the Sacred Host might have the appearance of irreverence. However, he was not long able to resist the inclination. He looked towards the altar and saw the Sacred Host as it always is, but it soon increased to the size of a mill-stone, and in the center of it there appeared the Good Shepherd with a lamb upon His shoulders. This sight did not perplex the man: he wished to convince himself of what he seemed to see. He accordingly closed one eye for awhile and thus looked at the apparition, and then again with both eyes, until he was fully satisfied that there was no illusion in the matter. Besides, it was a clear noon-day, and he was standing scarcely two steps from the altar.

After the lapse of about five minutes, the vision disappeared, and the Sacred Host resumed its original appearance. On leaving the church, Pollworth asked some of his neighbors whether they had seen nothing singular during the divine service, but when he perceived that they knew nothing of the apparition, he said no more. The next day he invited the priest to pay him a visit, and as soon as Rev. Mr. Urbanek entered the house, Pollworth said: "Now, indeed, is the lost sheep at last found, after its long straying among the briars. I wish to become a Catholic." A few days later he was received into the Church, and after he had made his Profession of Faith, he solemnly attested by oath to the truth of the vision above related. On the same day a bigoted Calvinist was baptized. Upon the simple assurance of Mr. Pollworth of what had taken place, he had been converted. The Right Rev. Bishop granted to the congregation of the church in which the wonder had taken place the privilege of having, on every 16th of July, the day of the apparition, a solemn procession with the Blessed Sacrament, exactly as on Corpus Christi. Pollworth and his family always go to Holy Communion on this day.

12. Towards the close of the last century, there lived a very impious man in Rottweil, a little town of Swabia, Germany. One day, when in the most solemn procession of Corpus Christi, the Blessed Sacrament passed by the house of this impious wretch, he had the diabolical audacity to scoff at the Blessed Sacrament in a most horrid manner. He placed himself before the window in his shirt sleeves, with his butcher's apron on and a white nightcap on his head. By appearing in this unbecoming dress, he wished

to show his contempt and disrespect to the Holy Eucharist.

What was still worse, as the Blessed Sacrament passed by him, he spat upon it. Only a few persons noticed his impiety; otherwise, it would have been immediately revenged. But what men failed to do God was not slow in accomplishing. This blasphemer soon after died the death of a reprobate.

This, however, was not all. The dreadful scandal which he had given and which had become generally known and the outrage which he had offered the Divine Majesty required a public act of reparation. God made use of the following means to effect this: Immediately after the death of this impious man, such horrible noises, such frightful groanings, lamentations and howlings were heard in his house that no one could stand it any longer. Every person easily guessed the cause of it; the difficulty was, how to remove it. At last, as if inspired by God, they had recourse to the following expedient: It was resolved that this man's portrait should be painted in the same dress and posture in which he had appeared, to scoff at the Blessed Sacrament, and that the painting should be placed in the opening of the wall, instead of the window, in order to show to all who should pass by how God punishes the scoffers of the Blessed Sacrament. Strange to say, no sooner was this painting placed in the wall, than the house became quiet. Some years afterwards, the wife of a Protestant preacher who lived opposite could no longer bear the sight of this horrid portrait. Accordingly, her husband went to the Civil Magistrate to obtain an ordinance for the removal of the picture. His petition was granted, but no sooner was the painting removed than the former frightful scenes returned and continued until the alarmed people of the house obtained permission to restore the painting to its place. One of our Fathers related this event to me, as an eye-witness of the fact.

13. In a procession at Valencia, when Blessed Nicholas Fattori was carrying the Blessed Sacrament, all at once a flock of birds came and formed a crown just above the canopy, singing most melodiously and steadily accompanying the procession, their warbling notes harmonizing beautifully with the ecclesiastical chant. When afterwards he was asked about this, he answered with a smile that they were Angels who came from Heaven to honor their Divine King. (His Life).

14. At the time when the modern heresies in relation to the Real Presence were arising, Our Lord was pleased to illustrate this doctrine by a miracle. A nobleman of Tyrol named Oswald Mulser, on coming to make his Paschal Communion, insisted on being communicated with a large host. This was an act of pride and unbelief, but the priest was induced through human respect to give him a large host instead of a small one, such as are ordinarily given; but in the very moment when the Host was placed on his tongue, the ground opened under his feet as if to swallow him. He had already sunk down to his knees when he seized hold of the altar, which yielded like wax to his hand. Seeing now the vengeance of God overtaking him, he repented of his pride and prayed for mercy. As God would not permit him to swallow the Sacred Host, the priest removed it and replaced it in the tabernacle. It was the color of blood. The author who records this, Tilman Breden-

bach, says that he himself saw the Host tinged with blood, the altar bearing the impress of Oswald's hands and the ground into which he was sinking still hollow and covered with iron bars. Witnesses testify to these visible evidences of the miracle, even to the present day.

15. Three years ago one of our priests received a letter from his father in Treves, Germany. In this letter a very melancholy example was related that occurred in that city on the occasion of the solemn procession of Corpus Christi. When the procession passed by the house of a certain Protestant gentleman, his servant girl, who was a Catholic, said to her master: "O come and see the splendid procession and the faith of the Catholics." In answer to this invitation, the gentleman uttered a most horrible blasphemy against the Blessed Sacrament. No sooner had it left the blasphemous lips than he fell to the ground dead. The whole city looked upon this instantaneous death as an evident chastisement of God for the horrible crime of blasphemy.

16. "One day," said the Curé d'Ars, when catechising the people, "two Protestant ministers who did not believe in the Real Presence of Our Lord in the Blessed Sacrament came to me. I said to them: 'Do you think a piece of bread could detach itself and of its own accord go and place itself on the tongue of a person who came near to receive it?' 'No,' said they. 'Well, then, it is not bread.'" The saintly Curate then related the following fact: "There was a man who had doubts about the Real Presence, and he said: 'What do we know about it? It is not certain what Consecration is! What happens on the altar at that moment?' But this man wished to

believe, and he prayed to the Blessed Virgin to obtain faith for him. Listen attentively to this: I do not say that this happened somewhere, but I say that it happened to myself. At the moment when this man came up to receive Holy Communion, the Sacred Host detached Itself from my fingers while I was yet a good way off, went of Itself and placed Itself upon the tongue of that man.'' (*Spirit of the Curé d'Ars*).

17. The same Curé relates also that a priest once, after Consecration, had some little doubt whether his few words could have made Our Lord descend upon the altar; at the same moment he saw the Host all red and the corporal tinged with blood.

18. Charles II, king of Spain, took a ride in his carriage at Madrid on the twentieth of January, 1685, accompanied by many personages of nobility and high rank and followed by a large concourse of the common people. Perceiving a priest approaching with the Blessed Sacrament, he quickly alighted from his carriage and knelt down to adore his Saviour in the Holy Eucharist, after which he begged the priest to take his place in the carriage. Taking his hat in his left hand and holding, like a coachman, the reins of the horses, he followed on foot with uncovered head to the house of the sick person. Here he again knelt down to adore his Lord and God in the Blessed Sacrament. He served the priest to the best of his power. Finally, he bestowed a rich present on the family in order that the sick man might die with less solicitude for those he was to leave behind him. (Bollandus).

19. It may excite surprise to hear that irrational animals can teach us lessons of reverence towards the Most Holy Sacrament, but such is the case. There

are not a few instances on record which prove that the Divine Author of nature has been pleased sometimes so to direct the instinct of brutes that, by their behavior, they might confound the pride of heretics and infidels or awaken the devotion of lukewarm and indifferent Catholics.

In the life of St. Anthony of Padua, a very striking miracle is recorded. As Almighty God by the prophet Isaias proposed the docility of the ox and the ass as a rebuke to the stubbornness of the children of Israel, so in this instance He made use of a brute beast to reprove the folly of those who reject the mystery of the Real Presence. In the time of St. Anthony of Padua, there lived at Tolosa, a city of Spain, a very obstinate heretic, Bovillus by name, who denied the Real Presence of Jesus Christ in the Blessed Sacrament. Although St. Anthony compelled him to acknowledge interiorly the truth of this doctrine, he persisted obstinately in his heresy. At last he professed his willingness to believe, provided he should see a miracle wrought in proof of it. "What, then, do you desire?" St. Anthony asked. "I will," said the heretic, "keep my mule without food for three days; afterwards, I will bring him to you. On one side I will place food before him, and on the other side you shall stand with the Blessed Sacrament. In case the mule leaves the food and goes to you, I will believe that Jesus Christ is truly and really present in the Blessed Sacrament."

St. Anthony having agreed to the proposal, on the day appointed a great concourse of people was assembled together in the public square to see the issue. St. Anthony, after having said Mass, took the Blessed Sacrament and carried It with him to the square. Then, when the hungry animal had been brought near and food put before him, St. Anthony, holding in his hands the Blessed Sacrament, thus spoke: "In the name of my Creator, Whom I am not worthy to hold in my hands, I command thee to draw near and prostrate thyself before thy God, to give due honor to Him, that the heretics may learn from thee how they ought to worship their God in the Blessed Sacrament." And behold, no sooner had St. Anthony thus spoken than the mule left his food, went before the Blessed Sacrament, and bowed his head to the ground as if to adore it! At this sight, Bovillus and many other heretics were converted and professed their faith in the Real Presence.

20. St. Francis of Assisi, whose power over irrational creatures almost carries us back to the days of man's original innocence, was followed by a sheep wherever he went. This sheep went even into the church and during the time of Mass would keep very quiet until the Consecration, when it would kneel down as if to adore its Creator.

21. The most striking fact of this reverence shown by animals, and one which would seem almost incredible, if its truth were not vouched by such authors as John Eusebius and Stephen Menochius, is related of a baker's dog at Lisbon. This dog, without ever having been taught to do so, seemed to exhibit towards the Most Blessed Sacrament all that devoted fidelity which so often distinguishes the attachment of these animals to their masters. As soon as the bell rang to announce that the Blessed Sacrament was to be carried to the sick, he would run to the church, and lying down at the door, he would wait till the priest came out with the Blessed

Sacrament, when he would join the procession, running from one side to the other, as if he was deputed to keep order.

Once, the bell was rung about midnight. The dog instantly jumped up to go in all haste to the church, but the doors of the house being all locked so that he could not get out, he went to his master's room, whining and barking in order to awaken him, but not being successful, he went to another person, whom he pulled by his clothes to the door of the house and held on to him till he opened it. Once in Holy Week, he watched for twenty-four hours successively when the Blessed Sacrament was exposed in the sepulchre. He would not permit the slightest indecorum in the presence of the Blessed Sacrament, and so long as he was in the church, no one dared to sit or stand.

On one occasion, as the Viaticum was being carried to a sick person, he found a peddler asleep on the roadside; he barked until the man awoke, uncovered his head and knelt while the Viaticum was passing. On another occasion he compelled a country woman, who was riding on an ass, to dismount and adore the Blessed Sacrament. Sometimes he was mistaken in the signal and would go to the church when the bell had rung for a funeral; in such cases he would return home immediately. No one, not even his master, was able to break him of this habit, and whether they tried to entice him with food or fastened him up, all was in vain. In the one case, he would snap at the meat once or twice, then as if fearing to be late, he would run off to the church. In the other case, he would howl so dreadfully that they were glad to release him. Thus has God been pleased to give us, through a creature devoid of understanding, a lesson in our duty.

22. There is no kind of miracle which, to our Catholic instincts, strikes us as less miraculous than a miracle wrought by the Blessed Sacrament. The miracles of our Blessed Lord in the Gospels, as compared to those of His Apostles and Disciples in the *Acts of the Apostles*, seem natural and obvious. Once acknowledge Our Blessed Lord's Divinity, and all distinction between the natural and the supernatural seems to cease in His regard, and miracles flow as the direct consequence of His Presence. In the same way, once grant the doctrine of the Real Presence in the Blessed Sacrament, and the wonder is that miracles are not of daily and hourly occurrence in our churches.

The word "miracle" is perhaps ill-selected to express what is here intended, since every offering of Holy Mass is in reality a far greater miracle than anything else in the world. Every Sacramental act of Holy Church is miraculous, inasmuch as it is supernatural. The supernatural order is as incidental to the ordinary working and life of the Church as the natural order is incidental to the government of the world. It is not the *supernatural* which is infrequent, but *manifestations* of the supernatural. These are only granted occasionally at rare intervals for the sake of encouragement or proof and generally as a reward for very deep and ardent faith. As the Archbishop of Westminster remarks in his prefatory commendation of this miracle, it is a manifestation of supernatural power to "confirm our consciousness of the operations of the Holy Ghost, both sacramental and miraculous, which like His presence, from which they flow, are perpetual in the Church."

The following miracle is introduced to us under the double warranty, so to speak, of the Curé of St. Martin at Metz, who narrates it, and the Bishop of Metz, who endorses the narrative with his imprimatur in the following words:

Bishop's Palace, Metz.

"Having considered the following narrative to be as edifying as we know it to be strictly conformable to truth, we have approved of its publication. It is scarcely possible to imagine anything more likely to awaken in the hearts of Christians earnest sentiments of faith, trust and love for Our Lord Jesus Christ in the Blessed Sacrament of the altar and to increase among us devotion to the Institution of the Perpetual Adoration than this simple recital of what took place in the Church of St. Martin during the religious services of that holy time. It would seem as if our Blessed Lord had wished to show by a signal favor how acceptable is this homage to His Divine Heart and had chosen for that token the sudden and miraculous cure of a young girl whose faith had led her to fall at His feet and to cry out with lively faith and humble confidence, 'Lord, if Thou wilt, Thou canst make me whole!'"

✠ Paul, Bishop of Metz
At Metz, 8th September, 1865

The statement of the Curé carries conviction to every candid reader by the truthful simplicity of its style.

"At the age of thirteen, Ann de Clery, who was the daughter of a distinguished member of the magistrature, still living, was sent to school at the convent of the Sacred Heart at Metz. Soon after she first went to school, her health gradually decayed, and after several serious attacks, her malady assumed the form of the disease which her Paris physician described as 'muscular and atrophical paralysis.' For more than nine years she lingered in a state of infirmity, pronounced by one doctor after another as incurable. In 1859 her physician had declared that she would be a cripple as long as she lived.

"From that time—that is, from the middle of the year 1859 up to the present time—Mlle de Clery has not been attended by any physician. Her mother alone watched over her health. Her infirmities kept increasing. She could hardly digest any food. Her thinness and weakness were pitiable. Violent headaches, three or four times a week, added to her prostration of strength. She could not be laid on the bed or the couch without suffering intense pain, and at such moments a strange effect of these paroxysms was visible in her face. Her eyelids became inflamed and of a purple color; this gave to her countenance an indescribable appearance of suffering. Paralysis was beginning to affect her arms, the only limbs she had hitherto retained the use of. It was feared that she would soon lose the principal means of occupation and amusement within her reach—the exercise of her skill in fancy works. The future prospects of this young lady seemed sad indeed to human prevision, but the time was at hand which God in His wisdom had fixed upon for the fulfillment of His merciful designs."

Her resignation to God's will was most complete. During several years, a priest brought her Holy Communion every week, and she spent her time in embroidering altar cloths or making artificial flowers for Corpus Christi.

She felt a great longing to be carried to the church of St. Martin for the forty hours' devotion, which was to take place on the 12th, 13th, and 14th of last June. The state of her health prevented the accomplishment of her wish until the third day.

"On the morning of the 14th of June, Ann received Communion in her bed. At twelve o'clock, which was the hour of adoration assigned by the parochial regulations to the inhabitants of the street in which the Hotel Coetlosquet is situated, she was carried to the church like a baby of a few months— she, a woman of twenty-three years of age—by her maid Clementine, who sat down on a bench on the left side of the nave and held her on her knees. Madame de Clery and Mlle Therese de Coetlosquet knelt, the one by her side and the other on the bench behind, in order, as much as possible, to screen her from observation. Madame and Mlle Paulin de Coetlosquet, who had preceded them, were kneeling in another part of the church. Neither the invalid herself nor any of her friends were expecting the extraordinary event about to take place.

"After a few moments' rest from the fatigue she had gone through and which was producing, as usual, a purple flush in her eyelids, Ann fixed her attention on the Blessed Sacrament; and after some instants' silent adoration, she said the prayer she often used at the moment of Communion: 'Lord, if Thou wilt, Thou canst cure me.' At the same instant, she felt so violent a pain in her whole body that it was all she could do not to scream out. She prayed earnestly for strength to bear it and then added: 'My God, if it is Thy Will that I should be carried back to my sick bed, give me grace at least to be always resigned to Thy Holy Will.'

"I cannot describe what then happened between God and her soul. She says she felt penetrated with faith and hope and, as she expresses it, became conscious that she was cured. She wanted to kneel. Her maid whispered to her: 'Mademoiselle, you will fall down.' But Ann threw herself on her knees, and said to those about her: 'Pray, pray; I am cured!' These words filled them with astonishment; tears and sobs mingled with their prayers. Madame de Clery, overwhelmed with emotion, in a state of bewilderment, not knowing what to think or to believe, led her daughter out of the church. She could not credit the evidence of her senses when she saw her standing on her feet, and then walking only with the help of her arm.

"They went into a summer house in the adjacent garden, and there the poor mother, whose fears made her incredulous, ascertained that the knots under her daughter's knees had entirely disappeared. Ann entreated to be allowed to return to the church, where she remained for three quarters of an hour kneeling before the Blessed Sacrament, without feeling the least tired and pouring forth praises and thanksgivings.

"When I was told what happened, I went to the summer house, but could not attend to any of the persons assembled around Ann. I could only look at her in silence and astonishment, while with intense gratitude to God she showed me that she could stretch out her limbs, walk, kneel, and hold up her head without effort. She was completely cured. God had done the work, and His work, accomplished in an instant, was perfect. All the ailments which had afflicted her had disappeared at the same time as the paralysis, and the weakness which follows long illness did not attend her recovery. Numerous proofs evinced it. The hour of vespers was at hand. Ann said she wished to be present at the service. Following the dictates of natural prudence—for I was not certain how far, in restoring her health, God had also given back to her her strength—I advised that she should rest, or at least if she were bent on coming to the church that day, that she should wait in the summer house till the time of Benediction. She complied with my request, but when the hymn *Pange lingua,* etc., resounded in her ears—'Sing, my tongue, the mystery of the glorious Body of Christ'—she could not sit still, and hastened to join the crowd which filled the church.

"The next day, which was the Feast of Corpus Christi, she heard a Mass in thanksgiving and went to Communion, kneeling at the altar among all the other communicants—a happiness she had not enjoyed for nine years. She was present during the whole of the High Mass, which is celebrated every Thursday in honor of the Blessed Sacrament, and in the afternoon was again in the church, kneeling before the altar and pouring forth the expressions of her ardent thankfulness. Three days afterwards—that is, on the Sunday on which the Feast of Corpus Christi is kept in France—Ann spent seven hours in the presence of the Blessed Sacrament, hearing Mass, attending Benediction, or visiting Our Lord at other times. When she was urged to moderate her devotion and to husband her strength, she replied that, far from feeling the least fatigue, she experienced an increase of strength and vitality whenever she approached our Blessed Lord.''

23. Having received information from many persons of the wonderful occurrence which I am now going briefly to relate, says St. Alphonsus in his book, *Visits to the Blessed Sacrament,* I endeavored to collect evidence sufficient to enable me to publish an account of it, and I first obtained a full relation of the fact written by a priest of the same town who was one of the eye witnesses of the miracle. But not satisfied with this, I myself read the authentic process which was drawn up by the Archiepiscopal Court of Naples, by order of his eminence Cardinal Sersale, the present Archbishop. The process is very long, consisting of 364 pages—a most careful investigation into the facts having been made by the officers of the court from the evidence of many priests and lay persons, all of whom, in perfect agreement, made their depositions on oath.

It happened, on the morning of the 28th of January in the past year 1772, at a place called S. Pietro á Paterno, in the diocese of Naples, that the tabernacle of the parish church in which the Blessed Sacrament was reserved was found open and that the two ciboria, a large and a small one, containing many Particles, had been taken away.

For several days the whole neighborhood was in the greatest distress and grief, and though the most diligent search was made, no tidings could be obtained either of the ciboria or of the Sacred

Particles. At length, on Thursday, the 18th of February, a certain youth, Giuseppe Orefice, of about 18 years old, as he was passing in the evening near the property of the Duke of Grottolelle, saw a number of lights, which had the appearance of bright stars. The following evening, he saw the same thing, and on coming home, he told his father what he had seen. His father, however, would not believe him.

On the following day, about an hour before sunrise, the father was passing by the same spot, with Giuseppe and his brother Giovanni, a child of 11 years, who, turning to his father, said: "See, father, the lights of which Giuseppe spoke to you yesterday evening, and you would not believe him."

On the evening of the same day, the same boys, on coming home, again saw the lights in the same place. D. Girolamo Guarino, the confessor of Giuseppe Orefice, was then informed of it, who in company with his brother, D. Diego, also a priest, went to the spot where the lights had been seen, and meanwhile sent for Orefice, who on coming there with his brother and a person called Tomaso Piccino, again saw the lights; but at that time the priests saw nothing.

On the evening of Monday, the 23rd of February, Orefice returned to the spot with Piccino and a man named Carlo Marotta and met on the road two strangers, who stopped and asked them what those many lights were which they had just distinctly seen and which twinkled like stars? They replied that they did not know; and taking leave of the strangers, they ran in haste to mark the spot where they had seen the lights. As soon as they had marked the spot, which was distant a few steps from the hedge, and in which was a poplar tree higher than the rest of the trees, they went to find the two priests already mentioned, told them what had occurred and returned all together to the spot.

When they were all there, with a child of five years, nephew to the two priests, the child cried out, "See, there are the lights, which look like two candles." (Here we must observe that the lights did not always appear in the same manner.) At the same moment, Orefice saw these two lights and said they shone like two stars; Carlo and Tomaso also saw them, and three other children of Signor Guarino, close to the poplar already mentioned.

After this they heard the shouting of many people, who from a stack of straw which was on the property were begging the priest to come and see in the stack a great light in the appearance of a flame. In the meantime, a woman named Lucia Marotta threw herself with her face to the ground on the spot where the light was seen.

The priests and many other persons ran up and, having lifted up the woman, commenced to dig in the ground, but then they found nothing. The two brothers, Giuseppe Orefice, with Tomaso Piccino and Carlo Marotta, then returned to the town and, going along the Strada Regia, they heard the cries of those who had remained on the spot. Going back there, Piccino fell suddenly upon his face, and after a few steps, Giuseppe felt himself pushed forward on the shoulders, and he also at once fell to the ground. In the same way and at the same moment, the other two, Carlo Marotta and Giovanni, Giuseppe's brother, also fell; and all four felt their heads wounded, as if they had received a severe blow with a stick.

Having got up, they went forward a few steps; and both Giuseppe, as also Carlo, Tomaso, and Giovanni, saw a brilliant light as of the sun coming forth from beneath the poplar tree; and they all four saw rising out of this light, to about four or five feet in height, a dove, which was almost as brilliant as the light itself. The dove, however, gliding down into the earth at the foot of the poplar from which it came out, disappeared, as also did the light. What the dove signified is not known, but it appears certain that it was something supernatural, and all the persons already mentioned gave evidence of the fact upon oath before the Vicar-General of Naples.

After this, remaining in the same place, they all cried out: "See, there are the lights!" And going on their knees, they began to seek for the Sacred Particles. While Piccino was scooping out the earth with his hands, they saw one Particle come out, white as paper. They then sent to call the priests. D. Diego Guarino came, and kneeling down, he took the Sacred Particle and put it in a white linen handkerchief, amid the tears and devotion of all the people, who wept bitterly.

He then began to search more carefully, and having removed some more earth, he saw a group of about forty Particles appear, which had not lost their whiteness, although they had been buried for nearly a month from the time they were stolen. They were placed in the same handkerchief, and the earth in which they were found was also removed.

It being now rumored about, other priests of the place came to the spot, bringing with them a ciborium, cotta [surplice], stole, canopy and torches. In the meantime, a priest and a gentleman went to

Monsignor the Vicar-General to know what was to be done. An order came that the Particles should be carried processionally to the church. They did so and arrived at the church about half-past eleven at night, when the particles were placed in the tabernacle.

This took place on the night of the 24th of February. The people were much consoled, but not fully so, because the greater part of the Particles, as was supposed, were still wanting.

But on the evening of the following Tuesday, the 25th, a small light, but very brilliant, was seen in the same place as at the first, by many persons, country people, gentlemen, as also by the priests D. Diego Guarino and D. Giuseppe Lindtner, who wrote for me an account of the whole affair, as I mentioned at the beginning. This priest, being much terrified, pointed to a mustard plant which was growing there, and cried out: "O Jesus, O Jesus! Look at the light there, look at it!" Upon which, the others also saw a most dazzling light, which rose about a foot and a half from the ground and formed itself on the top into the figure of a rose. Guiseppe Orefice, who was there, affirmed that the light was so brilliant that his eyes remained for some time dazzled and dimmed.

They began, therefore, to seek the remainder of the particles in that place, but found none; but on the evening of the following day, the 26th of February, a number of lights were seen round the stack of straw by three cavalry soldiers of the regiment called Borbone, Pasquale de S. Angelo of the diocese of Atri and Penne, Giuseppe Lanzano, and Angelo Di Costanzo of Acerra, who were all examined before the Archiepiscopal court. These deposed before Monsignor the Vicar-General that as they were riding round the royal villa of Caserta, where His Majesty the King then resided, they saw on the property above mentioned "several lights like shining stars." These are the very words of the soldiers as taken down in the process.

Moreover, on the same evening of the 26th, Signor D. Ferdinando Haam, a gentleman of Prague in Bohemia, Chancellor and Secretary for letters to the Embassy of His Imperial and Royal Apostolic Majesty, was returning from the city of Caserta at about nine at night, along the Strada Regia near to the above-mentioned property. He got down from his carriage to go and see the place where he had heard the stolen Particles had been found two days before. On arriving there, he found many persons, and among them the priest D. Giuseppe Lindtner, with whom he was acquainted, who told him the whole history, both of the sacrilege and of the miraculous discovery of the Particles.

Signor Haam, after having heard the priest, related that he also, eight or nine days before, on the 17th or 18th of the month, not having then heard either of the Particles that had been stolen or of the lights that had been seen, was passing by this place about nine at night and that he saw "a great number of lights amounting to about a thousand," and at the same time a number of persons who were standing in silence and with devotion round the lights. Being much frightened at what he saw, he asked the driver what those lights were; he replied that "perhaps they were accompanying the Most Holy Viaticum to some sick person." "No," replied Signor Haam, "that cannot be, otherwise we should at least hear the bells."

Hence, he suspected that these lights were the effect of some diabolical sorcery, and so much the more as the horse had stopped and would not go on a step; he therefore made the driver get down, but it was impossible to make the horse go on; it trembled all over and foamed at the mouth. At length, after many attempts, the horse, drawn away as by force out of the road which led to the ground, set off with such speed that the driver cried out: "O Jesus! What will come of this?" And so Signor D. Ferdinando returned to Naples seized with great fear. He himself deposed the whole of this in the Archiepiscopal Court, as may be read in the process (page 60, ff.).

On the evening of Thursday, the 27th, about 7 o'clock, Giuseppe Orefice and Carlo Marotta went to the place where the stack of straw was, which they found had been burned by the priests D. Girolamo Guarino and Giuseppe Lindtner, in order that they might more easily search for the missing particles. They found also Giuseppe Piscopo, Carmine Esposito and Palmiero Novello prostrate on the ground and weeping because they had seen a little light appearing and then disappearing before them several times. When Orefice heard this, he knelt down and began to recite the Acts of Faith, Hope and Charity. When he had finished, he returned with the others to see what the light was, which according to the deposition of Orefice, rose up about four fingers from the earth and then disappeared, as it were in the ground. After this, having put a mark over the place where the light had appeared, so as not to be mistaken, Orefice and Marotta went to inform the priest, D. Girolamo Guarino, who came immediately to the place and found many persons kneeling there. He began to search with care about the ground on which the mark had been placed.

At this moment, many persons again saw the light, and Guarino, who did not see it, made the Sign of the Cross upon the ground and ordered his brother Giuseppe to scoop out the earth on which the stack of straw had stood to the left of the cross, using a pick-axe which he had in his hand. But he found nothing. However, just as they were thinking of digging in another part, Giuseppe Orefice, who was on his knees all the time, put his hand on the ground and, finding that it was soft and yielding, mentioned it to the Rev. Guarino, who taking a knife from his brother, stuck it into the ground on the spot which had been marked with the cross. And when it was at its depth, he heard a noise as if several hosts united together were broken.

He drew the knife out of the ground and with it a little ball of earth, to which he saw many Particles were attached. Struck with fear at what he saw, he cried out in astonishment: "Oh, oh, oh!" and then fainted away, so that as he himself deposed, his sight failed him and, losing all power over himself, the knife, with the ball of earth and the Particles, fell from his hand.

As soon as Guarino recovered his senses, he put the Particles in a white linen handkerchief, covered them up and laid them in the hole in which they had been found; for on account of the trembling which had come over him, and especially in the arms, he was not able to stand upright. The parish priest, being informed of what had happened, came quickly to the spot, where he found all kneeling before this

Hidden Treasure. And having taken better information of the event, he went back to his church and
sent a canopy, veil, a number of wax-tapers and a
chalice, in which the Sacred Particles were put.

The assistants spread the veil over a little table
covered with silk, on which the Blessed Sacrament
reposed; around this a number of persons knelt with
lighted torches, and many people arrived, not only
from the town, but also from the surrounding vil-
lages, with their priests, all of whom shed tears of
tender devotion. In the meantime, the priest Lindtner
and Signor Giuseppe Guarino went off to find Monsignor the Vicar-General and returned about 10
o'clock with orders to carry in procession to the parish church of S. Pietro á Paterno the Particles that
had been found. They did so, and along the way they
all sang, praising and thanking Almighty God. As
soon as they arrived at the church, Benediction was
given with the chalice in the midst of the tears and
cries of devotion of the whole people, who could not
leave off weeping and thanking the Lord for the great
consolation they had received.

We read in the history of olden times of many
suchlike prodigies in confirmation of the truth of the
most Holy Sacrament. I myself, in my *History of
Heresies,* have related many examples on this matter
in the time of the impious Wickliffe, who was the
first of modern heretics to deny the truth of this
venerable Sacrament. At that time Almighty God
was pleased to work many miracles to confound their
incredulity, which I have inserted in the book just
mentioned (Chapters 36 and 37).

Nevertheless, there are not wanting certain critical

spirits who altogether refuse to believe these ancient accounts and say, "But who saw them?" Now, if such a one should doubt the fact which I have just now related and which was proved with such exactness in the Archiepiscopal court of Naples, he can easily certify himself of the truth of it by going himself to the town of S. Pietro á Paterno, which is not far from the city, where he will find many lay persons and ecclesiastics who will assure him that they beheld, with their own eyes, the prodigies here related.

For the rest, let others say what they please; for my own part, I hold the fact to be more than certain, and therefore I wished to make it known by publishing an account of it. It is true that the miracle here described does not call for any other than mere human faith; nevertheless, of all such facts grounded on human faith, I do not know if there be one that is more deserving of belief than this that I have just related, considering the extreme care with which the information was taken by the Neapolitan court and the evidence, not of credulous women, but of 17 men, lay and ecclesiastics, who judicially deposed on oath all that they had seen with their own eyes. All these circumstances, which are so many marks of truth, make the fact more than morally certain. Hence, I hope that all those who read this account will not be disinclined to believe it, but will do what they can to make it known—for the glory of the Most Holy Sacrament of the Altar.

CHAPTER 15

The Most Holy Sacrifice of the Mass

BEFORE speaking of the Most Holy Sacrifice of the Mass, I must first explain to you what is meant by sacrifice. A sacrifice, or oblation, in its most general sense is anything that is offered to God. In this sense, a sacrifice may consist of the internal motions of the heart, as Holy Scripture for instance calls a contrite heart "a sacrifice to God." But, in its strict sense, a sacrifice is an offering to God of some sensible object, to acknowledge, by the destruction or change of this object, the sovereign power of God and His absolute dominion over all creatures, as also to render Him the homage due to His Divine Majesty.

All nations have agreed upon the propriety of making such oblations to the Being to whom they give supreme honor. The Holy Scripture, the most ancient of all histories, tells us that Cain and Abel offered sacrifices to God soon after the Fall of our first parents. At the time of the Deluge we find Noah offering clean animals to God, and the same was often done by Abraham and his posterity. Now, how are we to account for so general an agreement of mankind about this mode of worshiping God? Reason alone must convince man of the necessity of expressing in some external way his obligation of dependence on God. We are composed of soul and body, and as we know that God has a right to the services of both, we cannot be satisfied until we have given an adequate expression to the emotions of our heart. It is not very probable, however, that natural reason dictated that particular species of oblation which has been in use among most nations: I mean *animal* sacrifice.

For, although the sense of guilt, which has weighed upon all men ever since the Fall of Adam, would naturally have suggested to them the necessity of some expiatory offering whenever they were about to approach God, yet we cannot see why they should have chosen to sacrifice an animal for that purpose. On the contrary, the offering to God of the life of a harmless creature, in expiation of the sins of men, considered apart from Divine Revelation, would seem to be even absurd. It is, therefore, most probable that God Himself instituted animal sacrifice in the beginning of the world to foreshadow the meritorious sacrifice of Christ and to give man a means of acknowledging his guilt.

Now, domestic animals have been generally chosen for sacrifice, chiefly for two reasons: first, because they stood in the nearest relation to man and consequently were the most fitting substitutes to bear the penalty which he had incurred; and secondly, because by their gentleness and innocence, they served to represent the meek and spotless Lamb of God. However, this original revelation concerning animal sacrifice, of which we find traces among all nations, became very much corrupted in the course of time. Supposing that *that* which they loved and prized the most would be the most acceptable offering to God, men went at last so far as to sacrifice their fellow men, nay, even the lives of their own children.

Of course *such* sacrifices were in the highest degree hateful in the sight of God. In order, therefore, to teach men how to worship Him properly, the Lord chose a particular people, to whom He gave express and minute directions about the sacrifices that they were to offer. This was the Jewish nation. Out of this nation He chose a particular family—the family of Aaron—who were to offer Him sacrifice. These sacrifices ordained by God were of various kinds: offerings of adoration, offerings of impetration, sin offerings, and thanksgiving offerings.

In some of these sacrifices the victim was only partially consumed by fire, while in others it was entirely consumed. The latter were called holocausts or burnt offerings. This system of worship lasted until the coming of our Saviour. It was then abolished because all these sacrifices were in themselves utterly incapable of appeasing the wrath of God. They were meritorious merely because they prefigured the death of Christ; consequently, after that event these sacrifices became entirely unmeaning and worthless. Ever since the death of Christ there has been no bloody sacrifice, for the death of Our Lord was the true propitiation for the sins of the world.

The Prophet, however, expressly foretold the institution of a new kind of sacrifice, a real sacrifice, though an unbloody one, which was to succeed the abrogated sacrifices of the Old Law and to be offered unceasingly in every part of the world. The passage to which I allude is very remarkable; it is from the prophet Malachy (1:10-11): "I have no pleasure in you, saith the Lord of hosts," addressing the Jewish people, "and I will not receive a gift of your hand. For from the rising of the sun even to the going down, my name is great among the Gentiles, and in every place there is sacrifice, and there is offered to my name a clean oblation: for my name is great among the Gentiles, saith the Lord of hosts." Here we have the promise that when the Jewish sacrifices should have ceased, another and far more precious sacrifice would be offered, visible indeed like them, but, unlike them, possessed of an intrinsic sanctity, a sacrifice that was to be offered from the rising to the setting of the sun—a sacrifice that was to be offered in every place, even to the End of Time.

Now all these attributes are found—and found only—in the Catholic sacrifice of the Mass. This is so evident that all the Fathers of the Church, with one accord, interpret this passage as a clear prophecy of this most adorable sacrifice. It is a real sacrifice in the proper sense of the word because Our Lord is not only really present in the consecrated Host, but He also truly offers Himself to His heavenly Father. It is not, however, a bloody sacrifice, because Our Lord is not really slain in the Mass; His death is merely represented in a mystical manner by the separation and destruction of the species. According to some of the Holy Fathers, the word Mass is derived from the Latin word "missa" or "missio," which signifies a "sending," because God sends His well-beloved Son to be our victim, and the priest sends Him back to the Eternal Father as our ransom and our intercessor.

But you may ask, does it not argue a want of perfection in the sacrifice of Christ on the Cross to continue thus to offer Himself in the Mass? By no means. The sacrifice of the Mass is the same that was offered on the Cross, the only difference being in the manner of offering. The victim is the same in both—it is Jesus Christ, the true Lamb of God, really slain on the Cross, mystically slain in the Mass; the priest, too, is the same: it is Jesus Christ, the true High Priest, who offered Himself *immediately* on the Cross and who offers Himself *mediately* by the ministry of His priests in the Mass. *In itself,* the sacrifice which our Saviour offered on the Cross is of infinite value, and it is more than sufficient for our redemption. But of what use will it be to *us,* unless it is applied to our souls? Of what use is it to a poor person to know that there is somewhere a sum sufficient for his ransom, if that sum be not really given to him?

Cardinal Hosius gives a beautiful illustration of this truth: "Suppose," he says, "that there were, in a certain city, a large fountain of water, sufficient to supply the wants of all the inhabitants. Suppose that this fountain was situated in the center of the city and entirely open to all; will the mere fact of the existence of such a fountain be sufficient to supply everybody's wants? Must not everyone that stands in need of this water either draw it himself or have it brought to him by some means or other? Now, there is a fountain of living water flowing from the open side of Jesus Christ; it is a never-failing fountain, a copious fountain, sufficient and more than sufficient to wash away the sins of the whole world and to impart life to all the children of men. In order, however, that we may experience the wonderful virtue of this living water, it must be applied to our souls.

"Now, Jesus Christ has established certain channels through which the waters of His grace come to us. Baptism is one of these channels; the daily Sacrifice, which we call Mass, is another. By this sacrifice, the fruit of the sacrifice accomplished on the Cross and the Precious Blood there shed for us are applied to our souls. How unjustly, then, do the Protestant ministers reproach us with obscuring the sacrifice of the Cross by our daily sacrifice of the Altar! Would it not be absurd to say that to desire Baptism and to place one's confidence in water, instead of in the blood of the Redeemer, would be to disparage the merits of Christ? Now, just as absurd is it to say that we, by our daily sacrifice, obscure the glory of the sacrifice of the Cross and detract from its dignity, since we, by this very means, only participate in the sacrifice of the Cross and make it available to our salvation." (*Confessio Cathol. Fidei in Synodo Petriconensi,* C. 41, Fol. 94.).

Moreover, our Divine Saviour instituted the sacrifice of the Mass in order that His religion might not be wanting in what even the Jewish religion possessed, a continual sacrifice, and that we might have an adequate means to worship Him properly. The sacrifice of the Mass, therefore, far from derogating from the sacrifice of the Cross, only brings it nearer to us and renews and extends its effects in a wonderful manner.

Our Blessed Lord instituted this sacrifice of the Mass at the Last Supper. On the very night in which He was betrayed, He changed bread and wine into His Body and Blood and gave to the Apostles and to their successors the power to do the same in commemoration of Him. In obedience to the commands of Our Lord, the Apostles frequently offered up the Holy Sacrifice of the Mass, as we see from the *Acts of the Apostles* (2:42) and from the writings of the

Fathers of the Church, especially of St. Ignatius the Martyr and St. Clement, both disciples of the Apostles.

The wooden altar on which St. Peter and the succeeding Popes—down to St. Sylvester—used to say Mass is still preserved at Rome. St. Matthew the Apostle was pierced with a lance in the very act of saying Mass. When St. Andrew the Apostle was required by the tyrant Aegeas to sacrifice to the gods if he wished to escape the punishment of the cross, he replied: "I daily offer up on the altar to the only true and Almighty God the Immaculate Lamb, which, though it is consumed, remains always living and entire. And indeed St. Paul expressly declares, in the Epistle to the Hebrews: "We have an altar, whereof they have no right to eat, who serve the [Jewish] tabernacle." (*Heb.* 13:10).

An altar implies a sacrifice, since an altar is used only for sacrifice. Now as there is no other sacrifice in the Christian religion than that of the Eucharist, it follows that the altar of which the Apostle speaks must have been an altar for saying Mass. The Fathers of the Church commonly speak of the Mass as "a salutary sacrifice." St. Cyprian, in the third century, calls it "an everlasting sacrifice." (*Lib. de coena*). St. Augustine, in the fourth century, declares it to be "a true and august sacrifice, and that it has supplanted all former sacrifices." (*De Civit. Dei,* Cap. xx). But no one has spoken of the subject in more sublime terms than St. John Chrysostom. "O wonder!" he exclaims in his homily *De Sacra Mensa*. "At this table, so magnificently furnished, the Lamb of God is immolated for thee; there the Cherubim are present; there the Seraphim attend; there all the Angels join with the priest in praying for thy welfare.''

And again, in his book *De Sacrificio* (Lib. iii), he says: "When thou beholdest the Lord immolated and lying upon the altar and the priest bending over the sacrifice and praying and all the assistants reddened with that precious blood, dost thou think that thou art still on earth? Does it not rather seem to thee that thou art rapt into Paradise and beholding with the eye of thy soul the things that are done in Heaven?" In his eighty-third homily, he says: "How surpassingly pure ought he to be who offers such a sacrifice? Ought not the hand that divides this sacred flesh, the mouth that is filled with this spiritual fire, the tongue that is dyed with this most sacred blood be purer than the light of the sun? Think how thou art honored, to what a banquet thou art admitted! That before which the Angels tremble and veil their faces is our food; we are united to Christ; we are made one body and one flesh with Him!" "Who shall declare the power of the Lord and set forth all His praises?"

These passages give us a very exalted idea of the dignity and value of the Sacrifice of the Mass, and yet they fall far short of the reality. Indeed, if all the learned and saintly men that ever lived, or ever will live, were to unite with the Angels and Saints of Heaven and with the Blessed Mother of God herself and were each to strive to the utmost of his power to set forth the dignity of the Mass, they would all be unable to praise it worthily.

None of the Doctors of the Church has written so fully and profoundly on this subject as St. Thomas Aquinas, and Our Lord Himself commended him for his efforts to explain and illustrate it; but even he did not receive the praise of having written *worthily* on the subject; Our Lord only said to him: "Thomas, *bene de me scripsisti*"—"Thomas, thou hast written *well* concerning Me." Not *worthily!* Nay, if Our Lord Himself were to appear to us and to describe the greatness of the Mass, we should not be able to understand Him, for the Mass is infinite in dignity, since it is God Himself who is the priest and victim.

St. Chrysostom was therefore right in applying to this glorious mystery the words of the Psalmist: "Who shall declare the power of the Lord and set forth all His praises!" But besides the great dignity of the Mass, there is another reason for which we should esteem this holy sacrifice: it is its great utility.

Mass is, in the first place, a sacrifice of adoration; secondly, a sacrifice of thanksgiving; thirdly, it is a sacrifice of propitiation; and fourthly, a sacrifice of impetation. I said, in the first place, that the Holy Mass is a sacrifice of *adoration,* that is to say, a sacrifice by which we render to God a worship corresponding to His greatness. It is evident that we are bound to worship God, for even our reason tells us that honor should be given to whom honor is due. We usually honor men according to their rank and acquirements. We honor a man of learning, for instance, more than an ignorant rustic; a saint more than a sinner; a prince more than a peasant; a priest more than a layman. Now God is infinite in all His perfections and consequently desires supreme honor and reverence. He alone is, as the Holy Scripture says, "Blessed and Mighty, the King of Kings, and Lord of Lords; who alone hath immortality and inhabiteth light inaccessible; whom no man hath seen nor can see; to whom be honor and empire everlasting.''

Now, how are we to render to God the honor that is due to Him? I have said already that *sacrifice* is the mode by which we acknowledge the supreme sovereignty of God, but where shall we find a sacrifice pure and precious enough to be offered to His Majesty? It is plain that we finite creatures have nothing of ourselves great enough to offer Him; even the sacrifice of our lives would be an inadequate homage. ''What shall I offer to the Lord that is worthy? Wherewith shall I kneel before the high God?'' (*Micheas* 6:6).

Almighty God Himself has furnished us with an offering, as He declared one day to one of His servants who was burning with love for Him and with an ardent desire to honor Him. ''Oh,'' said this fervent soul, ''I would that I had a thousand tongues that I might praise God always! Oh, that I had hearts without number wherewith to love Him! Oh, that the whole world were mine that I might see Him loved and served by all men!'' ''My daughter,'' replied an inward voice, ''thy zeal and love are extremely pleasing to Me, but know that I am more honored by a single Mass than by all the honors that thou couldst ever conceive or desire.''

The reason for this is plain. The victim which is offered to God in the Mass is Our Lord Jesus Christ Himself, the well-beloved Son of His Father, equal to Him in all things; and therefore, this sacrifice must be of infinite dignity and value. In this sacrifice we offer to the Eternal Father all the honor which Jesus Christ gives Him and thereby make up for our natural poverty. Hence Father Paul Segneri well says in his *Homo Christianus* (P. 1, diss. 12): "If, on the one hand, the Blessed Mother of God and all the Saints and Angels of Heaven were to prostrate themselves before God in the deepest humility and reverence and, on the other hand, the humblest priest on earth were to offer but one Mass, the offering of the priest would give more honor to God than the united adoration of all those Angels and Saints."

In the second place, we need a sacrifice of thanksgiving, for we are bound to return thanks to God for all the benefits He has bestowed on us. How many blessings have we not received from God? Creation, preservation and all the blessings of His Providence; redemption by vocation to the True Faith; the grace of repentance, deliverance from [going to] Hell, the promise of Heaven, the Sacraments, holy inspirations, the examples and intercession of the Saints. What a debt of gratitude do we owe for so many favors! Solomon, the wise man, requires us to "give to the Most High according to what He has given to us." (*Ecclus.* 35:12). But what can we render to God for all that He has done for us?

We cannot pray always; we cannot, like David, compose a whole book of inspired hymns in praise of God's wonderful dealings with us; and even if we could, our thanksgiving would be insufficient and unworthy of God. Now God in His mercy has given the devout soul a means of paying this immense debt of gratitude. The Mass is a *Eucharistic* sacrifice, that is to say, a sacrifice of thanksgiving. Jesus Christ has left us Himself to be offered therein by way of thanksgiving to His heavenly

Father.* He gives thanks to the Eternal Father for us, and thus we are enabled to return to God even more than we have received from Him.

Two pious souls were one day discoursing about the graces they had received from God. One of them complained of her inability to give due thanks to God for all she had received; the other smiled and said: "I give to God every day more than I ever received from Him." This answer naturally surprised the former, and she asked how this was possible. "Oh," replied the latter, "I go to Mass every day and offer up Jesus Christ to my heavenly Father for all the graces He has bestowed upon me; and Jesus Christ, the well-beloved Son of God, is certainly of greater worth than all the benefits which I have ever received, or ever will receive."

In the third place, the Mass is a *propitiatory* sacrifice, that is to say, a sacrifice by which God is intended to forgive us our sins and to remit the temporal punishments due to them. Such a sacrifice is very necessary, for we are bound not only to adore and thank God, but also to beg of Him new graces. Now the most important grace that we can ask of God is the pardon of our sins. Sin is an offense against the Majesty of God. Were all the men that ever lived to unite, they could not repair the outrage that is done to God by one venial sin. Hence

---

*Note: It is a doctrine of the Catholic Church that Mass can be offered to God alone. This is indeed implied in the very nature of a sacrifice. When therefore Catholics speak of the Mass of such and such a Saint or of offering Mass in honor of a Saint, they mean a Mass offered to God in thanksgiving for the graces bestowed on that Saint or for the graces obtained through his intercession.

Almighty God, who is in a certain sense infinitely offended by sin, instituted the Sacrifice of Mass, by which an infinite satisfaction is continually rendered to Him.

The Council of Trent declares (Sess. 12, C. 1) that the same Jesus Christ who offered Himself up on the Cross for the sins of the whole world is daily offered up by the priest in the Holy Mass. The Sacrifice of the Mass is the same as the sacrifice of Calvary, the only difference being that on the Cross He really suffered and shed His blood in a visible manner, while in the Mass He offers Himself without suffering and sheds His blood in a mystical manner. Our sins, indeed, are not directly and immediately remitted by the Mass, but Almighty God is moved by this mystical sacrifice to impart to us the fruits of the meritorious death and Passion of Christ, especially the grace of a true sorrow for our sins.

The Council of Trent says (Sess. 22, C. 3) that God, appeased by the sacrifice of the Mass, forgives even the most enormous sins by granting to the sinner the grace of doing penance for them. The Holy Sacrifice of Mass, then, obtains for us the grace to do penance for our sins. Without doubt it is to this efficacy of the Mass that we must attribute the less frequent occurrence in later times of those terrible punishments which God formerly inflicted on the wicked. The whole world was once destroyed by a deluge on account of sin. Seventy thousand men fell victims to a pestilence sent by God to punish the vanity of King David. Fifty thousand of the Bethsamites were punished with death for the irreverent curiosity with which they gazed upon the Ark of the Covenant. Why are there so few instances of such punishments since the coming of Jesus Christ? Sin has lost none of its inherent wickedness; on the contrary, it has become much more malicious by reason of the more abundant graces of God. The holy Fathers tell us that without doubt it is because, in all countries, and at all times, every hour, Jesus Christ is offered up by the priests of the Catholic Church, and the hands of God are bound. The voice of the blood of the Lamb of God prevails over the sins which cry to Heaven for vengeance, and benedictions descend where punishments are due. How could it be otherwise?

Through the Blood of Christ visibly shed on the Cross, the dying malefactor obtained the grace of conversion. Now, why should not they receive the same grace who with a good will assist at Mass, where the same Blood is shed in a mystical manner? Will God the Father refuse to grant us true contrition for our sins when we offer Him the Blood of His beloved Son Jesus Christ in satisfaction for them and beseech Him, by the merits of this Blood, to have mercy on us? A nobleman named Alphonsus of Albuquerque was once on the point of being shipwrecked. He had given himself up for lost, but happening to see a child crying near him, he took it into his arms and raising it towards Heaven, he exclaimed: "Lord, if I do not deserve to be heard, at least hear the cries of this innocent babe and save us." No sooner had he uttered these words than the storm subsided, and he was saved.

Let us imitate his example. We are in peril; we have offended God and are in danger of losing our immortal souls. Should we despair? No. Let us offer to God the Divine Infant in the Mass and say:

"Lord, we have grievously sinned against Thee and are undeserving of pardon, but look upon the sufferings of this Thine innocent Son and have mercy on us!" This is what St. Anselm exhorts us to do. He says that Jesus Christ, desirous to save us from eternal death, encourages us all and says, "Fear not, O sinner; if by your sins you have made yourself the slave of Hell and are unable to deliver yourself, offer Me to My Eternal Father, and you shall escape death." And the Mother of God gave the same advice to Sister Frances Farnese. She put the Infant Jesus into her arms and said: "Behold, here is my Son; endeavor to save your soul by offering Him frequently to God."

Besides the remission of the eternal punishment due to sin, we also obtain by the holy Sacrifice of the Mass the remission of the temporal punishment. This grace we obtain in proportion to our good dispositions. On this account, the Saints, who have always been desirous to render to God a full satisfaction for their sins, have made it a point to hear as many Masses as possible. St. Margaret of Cortona, reflecting on her many grievous sins and wishing to atone for them, went to her confessor once and asked him what was the best way for her to make satisfaction to God for her sins. He told her the easiest way was to hear as many Masses as possible. From that time forward she was very careful to assist at all the Masses she possibly could.

There is still another way in which the Mass is beneficial to us. We need not only forgiveness of sins, but also numberless other blessings, both for soul and body. By the Sacrifice of the Mass we can obtain all these favors. Mass is also an *impetratory* sacrifice.

St. Porphyrus, Bishop of Gaza, was once going to Constantinople to ask a favor of the Emperor Arcadius. On his way, he met the servants of the Emperor carrying with them his infant son, Theodosius. The holy man immediately drew near and placed his petition in the hands of the young prince. The Emperor, agreeably surprised at this singular artifice of the bishop, readily granted his petition through love for the little bearer. (Schmid's Historical Catechism).

We must adopt a similar means in order to obtain favors from God. We need numberless and continual blessings of Providence: blessings on our daily labors; strength to resist sin and to bear patiently the manifold trials and contradictions of this life; steadfastness in faith, hope and charity. Now in the Mass, Jesus Christ, the Son of God, is ever ready to carry up our desires to the throne of His heavenly Father. Let us then with confidence charge Him with our petitions, and let us rest assured that His heavenly Father will, for His sake, grant us all we ask. There are innumerable examples of the efficacy of the Mass in obtaining from God every possible grace.

St. Augustine relates (*De Civitate Dei,* Lib. II, C. 8) that the house of a man named Hesperius was dreadfully disturbed day and night by evil spirits. But no sooner had Mass been celebrated in it than all the disturbance ceased, and nothing of the kind ever occurred there afterwards. St. Gregory relates that on certain days the fetters used to fall from the hands of a Christian captive who had been taken prisoner by the barbarians, and after his deliverance he found out that on those days his relatives had offered Mass for him.

In the life of St. John the Almoner, an instructive narrative is told of two tradesmen, Peter and John, one of whom had a large family to support, while the other had to provide only for himself and his wife. Peter, although he was accustomed to hear Mass every day, managed to maintain his family very comfortably, while John could scarcely gain a subsistence, although he labored so hard that he very seldom found time to hear Mass and was sometimes even obliged to work on holy days of obligation. One day John asked his more prosperous neighbor how it happened that with so large and helpless a family he always managed to live comfortably, while he himself and his wife were always in want, although he worked day and night. Peter promised to show him the place where he always found everything he needed. Next morning he called on John and led him to the church, where they both heard Mass. After Mass, Peter took leave of him and went home. He did the same the next day, but upon his calling the third day for the same purpose, his friend said: "If I had wished to go to Mass, I would not have needed you to lead me there, as I know the way myself; what I wanted was to know where you find your wealth, that I also might become rich." "I know no place," answered the pious tradesman, "where there is so much to be obtained for this world and for the next as in the Church," and in proof of what he said, he added the words of Our Lord: "Seek ye, therefore, first the kingdom of God and His justice, and all these things shall be added unto you." (*Matt.* 6:33). John immediately understood the good lesson which his friend wished to teach him, and enlightened by the Holy Ghost, he resolved to change his life and to hear Mass every day. He did so. In a very short time, he found himself greatly improved temporally and spiritually.

In the year 817 the Danes invaded England, and Ethelred, the King of England, having collected a small army, went out to meet them. But trusting more in the protection of God than in the valor of his arms, he went first to hear Mass. While he was assisting at Mass, messengers came to tell him that the Danes were at hand and that he must prepare immediately for battle, but he answered that he would not go until he had received his Saviour in Holy Communion. He stayed in the church till Mass was over, and then went forth to attack his enemies. After a short conflict he succeeded in putting them to flight. (Baronius).

One day as St. Bernard was about to say Mass in the church of St. Ambrose at Milan, the people brought to the church a lady of high rank who had been sick for many years. She had lost her sight, her hearing and her speech, and her tongue had become so long that it protruded out of her mouth. St. Bernard, having exhorted the people to join him in praying for her, began to celebrate Mass, and as often as he made the Sign of the Cross over the Host, he made it over the sick woman also. As soon as he had broken the Host and said, *"Pax Domini sit semper vobiscum,"* she was instantly cured. The people, filled with joy and astonishment, began to ring the bells, and soon the whole city hastened to the church to witness the miracle and to give thanks to God. (Life of St. Bernard).

St. Philip Neri used to have recourse to the sacrifice of the Mass in all matters of importance. By means of this holy sacrifice he succeeded in converting many Jews and heretics.

We see from these examples the great power of the Mass as an impetratory sacrifice and that it is not in vain that the priest prays that through it "we may be filled with every heavenly blessing and grace."

But I have yet one more grace to speak of which we can obtain through this sacrifice. The Mass is a very efficacious means of obtaining relief for the souls in Purgatory. This is the common doctrine of the Fathers. St. Jerome says that by every Mass, not only one, but several souls are delivered from Purgatory, and he is of the opinion that the soul for which the priest says Mass suffers no pain at all while the Holy Sacrifice lasts. (*Apud* Bern. de Busto, Serm. 3, *de Missa*.). The Fathers of the Council of Trent declare that by the Sacrifice of the Mass, the souls in Purgatory are most efficaciously relieved. This was clearly the belief of St. Monica, the mother of St. Augustine, when she replied on her deathbed to her son's inquiries concerning her place of burial. "Bury me," said she, "wherever you please; all that I ask of you is to remember me at the altar of the Lord."

In the time of St. Bernard, a monk of Clairvaux appeared after his death to his brethren in religion to thank them for having delivered him from Purgatory. On being asked what had contributed most to free him from his torments, he led the inquirer to the church, where a priest was saying Mass. "Look," said he, "this is the means by which my deliverance has been effected; this is the power of God's mercy; this is the salutary sacrifice which takes away the sins of the world." Indeed, so great is the efficacy of this sacrifice to obtain relief for the souls in Purgatory that the application of all the good works which have been performed from the beginning of the world would not afford so much assistance to one of these souls as would be imparted by a single Mass.

I will illustrate this by an example drawn from the history of St. Dominic. The Blessed Henry Suso made an agreement with one of his brethren in religion that as soon as one of them died the survivor should say two Masses every week, for one year, for the repose of his soul. It came to pass that the religious with whom Henry had made this contract died first. Henry prayed every day for his deliverance from Purgatory, but forgot to say the Masses which he had promised. The deceased appeared to him with a sad countenance and sharply rebuked him for his unfaithfulness to his engagement. Henry excused himself by saying that he had often prayed for him with great fervor and had even offered up penitential works for him. "O my brother," exclaimed the soul, "blood, blood is necessary to give me some relief and refreshment in my excruciating torments! Thy penitential works, severe as they are, cannot deliver me. There is nothing that can do this but the Blood of Jesus Christ, which is offered up in the Sacrifice of the Mass. Masses, Masses, these are what I need."

If, then, dear Christian, you wish to offer the Divine Majesty a fitting worship; if you wish to thank Him as you ought for the innumerable benefits He has conferred on you; if you wish to expiate the sins you have committed against Him; if you wish to obtain for yourself and others all the blessings you need for soul and body; if you wish to practice charity toward the suffering souls in Purgatory, you will find a suitable means to do all this in the Sacrifice of the Mass. You have but to unite your homage, your thanksgiving, your contrition, and your petitions to the fourfold offering which Jesus Christ therein makes for you; you have but to offer to the Eternal Father the Victim that is mystically immolated on the altar, and your worship becomes infinitely pleasing to God and infinitely profitable to you.

The Mass *in itself* is indeed always of the same value, whether those who assist at it be devout or indevout; but the *fruit* we derive from it is greater or less according to our dispositions. When Our Lord offered His life on the Cross as a sacrifice for the sins of the world, those who were present received the fruits of that sacrifice in very different degrees. Some received no grace at all, but went away as hardened as they had come, while others received great and special favors. The good thief obtained an entire remission of all his sins and of the punishment due to them; St. Mary Magdalene received a large increase of sanctifying grace. So it is also at Mass.

The Council of Trent says that God gives the grace of contrition and forgiveness of sins to those who assist at this Sacrifice with a sincere heart, with faith and reverence. The same may be said of all other blessings—they are given more or less in proportion to the devotion and purity of intention of those who assist at Mass. In one of the prayers which the priest recites in the canon, he says: "Be mindful, O Lord, of all here present, whose faith and piety are known to Thee." It follows from this that one person may gain more graces from a single Mass than another would gain from 20 or 30. When you go to the well to draw water, you can only take as much as your vessel will hold; if it be large, you can draw much water; if it be small, you can draw but little. Now the Mass is an inexhaustible fountain of blessings; it is, to use the language of Scripture, the Saviour's fountain, from which the precious graces He has merited for us gush forth upon our souls; and the vessel in which we receive these graces is our faith and devotion.

If our faith be lively and our devotion ardent, the blessings of Heaven will fill our hearts; if our hearts be filled with the thoughts of this world, we shall receive but a small share of these blessings. All this was once shown in a vision to Nicholas de la Flüe, a holy hermit of Switzerland who was greatly enlightened by God in spiritual matters. While this good man was one day present at Mass, he saw a large tree full of the most beautiful flowers. He soon noticed that the flowers began to fall down upon those who were present. But some of the flowers, as soon as they fell, became withered and dry, while others retained their freshness and fragrance.

After Mass, he related this vision to his brother and requested him to explain its meaning. The brother replied that he too had seen the vision, and he explained it as follows: "The tree," said he, "is the Holy Mass; the beautiful flowers which it bears are the fruits of the Holy Mass; the withering of many of the flowers signifies that many of the graces which Our Lord distributes in the Mass are lost because Christians are not recollected and devout while they assist at this sacrifice, or because they afterward allow worldly thoughts to stifle all the good inspirations which they have received; the flowers which retained their odor and beauty signify the permanent fruits which those Christians derive from the Mass who assist at it with reverence and devotion and who, after having left the church, are still mindful of the great blessings which they have received from this holy sacrifice." (Dr. Herbst, Vol. II, p. 409).

After having seen of what great importance it is to hear Mass devoutly, you will not be surprised to learn that the devil makes every effort to distract Christians while they are assisting at this Holy Sacrifice. It has been often remarked that infidels and idolaters never behave disrespectfully at the sacrifices which they offer to their false gods. Now, this is not strange, for as Picus Mirandola justly remarks, there is no reason why the devil should tempt them to irreverence since it is he himself who is honored by their superstitious ceremonies; but as he knows how highly God is honored by the great sacrifice of the Christians, he does all in his power to keep the faithful from church, or at least to make them indevout or irreverent when they are there.

Once, when the Israelites were fighting against the Philistines and were on the point of being defeated, they had the Ark of the Covenant brought to the camp. As soon as it came, they all raised a great shout, so that the earth rang again. The Philistines heard the shout and were struck with terror on learning that the God who had done such wonderful things against the Egyptians was come into the camp of their enemies. "Woe, woe to us!" they cried; "who shall deliver us from the hands of these high gods?" However, driven to desperation by the greatness of their danger, they exhorted one another to fight manfully: "Let us take courage," they cried;

"let us behave like men, O Philistines, lest we become the servants of the Hebrews, as they have served us! Let us take courage and fight bravely." (*1 Kings* 4:8-9).

In like manner, when the signal is given for beginning Mass, the great adversary of mankind is seized with rage and terror. "Woe! woe!" he cries, "what shall we do! This is that sacrifice which every day snatches so many souls from our grasp; this is the weapon with which Antony and Francis and so many others have defeated us and weakened our power. What shall we do?"

Then, urged on by the rage he feels at his own impotence, he employs all his cunning to destroy at least some part of the good fruits of the Mass; he prevents the sinner from escaping from his power by placing before him some dangerous object on which his eyes may rest; he deprives the devout Christian of the strength and consolation which he would have received during Mass by filling his mind with vain thoughts and worldly cares, so that he cannot attend to what is going on; and thus he gradually leads him into mortal sin. It is thus that, notwithstanding the presence of God on our altars and the infinite value of the Sacrifice, so many precious graces are lost during Mass.

In order to reap all the fruits of the Mass, you should unite your intention at the beginning with that of the priest who offers the Holy Sacrifice. You may do this briefly, thus: "O my Lord, I offer up to Thee this Sacrifice for the same ends for which Thou didst institute it and for which Thy priest now celebrates it, beseeching Thee to grant that the souls of the living as well as the souls in Purgatory may share in its fruits." After this you may spend the time of Mass in such prayers as your devotion may suggest.

According to Saint Leonard of Port Maurice, it is a very good plan to divide the whole Mass into four parts, corresponding to the four principal objects for which Mass is offered, that is to say: to consider the Mass from the beginning to the Gospel, as a sacrifice of propitiation; from the Gospel to the Elevation as a sacrifice of impetration; from the Elevation to the Communion as a sacrifice of adoration; and from the Communion to the end as a sacrifice of thanksgiving.

In the first part you will consider the holiness of God and the enormity of sin, and bewailing your offenses, you can offer the Immaculate Lamb to the Father and ask in the name of that Immaculate Lamb a more complete forgiveness of your sins and of the temporal punishment due to them and a more profound spirit of penance. In the second part, you can offer this sacrifice to obtain special graces from God for yourself and others; pray for the welfare of Christendom, for the propagation of the Catholic faith, for the extirpation of heresy, for peace among Christian rulers, for grace to fight against your besetting sin; and be not unmindful of the poor souls in Purgatory. In the third part, you will consider your own nothingness and God's greatness; then offer up to Him the homage of His well-beloved Son, and in union with this same sublime homage of Jesus Christ, offer up your own acts of adoration to the Heavenly Father. You can rejoice in His glory and desire that all men should render Him due honor.

In the fourth part, you may consider what God

is in Himself and what He is in His Saints, and offering to Him the thanksgiving which Jesus Christ makes in the Mass, you may add an affectionate oblation of yourself and of all you have, in return for the great mercies He has shown you. You may here make a special acknowledgment of the graces which the Lord has bestowed on the Blessed Virgin Mary, our Mother, and on your Angel Guardian; or at the beginning of Mass, you may briefly make these intentions and spend the rest of the time in meditating on the Passion of Jesus Christ, or on some eternal truth; or you may here make use of your Book of Devotions; or you may say the Rosary of the Blessed Virgin. In case you say the Rosary, it is good, *after the word "Jesus" in each Hail Mary, to add:* "Who offers Himself in this sacrifice to His Heavenly Father." By these means the time of Mass will never seem irksome, and you will derive great fruit from the Most Holy Sacrifice.

After all these reflections on Mass, no one will find it strange if the Holy Church obliges her children under pain of mortal sin to assist at this Holy Sacrifice on Sundays and festivals of obligation. On other days, it is true, the faithful are not bound to hear Mass, but our holy Mother the Church earnestly wishes that all her children should and would assist at this salutary sacrifice as often as possible. In most churches, Mass is said every day; in some, several times a day; and wherever it is offered, the people are invited to assist.

The good Catholic then will feel himself impelled always to assist at this Holy Sacrifice, unless an important reason prevents him from so doing. I could cite you many interesting examples which would show you how anxious pious Catholics have always been to hear Mass. St. Louis, King of France, used to hear two Masses every day, sometimes even three or four. Some of his courtiers murmured at this, but the King gave them a sharp reprimand, saying: "If I were to ask you to play or to go hunting with me three or four times a day, you would find no time too long, and now you feel weary of staying in the church during one or two Masses for the honor of Our Lord and Saviour." (Raivenius in Annal. 1270, No. 19).

In the time of Queen Elizabeth of England, when the severe prohibitions against the exercise of the Catholic religion were in force, a rich Catholic was condemned to pay five hundred *scudi* in gold for having dared to assist at Mass. The nobleman selected the brightest and most beautiful pieces of Portuguese gold, on which the cross was stamped. When he was presenting them to the officers, one of them, a Protestant, smiled and made some jocose remark with reference to the beauty of the coins. "I would have considered it a sort of sacrilege," said the Catholic, "to offer a baser coin to pay for the privilege of adoring my Saviour in the Blessed Sacrament. This cross," pointing to the crest on the piece, "reminds me of the Cross of my Lord, which I shall ever be willing to bear for His sake; the purity of the gold recalls to my mind the purity of His love, which I shall ever seek and treasure up." (Schmidt's Example-book).

Gillois relates that in the beginning of the present century there lived in Roibon, a town in the diocese of Grenoble, a peasant who, by his great devotion at Mass, edified everyone who saw him. He lived three miles from the church, and yet he never failed to be one of the first worshippers in the morning. In the latter years of his life, he was subject to severe pains in his legs, which prevented his walking so far in the Winter season, but as soon as the Spring came on, he used to rise about one o'clock in the morning, and dragging himself by means of crutches, reached the church after a painful and laborious walk of four hours.

Sir Thomas More, Martyr and Chancellor of England, daily assisted at Mass with the greatest reverence and devotion. On one occasion while hearing Mass, he was sent for by the King, apparently on urgent business, but he did not stir; soon after a second messenger came, and after a while a third, with the express command to leave the church immediately and come to the royal chamber, where the King awaited him. He replied: "I am now serving the Lord of lords, Whose service I must first perform." (Stapleton's *Life of Sir Thomas More,* Chap. 6). Would to God that you too would imitate such fervent Christians. The Apostle St. Paul, speaking of the blessedness of those who believe in Christ, says: "I give thanks to my God always for you, for the grace of God that is given you in Christ Jesus: that in everything ye are made rich in Him in all utterance and in all knowledge. . .so that nothing is wanting to you in any grace." (*1 Cor.* 1:4-7).

Mass alone of itself is an inexhaustible treasure of graces. Be careful to profit well by it. Resolve, if possible, to hear Mass every day. Do not imitate those lukewarm Christians who stay away from church for the most trivial reasons. For them a little rain, a damp mist, the slight inconvenience of heat, a little moisture underfoot rise up as a sufficient excuse. Early in the morning, when angels are descending from Heaven to take their stand around the altar of the Most High, do you too set out to assist at the Holy Sacrifice and emulate their devotion during the performance of this stupendous mystery.

Do not think the time is lost which you spend in hearing Mass; it will prove most profitable to you in this life and in the next also. See how many sins you will expiate by it! How many punishments you will avert! How many graces you will draw down upon yourself and others! How many merits you will store up for Heaven! This I can promise you: be diligent in hearing Mass, and you will find in it all that you need, your happiness here below and your happiness hereafter. Amid all the vicissitudes of life, at the Altar you will find true peace and support.

At one time it will be Mount Calvary for you, where you will weep tears of sympathy for your Saviour and of grief for your sins and for those of others; at another time it will be Mount Thabor, where heavenly joy will be poured into your sorrowing heart and tears will be wiped away from your eyes. Again, that same Altar will be a Crib of Bethlehem for you, where you will gather strength to bear contempt, poverty, pain and desolation. Yes, at the Altar you will find that Mount of Beatitudes where you will learn the vanity of all earthly things and the way to true and lasting pleasure; and in fine, it will be to you Golgotha, where you will learn to die to yourself and to live to Him who died for you. All this and much more you will find in the Mass, if you cherish a tender devotion to it. Persevere in this devotion and you will soon experience the truth of what

I have said, tasting the sweets of those inspired ejaculations: "How lovely are Thy tabernacles, O Lord of Hosts! Thou hast prepared a table before me against them that trouble me. Better is one day in Thy courts above thousands! Blessed are they that dwell in Thy house, O Lord: they shall praise Thee forever and ever."

CHAPTER 16

On the Ceremonies of the Mass

YOU may ask, dear Reader, if Our Lord also ordained the ceremonies of Mass. I answer, "No." He instituted only the essential parts of the Mass. He left it to His Church to prescribe the rites and ceremonies to be observed in its celebration. However, most of the ceremonies of Mass are of great antiquity, and many of them are without doubt of Apostolic origin. It is principally for two reasons that the Church has prescribed so many ceremonies in the celebration of Mass: first, because Mass being the highest act of religious worship, the Church desires that it should be celebrated with a solemnity and reverence corresponding in some degree to the greatness of the sacrifice; secondly, because, if the various ceremonies of Mass are well understood, they will greatly excite and foster a reverence and spirit of devotion in the hearts of the faithful. They all refer to our Saviour's Passion and death, of which the Mass is a commemoration. Hence the ritual of the Mass is arranged in accordance with the awful tragedy of Calvary.

The priest, the representative of Christ, is clad in garments like those in which the Redeemer was attired on the day of His cruel death. The amice, or white cloth worn around his neck, represents the handkerchief with which Our Lord was blindfolded; the alb, or long white garment, signifies the white robe which Herod put on our Saviour in mockery; the cincture or girdle, the maniple on the left arm, and the stole passing round the neck and crossed upon the breast represent the cords and strings with which Our Lord was bound, and by which He was dragged through the streets of Jerusalem; the chasuble, worn over all the others, signifies the scarlet robe in which He was arrayed when Pilate showed Him to the people, saying: "Behold the man!" The altar, with its crucifix, represents Mount Calvary; the chalice signifies the Saviour's tomb; the paten, His tombstone; and the purifier, with the pall and corporal, the linen cloths in which His Sacred Body was wrapped when it was laid in the tomb.

When the priest begins Mass, he says with the server some prayers at the foot of the altar, during which he bows very profoundly. This signifies Our Lord's entering upon His Passion in the Garden of Gethsemani, where He sweat blood and prayed prostrate on the ground. These prayers of the priest are a kind of preparation for Mass. He begins by saying: *In nomine Patris et Filii et Spiritus Sancti*—"In the name of the Father, and of the Son, and of the Holy Ghost." It is as much as to say: "I act now by the authority of God the Father, whose priest I am; and of God the Son, in whose place I am priest; and of God the Holy Ghost, by whom I am priest." Or, "I offer this sacrifice in the name of the Father, to whom I offer it, and of the Son, whom I offer, and of the Holy Ghost, by whom I offer it."

Then he recites a Psalm expressive of humble trust in God, which is followed by the *Confiteor* and the Ordinary prayers accompanying it. After this he ascends the altar and kisses it. This part reminds us of the seizure of Our Lord by the Jewish multitude, into whose hands He was betrayed by the perfidious kiss and cruel treachery of Judas.

And now begins what may be called the preliminary part of the Mass, which answers to the time when Our Lord was interrogated about His doctrine before the tribunals of Caiphas and Pilate; it lasts till the end of the Creed. Having read the Introit, or short verses from Scripture, the priest says nine times, *Kyrie eleison,* "Lord have mercy on us," thereby giving us to understand how constant and persevering we ought to be in prayer. Immediately after the *Kyrie* follows the *Gloria in excelsis,* the hymn which the angels sang at the birth of Jesus Christ. Surely if such a hymn of praise was sung by the heavenly choirs when our Saviour commenced the work of our redemption, we ought to render to Him a tribute of gratitude no less fervent when at Holy Mass we commemorate and participate in all His benefits and merits.

Therefore, everyone should recite this divine hymn along with the priest, or at least join his intention with him and say some *Gloria Patri,* by way of thanksgiving. After the *Gloria,* the priest turns to the people and says, *Dominus vobiscum,* and the server, in their name, replies, *Et cum spiritu tuo,* a salutation and response which occur very often during Mass. The meaning of the former is, "The Lord be with you," and of the latter, "And with thy spirit," and the Church intends by this frequent interchange of holy affections between the priest and the people to excite devotion, and to teach us how we should desire above all things to remain always in the peace of God.

The priest extends his arms when he says these words to express the exceedingly great charity which Jesus Christ bears towards the faithful and to show how He wishes them ever to remain united to Him in the bonds of true love and obedient to His commandments. The outstretched hands of the priest at the *Dominus vobiscum* signify also the outstretched arms of our dying Lord on the Cross, who, dying for all mankind, wished to receive them in His arms and press them to His heart in token of His undying love for them.

The *Dominus vobiscum* is followed by the Collect [Prayer] of the day, and after that follow the Epistle and the Gospel. These vary according to the season, and may be found translated in many of the ordinary prayer books.

When the Epistle is ended, the server says, *Deo Gratias,* "Thanks be to God," that is to say, for the good instruction contained in the Epistle. The server then carries the Missal to the other side of the altar for the reading of the Gospel—at the left. This signifies that, after Our Lord had been taken prisoner, He was led about from one iniquitous judge to another: from Annas to Caiphas, from Caiphas to Pilate, from Pilate to Herod and from Herod back again to Pilate. This ceremony signifies also that when the Jews had rejected the Gospel, it passed over to the Gentiles, who received it with joy.

When the priest begins the Gospel, he makes the Sign of the Cross on the book to remind us that Our Lord died for the truth of the doctrine which He taught and that we also should ever be ready to lay down our lives for the same truth. After that, the priest makes the Sign of the Cross on his forehead, on his lips and on his heart, and the people do the same. This action is very significant and should never be omitted. By signing the forehead with the Sign of the Cross, we declare that we entirely submit our minds to the teaching of faith; by signing the lips, we testify our readiness to profess our faith before men; and by signing the heart, we remind ourselves of the duty of carefully preserving the word of God in our hearts.

At the end of the Gospel the server says, *Laus tibi, Christe,* "Praise be to Thee, O Christ!" viz., for His love, shown in the work of Redemption, which the Gospel makes known to us. The Gospel is followed by the Creed, or explicit confession of the truths which our Saviour has taught us; and when the priest says *Et incarnatus est* ["And was incarnate"], etc., all kneel down in adoring gratitude to the Son of God for having become man for us.

Now begins the Offertory, or the first [principal] part of the Mass, with which Mass may properly be said to commence. The priest uncovers the chalice, and taking the paten with the host upon it in his hands, he solemnly offers it to God the Father. He afterwards does the same with the chalice, into which he has poured the wine; but before offering the chalice, he drops into it a little water, in remembrance of the water that flowed from our Saviour's side, and also to signify that as the water becomes inseparably incorporated with the wine, so are we closely united to Jesus Christ in Holy Communion.

Then, turning to the people he says, *Orate, Fratres,* etc., "Pray, my brethren," thereby inviting them to join with him in more instant supplications that the sacrifice which he is about to complete may be offered with suitable devotion. We have seen that St. Chrysostom, speaking of the moment in which this tremendous sacrifice is consummated, says, "So great is then the abstraction of the pious mind from all sublunary things, that it seems as if one were caught up into Paradise and saw the things that are done in Heaven itself."

It is possible that when he wrote these words he may have had in his mind the part of the service which comes next in order; for now the priest calls upon the people to banish all earthly thoughts and to think of God alone, saying, *Sursum Corda*—"Lift up your hearts!" And the people, in obedience to the call, answer by the server, *Habemus ad Dominum*— "We have lifted them up to the Lord." Then once more he appeals to them, saying, in view of the countless mercies of God, *Gratias agamus Domino Deo nostro*—"Let us give thanks to the Lord, our God." And they answer as before, *Dignum et justum est*—"It is meet and just." Whereupon, taking up the words which they have just uttered, he proceeds: "It is very meet, just, right and salutary that we should always and in all places give thanks to Thee, O holy Lord, Father Almighty, Eternal God, through Christ, Our Lord."

This part of the service is called the Preface, and it includes a particular thanksgiving for the special blessings which Holy Church commemorates. The Preface ends with a petition that our praises be accepted before the altar of the Most High, in union with the adoration of the Angels, who rest not day or night, saying, "Holy, holy, holy, Lord God of hosts!" At these words the *Sanctus* bell is rung to give notice of the approaching Consecration. Here all should kneel and keep as quiet as possible, avoiding even coughing or moving unnecessarily, for now the *Canon* or most solemn part of the Mass begins, and the *Consecration,* or the second [of the three principal parts] and *most essential* part of the Mass, soon takes place.

In the act of consecrating, the priest performs the same action which Jesus Christ performed at the Last Supper. He takes the host into his hands, and lifting up his eyes to Heaven, he repeats the words which Our Lord made use of; and by the divine power of those words, the bread is changed into the true body of our Saviour. After this he pronounces the words of Consecration over the wine in the chalice. The bell is rung three times at each Consecration as a warning to the people to adore Jesus Christ present on the altar. This is done according to the ancient usage of the Church. "No one," says St. Augustine, "eats of this flesh—the Holy Eucharist—without having first adored it."

The priest elevates the Host after he has consecrated it, and so he does with the chalice, in order that the faithful may compensate in some degree by the loving adoration of their hearts for the insults, mockeries, and injuries which Our Lord received when He was lifted up on the Cross. The priest also makes the Sign of the Cross very often over the sacred species. This is to remind us of the many pains and sorrows which Our Lord Jesus Christ endured for us during His crucifixion.

All the prayers of the Canon are said by the priest in such a low tone of voice that they cannot be heard. This is in memory of those awful hours during which Jesus Christ hung on the Cross and bore in silence the scoffs and blasphemies of the Jewish multitude. But at the *Pater Noster* the priest raises his voice; this is to remind the faithful of the last seven words which our Saviour spoke in a loud voice when hanging on the Cross. After the *Pater Noster,* the priest breaks the Host, signifying thereby the death of Christ, or the separation of Our Lord's soul from His body; at the same time, he drops a small particle of the Host into the chalice, to signify that Our Lord's soul descended into Limbo to announce to the Patriarchs their redemption. At the Communion of the priest, or the third [principal] part of the Mass, the bell is rung again in order that the faithful may be reminded also to receive Communion, at least spiritually.

The act of Communion represents the burial of Christ. At this moment we should offer our hearts as a sepulchre to Our Lord; that is to say, we should resolve to close them against the world and to keep them pure and incorrupt that they may be the resting place of Him who died for love of us. After Communion [including that of the people, if they are present], the priest says some prayers in thanksgiving, after which he turns and says, *"Ite Missa est."* This means that the Mass is ended; accordingly, immediately afterwards he dismisses the people with his benediction by making over them the Sign of the Cross, to remind them once more that every blessing comes from the death of Christ. Then the Gospel of St. John is read, at the end of which the server says, *Deo Gratias*—"Thanks be to God"—for His great mercy in having permitted us to assist at so precious and so holy a sacrifice.

Thus the ceremonies of Mass evince the deep

wisdom of our Holy Mother, the Church, and if one has but a little good will, they will be a powerful means of leading the mind on to the great and inestimable mysteries which the Holy Sacrifice contains. When our Saviour was crucified on Mount Calvary, the sun was darkened, the rocks were rent and the whole earth quaked; the Roman centurion, seeing the things that were done, was greatly afraid and said, "Indeed, this was the Son of God." So the mystical renewal of the sufferings of Christ which is made at Mass continually excites emotions of faith and love in those who assist at it with sincere hearts.

Truly, Mass is the most powerful means to foster faith and fervor. For this reason, the devil persuaded Luther to attack this holy sacrifice, as the most infallible means of preparing the high road to Protestantism, that is to say, a general apostasy from Christianity. As soon as God would permit the Mass to be abolished, the gates of Hell would exert a fearful power against the Church and even threaten destruction to the Christian religion. Nevertheless, it is possible to remain indevout and cold, even with so great a means of grace at our command. In the very temple of God, Our Lord found those that sold oxen, sheep and doves, and the changers of money sitting.

St. Chrysostom says of some Christians in his days that they committed greater sins by their irreverence in church than they would have done by remaining away altogether. It was on account of sacrileges perpetrated in church that the Kingdom of Cyprus fell into the hands of the Turks. But I need not go to history for instances of irreverence; modern times furnish, alas, too many, which prove how easy it is for one whose heart has grown hard and cold to treat the most holy things with disrespect. Be, then, always on your guard against the spirit of unbelief.

The love of the world soon deadens our appreciation of spiritual things. Strive to cherish a tenderness of heart for the greatest and most lovely mystery of our Holy Religion. When you go to Mass, say with St. Francis: "Now, ye worldly affairs and thoughts of business, leave me and remain outside, while I go into the Sanctuary of the Most High to speak to the great Lord of Heaven and earth." Be reverent while you are assisting at Mass, and when it is over, leave the church with such sentiments of humility and piety as if coming from the awful scene of the death of Jesus Christ on Mount Calvary. In fine, go forth to your duties with the same resolution with which you would have gone had you stood with Mary and St. John beneath your Saviour's Cross: namely, to merit Heaven by fulfilling the obligations of your state of life and by bearing with patience all sufferings, trials, hardships and injuries for the love of Jesus Christ, who loved us to such an excess and whom we shall never be able to thank sufficiently, nor repay His ever-burning love.

CHAPTER 17

An Exhortation To Hear Mass Devoutly

"ALL good works together," says the saintly Curé of Ars, "are not of equal value with the Sacrifice of the Mass, because they are the works of men, and the Holy Mass is the work of God." Martyrdom is nothing in comparison; it is the sacrifice that man makes of his life to God. The Mass is the sacrifice that God makes of His Body and of His Blood for man. Yet how little is this most august sacrifice valued by most of men! If someone were to say to us, "At such a place and at such an hour a dead person will be raised to life," we should run very fast to see it. But is not the Consecration which changes bread and wine into the Body and Blood of God a much greater miracle than the raising of a dead person to life? Ah, if Christians knew better the value of the Holy Sacrifice of the Mass, or rather, if they had more faith, they would be much more zealous to assist at it with reverence and devotion!

To increase your zeal and fervor in hearing Holy Mass with greater devotion, let me relate a marvelous vision in which St. Gertrude saw our Lord Jesus Christ celebrate Mass in a mystical manner: On Gaudete Sunday [Third Sunday of Advent (*Gaudete* means "Rejoice")], as Gertrude prepared to communicate at the first Mass—which commences "Rorate"—she complained to Our Lord that she could not hear Mass; but Our Lord, who compassionates the afflicted, consoled her, saying: "Do you wish, My beloved, that I should say Mass for you?" Then, being suddenly rapt in spirit, she replied: "I do desire it, O Beloved of my soul, and I most ardently beseech Thee to grant me this favor." Our Lord then intoned the *Gaudete in Domino semper* ["Rejoice in the Lord always"] with a choir of Saints to incite this soul to praise and rejoice in Him; and as He sat on His royal throne, St. Gertrude cast herself at His feet and embraced them. Then He chanted the *Kyrie eleison* ["Lord, have mercy"] in a clear and loud voice, while two of the princes of the choir of Thrones took her soul and brought it before God the Father, where she remained prostrate.

At the first *Kyrie eleison,* He granted her the remission of all the sins which she had contracted through human frailty, after which the Angels raised her up on her knees. At the second, He pardoned her sins of ignorance, and she was raised up by these princes so that she stood before God. Then two Angels of the choir of Cherubim led her to the Son of God, who received her with great tenderness. At the first *Christe eleison* ["Christ, have mercy"], the Saint offered Our Lord all the sweetness of human affection, returning it to Him as to its Source; and there was a wonderful influx of God into her soul and of her soul into God, so that by the descending notes the ineffable delights of the Divine Heart flowed into her, and by the ascending notes, the joy of her soul flowed back to God. At the second *Christe eleison,* she experienced the most ineffable delights, which she offered to Our Lord. At the third *Christe eleison,* the Son of God extended His hands and bestowed on her all the fruits of His most holy life and conversation.

Two Angels of the choir of Seraphim then presented her to the Holy Spirit, who penetrated the three powers of her soul. At the first *Kyrie eleison* [of the second series], He illuminated her reason with the glorious light of divine knowledge, that she might always know His will perfectly. At the second *Kyrie eleison,* He strengthened the irascible part of her soul to resist all the machinations of her enemies and to conquer every evil. At the last *Kyrie eleison,* He inflamed her love, that she might love God with her whole heart, with her whole soul and with her whole strength. It was for this reason that the choir of Seraphim, which is the highest order in the heavenly hosts, presented her to the Holy Ghost, who is the Third Person of the Most Holy Trinity, and that the Thrones presented her to God the Father, manifesting that the Father, Son and Holy Ghost are one God, equal in glory, co-eternal in majesty, living and reigning perfect Trinity through endless ages.

The Son of God then rose from His royal throne and, turning towards God the Father, entoned the *Gloria in excelsis Deo* ["Glory be to God in the highest"] in a clear and sonorous voice. At the word *gloria* He extolled the immense and incomprehensible omnipotence of God the Father; at the words *in excelsis* He praised His profound wisdom; at *Deo* He honored the inestimable and indescribable sweetness of the Holy Ghost. The whole Celestial Court then continued in a most harmonious voice, *Et in terra pax hominibus bonae voluntatis* ["And on earth peace to men of good will"]. Our Lord being again seated on His throne, St. Gertrude sat at His feet, meditating on her own abjection, when He inclined towards her lovingly; then she rose and stood before Him, while the Divine splendor illuminated her whole being. Two angels from the choir of Thrones then brought a throne, magnificently adorned, which they placed before Our Lord; two princes from the choir of Seraphim placed Gertrude thereon and supported her on each side, while two of the choir of Cherubim stood before her bearing brilliant torches. And thus she remained before her Beloved, clothed in royal purple. When the heavenly hosts came to the words *Domine Deus Rex Caelestis* ["O Lord God, Heavenly King"], they paused, and the Son of God continued alone, chanting to the honor and glory of His Father.

At the conclusion of the *Gloria in excelsis,* the Lord Jesus, who is our true [and eternal] High Priest and Pontiff, turned to St. Gertrude, saying *Dominus vobiscum, dilecta*—"The Lord be with you, beloved," and she replied, *Et spiritus meus tecum, praedilecte*—"And may my spirit be with Thee, O my Beloved." After this she inclined towards the Lord to return Him thanks for His love in uniting her spirit to His Divinity, whose delights are with the children of men. The Lord then read the Collect, *Deus, qui hanc sacratissimam noctem...* ["God, who this most holy night..."], which He concluded with the words, *Per Jesum Christum filium tuum* ["Through Jesus Christ, Thy Son"], as if giving thanks to God the Father for illuminating the soul of Gertrude, whose unworthiness was indicated by the word *noctem* ("night"), which was called "most holy," because she had become marvellously ennobled by the knowledge of her own baseness.

St. John the Evangelist then rose and stood between God and her soul. He was adorned with a yellow garment which was covered with golden eagles. He commenced the Epistle, *Haec est sponsa* ["This is the bride"], and the Celestial Court concluded, *Ipsi gloria in saecula* ["To Him be glory forever"]. Then all chanted the gradual *Specie tua,* adding the versicle, *Audi filia et vide.* After this they commenced the *Alleluia.* St. Paul, the great Doctor of the Church, pointed to St. Gertrude, saying, *Aemulor enim vos*—"For I am jealous of you..." (*2 Cor.* 11:2); and the heavenly choir sang the prose, *Filiae Sion exultent.* At the words *Dum non consentiret,* St. Gertrude remembered that she had been a little negligent in resisting temptations, and she hid her face in shame; but Our Lord, who could not bear to behold the confusion of His chaste queen, covered her negligence with a collar of gold, so that she appeared as if she had gained a glorious victory over all her enemies.

Then another Evangelist commenced the Gospel, *Exultavit Dominus Jesus,* and these words moved the Heart of Jesus so deeply that He arose and, extending His hands, exclaimed aloud, *Confiteor tibi, Pater* ["I confess to Thee, Father"—cf. *Matt.* 11:25], manifesting the same thanksgiving and gratitude to His Father as He had done when He said the same words on earth, giving special thanks for the graces bestowed on this soul. After the Gospel He desired Gertrude to make a public profession of faith by reciting the Creed in the name of the whole Church. When she had concluded, the choir chanted the Offertory, *Domine Deus in simplicitate,* adding *Sanc-*

tificavit Moyses. The Heart of Jesus then appeared as a golden altar, which shone with a marvellous brightness, on which the angel guardians offered the good works and prayers of those committed to their care. The Saints then approached, and each offered his merits to the eternal praise of God and for the salvation of St. Gertrude. The angelic princes, who had charge of the Saint, next approached and offered a chalice of gold, which contained all the trials and afflictions which she had endured, either in body or soul, from her infancy, and the Lord blessed the chalice with the Sign of the Cross as the priest blesses it before Consecration.

He now intoned the words *Sursum corda* ["Lift up your hearts"]. Then, all the Saints were summoned to come forward, and they applied their hearts in the form of golden pipes to the golden altar of the Divine Heart; and from the overflowings of this chalice, which Our Lord had consecrated by His benediction, they received some drops for the increase of their merit, glory and eternal beatitude.

The Son of God then chanted the *Gratias agamus* ["Let us give thanks"] to the glory and honor of His Eternal Father. At the Preface, He remained silent for an hour after the words *Per Jesum Christum,* while the heavenly hosts chanted the *Dominum nostrum* with ineffable jubilation, declaring that He was their Creator, Redeemer and the liberal Rewarder of all their good works and that He alone was worthy of honor and glory, praise and exaltation, power and dominion from and over all creatures. At the words *laudant angeli* ["the angels praise"], all the angelic spirits ran hither and thither, exciting the heavenly inhabitants to sing the Divine praises. At the words *Adorant Dominationes* ["the Dominions worship"], the Choir of Dominations knelt to adore Our Lord, declaring that to Him alone every knee should bow, whether in Heaven, on earth or under the earth. At the *Tremunt Potestates* ["the Powers are in awe"], the Powers prostrated before Him to declare that He alone should be adored; and at the *Caeli caelorumque* ["the heavens and the heavenly hosts"], they praised God with all the angel choirs.

Then all the heavenly hosts sang together in harmonious concert the *Cum quibus et nostras* ["with whose (voices) and ours"], and the Virgin Mary, the effulgent Rose of Heaven, who is blessed above all creatures, chanted the *Sanctus, sanctus, sanctus* [Holy, holy, holy], extolling with the highest gratitude by these three words the incomprehensible omnipotence, the inscrutable wisdom and the ineffable goodness of the Ever Blessed Trinity, inciting all the celestial choirs to praise God for having made her most powerful after the Father, most wise after the Son and most benign after the Holy Ghost. The Saints then continued the *Dominus Deus Sabaoth* ["Lord God of hosts"]. When this was ended, Gertrude saw Our Lord rise from His royal throne and present His blessed Heart to His Father, elevating it with His own hands and immolating it in an ineffable manner for the whole Church. At this moment, the bell rang for the Elevation of the Host in the church, so that it appeared as if Our Lord does in Heaven what the priests do on earth; but the Saint was entirely ignorant of what was passing in the church or what the time was.

As she continued in amazement at so many marvels, Our Lord told her to recite the *Pater noster* ["Our Father"]. When she had finished, He accepted it from her and granted to all the Saints and Angels for her sake that by this *Pater noster* they should accomplish everything which had ever been accomplished for the salvation of the Church and for the souls in Purgatory. Then He suggested her to pray for the Church, which she did, for all in general and for each in particular, with the greatest fervor; and the Lord united her prayer to those which He had offered Himself when in the flesh, to be applied to the Universal Church.

Then she exclaimed: "But, Lord, when shall I communicate?" And Our Lord communicated Himself to her with a love and tenderness which no human tongue could describe, so that she received the perfect fruit of His most precious Body and Blood. After this, He sang a canticle of love for her and declared to her that had this union of Himself with her been the sole fruit of His labors, sorrows and Passion, He would have been fully satisfied. Oh, inestimable sweetness of the Divine condescension, who so delights in human hearts that He considers His union with them a sufficient return for all the bitterness of His Passion! And yet, what should we not owe Him had He only shed one drop of His Precious Blood for us!

Our Lord then chanted *Gaudete justi* ["Rejoice, ye just"], and all the Saints rejoiced with Gertrude. Then Our Lord said in the name of the Church Militant, *Refecti sibo, etc.;* He then saluted all the Saints lovingly, saying, *Dominus vobiscum,* and thereby increased the glory and joy of all the Blessed. The Saints and Angels then sang for the *Ite Missa est*

["Go, it is finished"], *Te decet laus et honor, Domine* ["To Thee belongs praise and honor, O Lord"], to the glory and praise of the effulgent and ever peaceful Trinity. The Son of God extended His royal hand and blessed the Saint, saying: "I bless thee, O daughter of eternal light, with this special blessing, granting you this favor, that whenever you desire to do good to anyone from particular affection, they will be as much benefitted above others as Jacob was above Esau when he received his father's blessing."

My dear Reader, were Our Lord to favor you but once with such a vision, how great would not your devotion be in hearing Mass! Ah, dear Reader, our vision must be our faith! Faith is the best of all visions because it is not subject to any illusion. In the light of a lively faith you will see in every Mass all these marvels of divine omnipotence, wisdom and goodness which St. Gertrude saw. This faith teaches us to do what St. James the Apostle says in his Mass: "When the moment of Consecration is arriving, everyone should be silent and trembling with reverential awe; he should forget everything earthly, remembering that the King of Kings and the Lord of Lords is coming down upon the altar as a victim to be offered to God the Father and as food to be given to the faithful; He is preceded by the Angelic choirs in full splendor, with their faces veiled, singing hymns of praise with great joy."

Of these hymns of praise St. Bridget writes thus: "One day, when a priest was celebrating Mass, I saw at the moment of Consecration how all the powers of Heaven were set in motion. I heard at the same time a heavenly music, most harmonious, most sweet. Numberless Angels came down, the chant of whom no human understanding can conceive nor the tongue of man describe. They surrounded and looked upon the priest, bowing towards him in reverential awe. The devils commenced to tremble and took to flight in the greatest confusion and terror." (*Lib.* 8, C. 56).

All this is in accordance with what other great Saints have seen or said on this subject. St. John Chrysostom says that whole choirs of Angels are surrounding the altar while Jesus Christ is as a victim upon it. St. Euthymius, when saying Mass, would often see many Angels assisting at the Sacred Mysteries in reverential awe. At other times he would see an immense fire and light coming down from Heaven and enveloping him and his assistant to the end of the Holy Sacrifice. (Life by Cyrillus). In the same manner the Holy Ghost would, in the form of a fiery flame, surround St. Anastasius whilst celebrating Mass. (Life by St. Basil). St. Guduvalus, Archbishop, who would always prepare himself for the celebration of this most august sacrifice by fasting, night watches and many fervent prayers, often saw how the Angels descended from Heaven during Mass, chanting hymns of praise with unspeakably great reverence; but he himself would be standing at the altar like a majestic column of fiery flame while he was celebrating the Holy Sacrifice.

Severus relates of St. Martin that when he was saying Mass a fiery globe would be seen above his head. Who shall not wonder at this behavior of the Angels during Mass and at the great preparations which the celestial spirits make when Mass is being celebrated, in order that this most august mystery may be performed with the greatest pomp and dignity possible. But we, wretched men as we are, see, for want of faith, but little of the supernatural that is going on during Mass. Were Our Lord to show us what He deigned St. Bridget and other Saints to see, what great marvels should we not witness? We should see how the whole of the heavenly host would be occupied in making most suitable preparations for renewing, in a mystical manner, the life, sufferings and death of Jesus Christ.

We should see, to our greatest surprise and astonishment, how a heavenly sun, moon and stars would shine upon this mystery during its celebration and how the Angelic choirs would glorify it by their music most sweet and their singing most enrapturing. We would see, moreover, how true it is what Our Lord once said to St. Matilda. (*Lib.* 3, Revel., C. 28). "At the moment of Consecration," said He, "I come down first in such deep humility that there is no one at Mass, no matter how despicable and vile he may be, towards whom I do not humbly incline and approach, if he desires Me to do so and prays for it; secondly, I come down with such great patience that I suffer even My greatest enemies to be present and grant them the full pardon of all their sins, if they wish to be reconciled with Me; thirdly, I come with such immense love that no one of those present can be so hardened that I do not soften his heart and enkindle it with My love, if he wishes Me to do so; fourthly, I come with such inconceivable liberality that none of those present can be so poor that I would not enrich him abundantly; fifthly, I come with such sweet food that no one ever so hungry should not be refreshed and fully satiated by Me. Sixthly, I come with such great light and splendor that no heart, how blinded soever it may be, will not be enlightened and purified by My presence. Seventhly, I come with such great sanctity and treasures of grace that no one, however inert and indevout he may be, should not be roused from this state."

Who should not exclaim, with St. Francis of Assisi, "Oh, wonderful greatness! Oh, most humble condescension, that the well-beloved Son of God should conceal Himself for man's sake under the small species of bread! Let entire man, the whole world and the heavens tremble at such a spectacle!" Not seeing these wonders with our eyes, we are accustomed not to appreciate them, and to assist at Mass with levity and indevotion. But the Angels see them and tremble. The devils see them and take to flight; we see them not, but believe them, and though faith is the best sight, yet we are present almost like marble blocks, looking at everyone who comes in or goes out; the least noise disturbs us and makes us forget Our Lord. We truly deserve the reproach which Jesus Christ made to St. Peter when He said, "O ye of little faith." Nowhere do these words come more true than when we are at Mass! How much is this our little faith confounded by the fervor and devotion of so many Christian Dukes and Monarchs.

Fornerus, formerly Bishop of Bamberg, relates (*Miser. conc.* 78) of the great Duke Simon de Montfort as follows: "This famous Duke was accustomed to hear Mass daily with great devotion, and at the Elevation of the Sacred Host, he would say with Simeon: 'Now Thou dost dismiss Thy servant, O Lord, according to Thy word in peace, because my eyes have seen Thy salvation.' (*Luke* 2:29-30). His regular attendance at Mass was known to the Albigenses, his bitterest enemies, against whom he had been waging war for 20 years. The Albigenses, being driven to despair, determined to make a sudden attack upon the Duke's army in the morning while he was at Mass.

"They executed their design and really surprised his soldiers. Officers came to him while he was hearing Mass, announcing to him the great danger in which the whole army was and begging him to come to their aid. The Duke answered, 'Let me serve the Lord now, and men afterwards.' No sooner were these officers gone than others arrived making the same most earnest request. The Duke replied, 'I shall not leave this place until I have seen and adored my God and Saviour Jesus Christ.'

"Meanwhile, he recommended his whole army to Our Lord, beseeching Him by the most august Sacrifice of the Mass to assist his people. At the Elevation of the Sacred Host, he poured out his heart in humble prayer to his Saviour, offering up to the heavenly Father the Body and Blood of His well-beloved Son, and making, at the same time, an oblation of his own life in honor of the Blessed Trinity. At the Elevation of the Chalice he prayed, 'Now Thou dost dismiss Thy servant, O Lord, according to Thy word in peace, because my eyes have seen Thy salvation.' Then, feeling inspired with great courage and confidence in the Lord, he said to his officers, 'Now let us go, and if God pleases, die for Him who has deigned to die for us on the Cross.'

"His whole army consisted of but 800 cavalry, with a small number of infantry. With this little force he attacked, in the name of the Blessed Trinity, the grand army of the Albigenses, commanded by the Count of Tolosa, who was supported by the army of Peter, King of Aragonia, his brother-in-law. Now, of this grand army Simon de Montfort, the Christian hero, killed 20,000 men on the spot, and the rest of his enemies he put to shameful flight. Everyone said and believed that Montfort had gained this glorious victory more by his fervent prayers at Mass than by the strength of his army, which counted but 16,000 men.''

Ah, how many and how great would be the victories which we should gain over the world, the flesh and the devil, were we always to hear Mass with as much faith, fervor and devotion as this Duke did! How great would be our humility to bear contempt and contradictions with a tranquil heart; how great our patience to carry the crosses and trials of this life until death; how great our confidence in the Lord under the most trying circumstances; how great our charity for our neighbor; how great the light of our understanding in religious matters, and the devotion of our hearts to relish the same, if we profited well by the gift of God in the holy Mass!

What the holy Patriarch Jacob said after his wrestling with the Angel of the Lord we too might say, but with more truth than he did: "I have seen God face to face, and my soul has been saved." (*Gen.* 32:30). For "As often as one hears Mass," said Our Lord Jesus Christ to St. Gertrude, "and looks with devotion upon Me in the Sacred Host, or has at least the desire of doing so, so many times he increases his merits and glory in Heaven, and so many particular blessings and favors and delights shall he receive."

(*Lib.* 4, *Revel.,* C. 25).

Yes, my dear Reader, for your sake and for mine the heavenly Father sends His well-beloved Son upon the altar; for your salvation and mine the Holy Ghost changes bread and wine into the Body and Blood of Jesus Christ; for your sake and mine the Son of God comes from Heaven and conceals Himself under the species of bread and wine, humbling Himself so much as to be whole and entire in the smallest particle of the Host; for your sake and mine He renews the mystery of His incarnation, is born anew in a mystical manner; for your sake and mine He offers up to His heavenly Father all the prayers and devotions which He performed during His life on earth; for your sake and mine He renews His Passion and death to make us partake of its merits, cancelling your sins and negligences and mine and remitting many temporal punishments due to the same.

One Mass which you have heard will do you more good than many which are said for you after your death. As many Masses as you have heard, so many consolations you will experience in the hour of your death, and so many advocates you will have before the tribunal of God to defend and plead for you. You can do nothing better for your parents, friends, for the poor and distressed, for your benefactors, for the dying, for the conversion of sinners, for the just, for the souls in Purgatory, than to hear and offer up for them the Holy Sacrifice of the Mass, nor can you give greater glory and joy to the Blessed Trinity, to the Blessed Virgin and all the Saints than by assisting at Mass with devotion.

Mass is the most powerful means for being

preserved from temporal and spiritual harm, for obtaining every gift from the Lord, both for this life and for that to come. In a word, Mass is, as St. Francis de Sales says, "the center of the Christian religion, the heart of devotion and the soul of piety; a mystery so ineffable as to comprise within itself the abyss of Divine charity; a mystery in which God communicates Himself really to us and in a special manner replenishes our souls with spiritual graces and favors." (*Intro. to the Devout Life,* Chap. 14). Hence, I can truly say and fairly conclude that there is no hour of the day so precious as that which you devote to hearing Mass. It is truly a golden hour, for the merit you gain therein is more precious than pure gold. The other hours of the day, although they are necessary, and have their use in the economy of Nature, in comparison, can only be esteemed as dross.

But you may say, "It is more necessary for us to labor than to hear Mass, because without work I cannot earn a subsistence for myself and family." I say otherwise: it is even more necessary to hear Mass than to labor, because it is a most powerful means to keep yourself in the state of grace and most difficult for you to obtain the blessings of God without it. I do not say neglect your work, but break off for a half-hour and give that short time to God, and you will find your business will succeed better, as it will have God's blessing upon it.

If you neglect to hear Mass, either for temporal interest or from slothfulness, you occasion to yourself a loss in comparison with which no worldly loss is to be compared, for you lose a hundredfold greater gain than you can make by your work during the whole day. This you may judge from the remarkable words which Christ used with so much emphasis: "What does it profit a man if he gain the whole world and lose his own soul." (*Matt.* 16:26). Can you hesitate for a trifling worldly profit to refuse to listen to and apply to yourself the trusty admonition of Christ Himself?

CHAPTER 18

Examples Relating to
The Holy Sacrifice of the Mass

1. St. Isidore was hired by a wealthy farmer to cultivate his farm. He would, however, never begin to work in the morning before he had heard Mass. He was accused by some of his fellow-laborers to his master of staying too long in the church and of being always too late at work. His master, to convince himself of the truth of the accusation, went out early in the morning to see whether Isidore came in due time to the farm—but how great was his astonishment when he beheld two Angels dressed in white, ploughing with two yoke of oxen, and St. Isidore in their midst. From this time forward Isidore was held in great veneration by the wealthy farmer and by all who heard of the fact.

2. The following event was related to me by one of our Fathers, in whose native country it took place: In the year 1828 or 1829, a young man travelled through Switzerland. When he came to Zurich, he fell dangerously ill. Being a Catholic, he begged the hotel-keeper to send for a Catholic priest. "I will send for one," said he. Meanwhile, he agreed with two other guests of his to play the priest with two servers. Accordingly, he went to the young man and heard his confession, after which he received from

him some money as a little present, with the request that he should say three Holy Masses. After this criminal action, he left the young man, went with the other companions into another room, saying to them: "Come, let us go and say the three Masses," meaning thereby that they would drink three bottles of wine.

They sat down at table, and having emptied one bottle, said: "Behold, one Mass already said." Having emptied the second bottle, they cried out with great laughter: "Now, two Masses are said." God did not long withhold His revenge. No sooner had they drunk the third bottle of wine than all three of them suddenly died—turning as black as coal. This dreadful event became known amongst the people. The civil magistrate interfered; they locked up the room, leaving therein the three black corpses for the space of 26 days, in order to make a minute examination of the case. This is a well known fact in that city, and in the neighboring provinces.

3. St. Anthony, Archbishop of Florence, relates that two young men went hunting on a holy day of obligation. Only one of them took care to hear Mass previously. Not long after they had started, a frightful thunderstorm came on, and a flash of lightning instantly killed the one who had not heard Mass. The other young man was panic-stricken at this, especially as he had heard at the same time a voice saying, "Strike him too." A little after, he felt encouraged by another voice, which said, "I cannot strike him, because he heard Mass this morning." (*Ant.* II, p. *Theologiae* ix., C. 10).

4. We read of St. Elizabeth, Queen of Portugal, that she gave orders to her almoner never to refuse

an alms to a poor person; besides, she herself would often give alms and employed several of her domestics to do the same. She especially chose for this charitable office one of her pages, because she had noticed in him a more than usual piety. He never omitted hearing Mass every day. Now it happened that another page, through envy, accused him to the King of too much familiarity with the Queen. The King became enraged; without further examination, he gave orders to a certain person who had the care of a furnace, to throw into it the first of his pages that would go to the place, and immediately make known to him the result. He then sent the page who had been accused to the place in which the furnace was. On his way, the page heard the bell for Mass and waited to assist at the Holy Sacrifice. Not hearing immediately what he expected from the person employed at the furnace, the King sent the other page to see what had happened. The miserable accuser, being the first who arrived, was cast into the furnace and burned alive. The innocent page afterwards appeared, and being reproved by the King for not having promptly obeyed his order, said that he had stopped on his way to hear Mass. The King began to suspect the accusation to be false, sought for better information, and discovered the innocence of the devout page. (*Chron. S. Fr.,* P. 2, *Lib.* 8, C. 28).

5. Three merchants prepared to travel together from the city of Gubbio. One of them wished to hear Mass before his departure, but the others refused to wait for him, and set out by themselves. But when they arrived at the river Corfuone, which had swelled to a great height in consequence of the rain that fell during the night, the bridge gave way, and they were

drowned. The third, who had waited to hear Mass, found the two companions dead on the bank of the river and thankfully acknowledged the grace which he had received on account of having assisted at Mass.

6. St. Anselm, Archbishop of Canterbury, when, on account of his old age, he was no longer able to say Mass, had himself carried daily to the oratory in order to hear Mass. (Life by Ediner).

7. In the Chronicles of Spain, it is related of Paschalis Vivas, a celebrated general, that while he was hearing Mass in the Church of St. Martin, he was seen at the same time fighting in the battle against the King of Corduba and gaining a most splendid victory over the enemies, although he was not present in person when the engagement took place, his guardian angel assuming his form and fighting in his place.

8. St. Basil would not finish Mass unless favored by a heavenly vision. Once this favor was denied him on account of a lascivious look of his assistant. The Saint then sent him away, whereupon the vision returned and he finished the Holy Sacrifice.

9. Paschasius relates that when St. Plegil said Mass, this holy priest would see Jesus Christ in the Consecrated Host under the form of a beautiful Child stretching out his arms as if to embrace him.

10. Once, at Easter, Pope Gregory I celebrated Mass in the Church of St. Maria Maggiore, and after he had said the words, *Pax Domini sit semper vobiscum* ["The peace of the Lord be with you always"], an Angel of the Lord answered in a loud voice, *Et cum spiritu tuo* ["And with your spirit"]. For this reason, when the Pope celebrates Mass on that day in the

church and says, *Pax Domini sit semper vobiscum,* no answer is made. (Life by John the Deacon).

11. We read in the life of St. Oswald, Bishop, that an Angel would assist him at Mass and make all the necessary answers.

12. "My children," said the Curé of Ars one day, "you remember the story I told you of that holy priest who was praying for his friend. God had made known to him, it appears, that this friend was in Purgatory; it came into his mind that he could do nothing better than to offer the Holy Sacrifice of Mass for his soul. When he came to the moment of Consecration, he took the Sacred Host in his hands and said: 'O, Holy and Eternal Father, let us make an exchange. Thou hast the soul of my friend who is in Purgatory, and I have the Body of Thy Son who is in my hands; well, do Thou deliver my friend, and I offer Thee Thy Son with all the merits of His death and passion.' In fact, at the moment of the Elevation, he saw the soul of his friend rising to Heaven, all radiant with glory. Well, my children, when we want to obtain anything from the good God, let us do the same. After the Consecration, let us offer Him His well-beloved Son, with all the merits of His death and His passion. He will not be able to refuse us anything."

At the moment when the mother of St. Alexis recognized her own son in the lifeless body of the beggar who had lived 30 years under the staircase of her palace, she exclaimed, "O my son! Why have I known thee so late?" Thus the soul, on quitting this life, will see Him whom it possessed in the Holy Eucharist, and at the sight of the consolations, of the beauty, and of the riches that it failed to recognize, it will also exclaim: "O Jesus! O my God! Why have I known Thee so late!"

13. During the reign of the Emperor Galerius, 30 men and 17 women were arrested in the city of Aluta in Africa for having heard Mass, contrary to the orders of the Emperor. While on their way to Carthage, they never ceased singing hymns of praise in honor of God. When they arrived at Carthage, where they were to be tried before the Emperor, an officer of the guard said: "Behold, O Emperor, these impious Christians, whom we have arrested at Aluta for having heard Mass, contrary to the orders of your Majesty." The Emperor at once had one of them stripped of his clothes, placed on the rack and his flesh torn to pieces. Meanwhile, one of the Christians, Telica by name, cried out in a loud voice, "Why, O tyrant, do you put but one of us to the rack, while we are all Christians, and all of us heard Mass at the same time." At once the judge treated this one just as cruelly as the other, saying, "Who was the author of your meeting?" "Saturninus, the priest," replied the Christians, "and we all together; but you, O impious wretch, act most unjustly towards us. We are neither murderers nor robbers, nor have we done any harm." The judge said, "You should have obeyed your orders and remained away from your false worship." Telica replied, "I obey the orders of the true God, for which I am ready to die." Then, by the Emperor's orders, Telica was taken off the rack and thrown into prison.

After this, the brother of St. Victoria came forth accusing Datiorus for having taken his sister, Victoria, to Mass. But the Saint replied, "Not by the permission of man, but of my accord I went to hear

Mass. I am a Christian, and as such I am bound to obey the laws of Christ." Her brother replied, "You are crazy and talk like a crazy woman." She said, "I am not crazy, but I am a Christian." The Emperor asked her, "Do you wish to return home with your brother?" She answered, "No, I will not; I take those for my brothers and sisters who are Christians like me and suffer for Jesus Christ." The Emperor said, "Save your life and follow your brother." She answered, "I will not leave my brothers and sisters, for I confess to you that I heard Mass with them and received Holy Communion." The judge then tried every means to make her apostatize, for she was very beautiful and the daughter of one of the noblest families of the city. When her parents wanted to force her to marry, she jumped out of the window and had her hair cut off. Then the judge addressed the priest Saturninus, saying, "Did you, contrary to our orders, call these Christians to a meeting?" The priest replied, "I called them in obedience to the law of God to meet for His service." The Emperor then asked, "Why did you do this?" Saturninus replied, "Because we are forbidden to stay away from Mass." "Are you, then, the author of this meeting?" asked the Emperor. "I am," said the priest, "and I myself said the Mass." Upon this, the priest was taken and put to the rack, and his flesh torn by sharp iron points, so much so that his entrails could be seen; finally, he was thrown into prison.

After this St. Emericus was tried. "Who are you?" he was asked. "I am the author of this meeting," he replied, "for the Mass was celebrated in my house." "Why did you," said the Emperor, "permit

them, contrary to our orders, to enter your house?''
''Because they are my brothers,'' said Emericus,
''and we cannot do without Mass.'' Then his flesh
was also mangled, after which he was led to prison
to the other martyrs.

The judge then said to the other Christians: ''You
have seen how your companions have been treated;
I hope you will have pity on yourselves and save your
lives.'' ''We are all Christians,'' they cried out with
one voice, ''and we will keep the law of Christ, being
ready to shed our blood for it.'' Then the iniquitous
judge said to one of them, named Felix, ''I do not
ask you whether you are a Christian, but whether
you were present at this meeting and heard Mass?''
''What foolish question is this,'' replied Felix; ''just
as if Christians could do without Mass. Incarnate
devil, I tell you that we were very devout at the meeting and prayed most fervently during the Holy Sacrifice.'' At these words, the tyrant felt so much
enraged that he knocked the holy martyr down and
beat him till he expired. The remainder of the Christians were also thrown into prison, where they died
from starvation. (Baronius).

14. It is related in the life of St. John a Facundo,
O.S.A., that he was unusually long in saying his
Mass. For this reason no one liked to serve it. His
Prior told him that he must not be longer in saying
his Mass than were the other priests. He tried to
obey, but finding obedience in this point so extremely
difficult, he begged his Prior to permit him to say
his Mass in the same manner as formerly. After hearing his reasons, the Prior most willingly granted this
permission. With John's leave, he told these reasons
to the brothers of the convent. They were the follow-

ing: "Believe me," he said, "that Father John's Mass lasts so long because God bestows on him the privilege of seeing the mysteries of the Holy Sacrifice, which are so sublime that no human mind can understand them. Of these mysteries he told me things so sublime that I was overwhelmed with holy awe and was almost beside myself. Believe me, Jesus Christ shows Himself to this Father in a most wonderful manner, converses with him most sweetly and sends forth upon him from His wounds a heavenly light and splendor so refreshing for both body and soul that he might live without any other nourishment. Father John also sees the body of Jesus Christ in its heavenly glory and beauty shining like a most brilliant sun. Now, considering how great and how unspeakably sublime the graces and favors are which men derive from saying Mass, or from hearing it, I have firmly resolved never to omit saying or hearing Mass, and will exhort others to do the same." (Mensehen in *Act. Sanct., Ad.* xii., *Diem Juni*).

15. Bollandus relates of St. Coleta that one day, when she was hearing the Mass of her confessor, she suddenly exclaimed at the Elevation: "My God! O Jesus! O ye Angels and Saints! O ye men and sinners, behold the great marvels!" After the Mass her confessor asked her why she had wept so bitterly and uttered such pitiable cries. "Had Your Reverence," she said, "heard and seen the things which I heard and saw, perhaps you would have wept and exclaimed more than I have done." "What was it that you saw?" asked her confessor further. "Although that which I heard and saw," she replied, "is so sublime and so divine that no man can ever find words to express it in a becoming manner, yet

I will endeavor to describe it to Your Reverence as well as my feeble language will permit.

"When Your Reverence was raising the Sacred Host, I saw Our Lord Jesus Christ as if hanging on the cross, shedding His blood, and praying to His heavenly Father in most lamentable accents: 'Behold, O My Father, in what condition I was once hanging on the cross and suffering for the redemption of the world. Behold My wounds, My sufferings, My death; I have suffered all this in order that poor sinners might not be lost. But now Thou wilt send them to Hell for their sins. What good, then, will result from my sufferings and cruel death? Those damned souls, when in Hell, instead of thanking Me for My passion, will only curse Me for it; but should they be saved, they would bless Me for all eternity. I beseech Thee, My Father, to spare poor sinners and to forgive them for My sake; and for the sake of My passion, preserve them from being damned forever.'"

16. A most remarkable miracle happened at Walduren in the year 1330: A priest named Otto, during the celebration of his Mass, accidentally upset the chalice after the Consecration, and the Sacred Blood was spilt upon the corporal. All at once there appeared upon the corporal the figure of Jesus Christ hanging on the cross, and around it twelve figures of the sacred head crowned with thorns and disfigured with blood. The priest was frightened almost to death and endeavored to conceal the accident by hiding the corporal in the altar. When the priest was lying on his deathbed, his agony was unusually great and horrifying. Thinking that his great sufferings were caused on account of his having so concealed the corporal, he called for a priest, to

whom he made his confession, asking him to look for the corporal, and giving him permission to reveal the miraculous fact. The corporal was found and forwarded to Pope Urban V, who confirmed the miracle as being authentic. This event is well known throughout Germany.

17. A similar miracle occurred during the time of Pope Urban IV, in the year 1263, at Vulsia, a town not far from Rome. A certain priest, having pronounced the words of Consecration over the bread at Mass, had a temptation against faith, the devil suggesting to him the doubt how Jesus Christ could be present in the Host when he could see nothing of Him. He consented to the temptation, but nevertheless continued saying the Mass. Now, at the Elevation of the Sacred Host, behold, he and all the people who were present saw blood flowing abundantly from the Host down upon the altar. Some cried out: "O Sacred Blood! What does this mean? O Divine Blood! Who is the cause of Thy being shed?" Others prayed: "O Sacred Blood! Come down upon our souls and purify them from the stains of sin!" Others beat their breasts and shed tears of sorrow for their sins.

When Mass was over, the people all rushed to the sacristy in order to learn from the priest what had happened during his Mass. He showed them the corporal all stained with the Sacred Blood, and when they beheld it, they fell upon their knees imploring the divine mercy. The miracle became known all over the country, and many persons hastened to Vulsia to see the miraculous corporal. Pope Urban IV called the priest thither, who came, confessed his sin, and showed the corporal. On beholding it, the Pope,

Cardinals and all the clergy knelt down, adored the Blood and kissed the corporal. The Pope ordered a church to be built at Vulsia in honor of the Sacred Blood and ordered the corporal to be carried in solemn procession on the anniversary of the day on which the miracle occurred. (Platinas' Life of Urban IV).

18. St. Dominic was once saying Mass in London, England, in the presence of the King and Queen and 300 other persons. As he was making the Memento for the living, he suddenly became enraptured, remaining motionless for the space of a whole hour. All present were greatly astonished, and did not know what to think or to make of it. The King ordered the server to pull the priest's robe, that he might go on with his Mass. But on attempting to do so, the server became so terribly frightened that he was unable to comply with the King's order.

After an hour's time, St. Dominic was able to continue the Mass, when, behold! At the Elevation of the Sacred Host, the King and all who were present saw, instead of the Host in the hands of the priest, the Holy Infant Jesus, at the sight of which all experienced great interior joy. At the same time they beheld the Mother of God in great brilliancy and splendor and surrounded by twelve bright stars. She took the hand of her Divine Infant to bless with it all those who were present at the Mass. At this blessing many experienced an ineffable joy and shed tears of tenderness. At the Elevation of the chalice, everyone saw a cross uprising from it, with Jesus Christ hanging upon it in a most pitiable condition and shedding all His blood. The Blessed Virgin was also seen sprinkling, as it were, the Sacred Blood over the people, upon which everyone received a clear knowledge of his sins and a deep sorrow for the same, so much so that everyone who saw them could not help weeping with them.

Mass being ended, St. Dominic ascended the pulpit and addressed the people as follows: " 'Sing ye to the Lord a new Canticle, because he hath done wonderful things.' (*Ps.* 97). You all have seen with your own eyes and experienced in your own hearts the wonderful things which Jesus Christ has done in the Most Blessed Sacrament. You have seen with your eyes, and it has been given to you to understand how Jesus Christ, the Saviour of the world and the Son of Mary, has been pleased to be born anew and to be again crucified for you. In this divine and tremendous mystery of holy Mass you have witnessed only things most holy, most sublime, most consoling and most touching. It is not only one or a few of you who have seen these wonderful things, but the entire 300 here assembled have witnessed them. Now if there be but one little spark of divine love in your hearts, sentiments of gratitude and hymns of praise in honor of the Divine goodness and Majesty ought to flow incessantly from your lips.'' (*Ex. lib. inter. B. Alanus rediv.,* Par. 3, Chap. 22).

19. It is related of Drahomira, the mother of St. Wenceslaus—a very impious Duchess of Bohemia—how she one day went in her carriage to Saes, in order to take a solemn oath on her father's grave to extirpate all the Christians in her dominions. Passing a chapel in which Mass was being said, the driver, hearing the bell ringing for the Elevation, alighted from his horse and knelt down reverently to adore

Our Lord Jesus Christ on the altar. At this the impious Duchess flew into a violent passion, cursing the driver and the Blessed Sacrament. In punishment for her horrible blasphemies, the earth opened and swallowed her and her whole escort. They cried for help, but in vain. In a moment they were gone forever. The driver rejoiced indeed for having alighted from his horse to adore the Blessed Sacrament, his faith and devotion saving him from destruction. (*Hagec. in Chronic. Bohemie,* ad. ann. 930).

20. The Albigenses, certain heretics who arose in the beginning of the twelfth century, forbade any priest, under great penalty, to say what they called a *private Mass.* Having learned that a certain priest had said Mass contrary to their orders, they arrested him, saying, "We have been told that you have said a private Mass, notwithstanding our strict orders to the contrary. Is this true?" Without fear the priest replied as did the Apostles when before the Jewish Council. "We must be more obedient to God than to men; for this reason I have said Mass in honor of God and the Blessed Virgin, notwithstanding your unjust orders." Enraged by this answer, they beat the pious priest and pulled out his tongue.

The servant of God suffered this most cruel pain very patiently. He went to the church and there he knelt before the altar of the Blessed Virgin, praying with his heart to the Mother of God to restore his tongue. The Blessed Virgin appeared to him with his tongue in her hand, saying, "On account of the honor which you have rendered to God and to me by saying Mass, I herewith restore your tongue, requesting you at the same time to continue to say Mass." He thanked the Mother of God for this blessing, and returning to the people, he showed them his tongue and confounded the enemies of Mass. (Cesarius of Heisterbach, who protests in his book that he has written nothing which he did not see himself, or hear from such witnesses as would be willing rather to die than tell a lie).

A Hymn to Jesus

Of Thanksgiving to Jesus Christ in the Blessed Sacrament

1. Sweet Jesus, hid for love of me,
   How shall I render thanks to Thee?
   Ah! Would that my poor love could be
   The half of that Thou'st shown for me!

2. What wondrous act is this of Thine,
   To make Thyself so wholly mine?
   My food, great God, Thou deign'st to be,
   To show how well Thou lovest me!

3. Lord Jesus, come, I beg of Thee,
   And with Thy grace, pray, strengthen me.
   For Thee alone my heart doth beat—
   Ah! Make of it Thy mercy-seat.

4. E'en as the thirsty stag doth fly
   To running brook, so, Lord, do I
   With longing heart pant after Thee;
   Then, come, sweet Jesus, come to me!

5. Ah! Hasten, Lord, make no delay!
   Come, wed my heart this very day,
   That thus united here below,
   I may not fear eternal woe.

6. With steadfast faith I cling to Thee,
   And press Thee, Lord, most tenderly
   Unto my weak and sinful heart,
   Well pleased to claim Thee as my part.

7. Now, Thou art mine and I am Thine!
   Ah! Mortal words can ne'er define
   My happiness thus close to be
   United, dearest Lord, with Thee.

8. By day and night I'll sing Thy praise,
   My voice in grateful anthems raise,
   To thee, dear Shepherd of my soul,
   Nor shrink beneath Thy meek control.

9. This passing life sufficeth not
   To thank Thee for my happy lot,
   So favor'd by Thy love to be—
   Ah! Lord, 'twill take eternity.

10. Had I a thousand lives to lay
    In sacrifice each dawning day,
    It would, most holy, gracious Lord,
    Be for Thy love a poor reward.

11. I cannot love Thee as I should,
    Nor even as my poor heart would.
    For pardon, then, I humbly crave,
    And beg Thee, still, my soul to save.

12. Lord Jesus Christ, for Thee I live,
    Lord Jesus Christ, I beg Thee, give
    Me grace to die thro' love of Thee,
    And be Thine own eternally!

ORDER FORM

1 copy	$9.00	
5 copies	5.00 each	25.00 total
10 copies	4.00 each	40.00 total
25 copies	3.00 each	75.00 total

U.S. & CAN. POST./HDLG.: If total order = $1-$5, add $1;
$5.01-$10, add $2; $10.01-$30.00, add $3;
$30.01-$50, add $4; $50.01-up, add $5.

Prices guaranteed through December 31, 1995.

Gentlemen:

Please send me _____ copy (copies) of
The Blessed Eucharist.

☐ Enclosed is my payment in the amount of

_____ .

☐ Please bill my credit card: ☐ VISA
☐ MasterCard   ☐ Discover

Credit Card No. _____

My Credit Card expires _____

Name _____

Street _____

City _____

State _____ Zip _____

TAN BOOKS AND PUBLISHERS, INC.
P.O. Box 424, Rockford, Illinois 61105
Toll-Free 1-800-437-5876   FAX 815-987-1833

GIVE COPIES OF THIS BOOK...

Give copies of this book to all your Catholic and non-Catholic friends to awaken in them the profound appreciation for the Blessed Eucharist we all need to have. And there is no better book to help achieve this goal than Fr. Michael Müller's *The Blessed Eucharist.* For, our Divine Master Himself has told us: "Amen, amen I say unto you: Except you eat the flesh of the Son of man, and drink his blood, you shall not have life in you. He that eateth my flesh, and drinketh my blood, hath everlasting life: and I will raise him up in the last day. For my flesh is meat indeed: and my blood is drink indeed. He that eateth my flesh, and drinketh my blood, abideth in me, and I in him. As the living Father hath sent me, and I live by the Father; so he that eateth me, the same also shall live by me. This is the bread that came down from heaven. Not as your fathers did eat manna, and are dead. He that eateth this bread, shall live forever." (*John* 6:54-59). There you have one of the most powerful, most shocking and most uncompromising statements ever uttered by Our Divine Lord. And we know He meant His words literally because "After this many of his disciples went back; and walked no more with him." (*John* 6:67). Nor did He stop them from leaving; therefore, we know He meant these words literally, and not in some sort of symbolic way. The world needs to heed them, to come to the Divine Master, to receive Him worthily in Holy Communion, and no other book presses home the urgency of this need and the glory of its call better than *The Blessed Eucharist—Our Greatest Treasure.* Therefore, it is incumbent upon all Catholics who read it to give this book to their friends and relatives—Catholic and non-Catholic alike—that they too may come to the profound understanding of the necessity of receiving frequently the Blessed Eucharist in Holy Communion, and that the non-Catholic may realize he must join the Church, so that he may receive the Eucharist, and thereby the graces necessary to save his soul. The majority of mankind is struggling in error and is being led to eternal perdition. Help stem this tide by giving extra copies of *The Blessed Eucharist.*